MAGNIFYING PRIESTHOOD POWER

MAGNIFYING PRIESTHOOD POWER

ROBERT L. MILLET

ISBN 13: 978-0-88290-779-6

Published by Horizon Publishers, an imprint of
Cedar Fort, Inc., 2373 W. 700 S., Springville, UT, 84663
Distributed by Cedar Fort, Inc., www.cedarfort.com

Cover design by Angela D. Olsen
Cover design © 2008 by Lyle Mortimer
Typeset by Angela D. Olsen

Printed in the United States of America

10 9 8 7 6 5 4 3 2 1

Printed on acid-free paper

Dedicated to Shauna
my sweetheart,
and companion in the Priesthood

PREFACE

We are the servants of the Lord. We are agents, and the Lord God is our Principal; those who have had the priesthood conferred upon them covenant to speak and act as they discern he would speak and act, to represent him in righteousness. President Ezra Taft Benson has instructed us that "the privilege of holding the priesthood which is the power and authority to act in God's name, is a great blessing, and one that carries with it equally great obligations and responsibilities. When I ponder what kind of men and boys we should be as priesthood holders, I cannot help but think of the Savior's questions to the Nephite twelve when He asked, 'Therefore, what manner of men ought ye to be? Verily I say unto you, even as I am' (3 Ne. 27:27)."[1]

All those who receive the Melchizedek Priesthood enter into covenant with God. President Benson described this covenant, as well as the accompanying oath sworn by Deity, as follows:

> When a priesthood holder takes upon himself the Melchizedek Priesthood, he does so by oath and covenant. This is not so with the Aaronic Priesthood. The covenant of the Melchizedek Priesthood is that a priesthood holder will magnify his calling in the priesthood, will give diligent heed to the commandments of God, and will live by every word which proceeds "from the mouth of God." (See D&C 84:33–44.) The oath of the Melchizedek Priesthood is an irrevocable promise by God to faithful priesthood holders. "All that my Father hath shall be given unto them." (See D&C 84:38.) This oath by Deity, coupled with the covenant by faithful priesthood holders, is referred to as the oath and covenant of the priesthood.[2]

In this work we shall speak at some length of the Holy Priesthood—of its necessity and purpose; of its nature, both here and hereafter; and of its transcendent rewards. More specifically, we shall discuss the Oath and Covenant which pertain to the Melchizedek Priesthood—the promises which man makes with God and the unspeakable blessings which God holds out to the faithful.[2]

---

1. *Teachings of Ezra Taft Benson* (Salt Lake City, Utah: Bookcraft, 1988), pp. 214–15.
2. *Ibid.*, p. 223.

In this writing I have sought to be in harmony with the standard works and the words of living apostles and prophets. The responsibility for the conclusions drawn from the evidence cited, nevertheless, is my own. The reader should not regard this book as an official publication of The Church of Jesus Christ of Latter-day Saints.

Robert L. Millet
Provo, Utah

CONTENTS

PREFACE vii

I. PRIESTHOOD: THE POWER OF GODLINESS 1

    Nature and Definition of the Priesthood 1

    Eternity of the Priesthood 3

    Earthly and Heavenly Powers 6

    Orders of the Priesthood 7

    Priesthood as a Source of Revelation 10

    Priesthood as a Source of Power 11

    Summary 12

II. OATHS AND COVENANTS 15

    The Purpose of Oaths 15

    The Place of Covenants in the Gospel 16

    Covenants Which Lead to Salvation 18

    The Oath and Covenant of the Priesthood 22

    Summary 27

III. OBTAINING THE PRIESTHOOD 29

    Worlds Without End 29

    The Councils in Heaven 31

    Election 35

    Foreordination 38

    The Word of Prophecy 40

    Receiving the Priesthood in Mortality 41

    Summary 42

IV. MAGNIFYING CALLINGS IN THE PRIESTHOOD . . 43

    Meaning of "Magnify" 43

    Learning the Duty 46

    Power in the Priesthood 48

    Latter-day Examples of Power in the Priesthood 50

    Blessing the Family 54

    Blessing the World 56

    Summary 57

V. BEWARE CONCERNING YOURSELVES 59

    Be Ye Clean 59

    Guarding the Thoughts 62

    Many Called, Few Chosen 63

The Things of This World 64

Aspiring to the Honors of Men. 66

Gratifying Pride and Vain Ambition 67

Exercising Unrighteous Dominion 68

Amen to the Priesthood 69

Governing the Saints: The Lord's Way 70

An Eye Single to the Glory of God 72

Summary. 75

VI. THE WORDS OF ETERNAL LIFE 77

Searching the Scriptures 78

Pondering and Meditation 81

Praying in Spirit 83

Growing in the Principle of Revelation 87

Unfolding the Mysteries 89

Knowledge by Faith. 92

Summary. 95

VII. RECEIVING THE LORD'S SERVANTS. 97

The Living Oracles 98

The Need for Modern Scripture 99

Living vs. Dead Prophets 101

Sustaining the Brethren. 104

Evil Speaking of the Anointed 107

Intelligent Obedience 108

Summary. 110

VIII. THE DOCTRINE OF ADOPTION 113

Man's Stages of Existence. 113

The Role of Christ in the Gospel Plan 115

Birth Into the Kingdom of God 117

Adoption Into the Royal Family 120

The Role of Abraham in the Gospel Plan 121

The Sons of Moses and Aaron 122

The Role of Joseph Smith in the Gospel Plan 123

Summary. 124

IX. HIGHER BLESSINGS TO THE FAITHFUL 127

Testimony and Conversion: A Contrast. 127

Except Ye Be Converted 130

The Just Shall Live by Faith. 131

Blessings of the Sanctified 133

Renewal by the Spirit. 134

Summary. 136

X. THE ROAD TO ETERNAL LIFE 137
    The Elect of God 138
    Receiving the Lord 141
    The Church of the Firstborn 143
    Joint Heirs Through Christ 144
    A Fulness of the Priesthood 145
    Summary 147

BIBLIOGRAPHY 149
    Latter-day Saint Scripture 149
    Latter-day Saint Historical and Doctrinal Source 149
    Periodicals 150
    Miscellaneous 151

ENDNOTES 153

LIST OF QUOTATIONS FROM MAJOR SOURCES 167

ALPHABETICAL INDEX 171

ABBREVIATION OF TITLES

CR . . . . .Conference Reports
D&C . . . . Doctrine and Covenants
HC . . . . History of the Church
IE . . . . .Improvement Era
JD . . . . .Journal of Discourses
JI . . . . .Juvenile Instructor
MS . . . . .Millennial Star
TPJS . . . . Teachings of the Prophet Joseph Smith

All references are direct quotations, except when ellipses (. . .) indicates that some material has been left out, or where brackets [   ] indicate that the author has added words not in the original source.

EXPLANATION OF FOOTNOTE AND REFERENCE PROCEDURES

Ibid.,—(for the Latin *ibidem,* "in the same place") means that the quotation is taken from the same source as the reference which precedes it.

Op. cit.,—(for the Latin *opere citato,* "in the work cited") means that the quotation is taken from the same book which has previously been quoted by that author.

PRIESTHOOD:
THE POWER OF GODLINESS

FEW MEN EVER COME to understand the divine nature and magnitude of the Priesthood of God. That such should be true is in part due to the solemn fact that few men come to a point of spiritual union with the Almighty, for "the things of God knoweth no man, but the Spirit of God."[1] In a similar vein, the Latter-day Seer Joseph Smith taught that ". . . the things of God are of deep import; and time, and experience, and careful and ponderous and solemn thoughts can only find them out."[2]

Before one can appreciate fully the Oath and Covenant that accompany the Melchizedek Priesthood, he must first grasp the simple yet profound and sacred nature of the Priesthood itself: it is to be exercised righteously through *simple faith*, but its *profundity* is only to be understood through a realization of its sacred character—it is God's own power.

From the statements of the Prophets we may ascertain that a knowledge and appreciation of the Priesthood only comes as man (1) is taught from on high through the medium of the Holy Ghost; and (2) gives himself to much meditation and soul-searching. As the Priesthood bearer comes to discover the powers within his grasp, gains valuable experience in the workings of these powers, and ultimately has his will swallowed up in the will of the Lord, he will eventually receive the glorious reward promised to the true and faithful of the Priesthood: ". . . then shall thy confidence wax strong in the presence of God; and the *doctrine of the priesthood* shall distil upon thy soul as the dews from heaven."[3] To this goal our eyes should ever be affixed.

NATURE AND DEFINITION OF
THE PRIESTHOOD

The conscientious student of the scriptures soon becomes aware of the fact that "Priesthood" implies many things. In a very real sense, Priesthood is a part of God's own power.[4] The exalted Man of Holiness and His Beloved Son are the sources of Priesthood power to man on the earth. President David O. McKay taught that "Priesthood is inherent in the Godhead. It is authority and power which has its source only in the Eternal Father and his Son Jesus Christ. In seeking the source of the Priesthood—we can conceive of no condition beyond God himself. In him it centers. From him it must emanate."[5] The

1

Godhead requires the Priesthood for its existence and operation; Godhood presupposes a fulness of Priesthood powers. That this unlimited power does center in Jesus the Christ, the Mediator of the New Gospel Covenant, is evident from the very title of God's power: the Holy Priesthood after the order of the Son of God.[6] President McKay's statement that "we can conceive of no condition beyond God himself," does not necessarily imply that all power has eternally centered in Elohim, our Eternal Father, and Jehovah, His Firstborn; on the contrary, Joseph Smith taught that "he was once a man like us; yea, that God himself, the Father of us all, dwelt on an earth, the same as Jesus Christ himself did...."[7] But the fact is, man has no need to be concerned with the existence of Priesthood prior to Elohim, inasmuch as his specific salvation and exaltation center in God through Jesus Christ.

Priesthood is the power by which the Gods manage and direct their innumerable creations. It is the governing force by which worlds are brought into being, peopled, redeemed, exalted and glorified. President Brigham Young stated that "the Priesthood of the Son of God is the law by which the worlds are, were and will continue for ever and ever. It is that system which brings worlds into existence and peoples them, gives them their revolutions, their days, weeks, months, years, their seasons and times and by which they ... go into a higher state of existence"[8] Elder Parley P. Pratt also explained that "... the priesthood is the government, or rather the source and fountain from which springs all things pertaining to his [God's] government on the earth."[9] The Priesthood of God is the means by which the heavens and the earth are governed. John Taylor thus spoke as follows: "What is this Priesthood? It is the rule, authority, administration, if you please, of the government of God on the earth or in the heavens: for the same Priesthood that exists upon the earth exists in the heavens...."[10] It is the source of power for the Government of God and Church on earth, and the means by which the Saints are brought to a unity of the faith. It is likewise the source of power for the government of affairs beyond the veil.

In a more personal manner, the Priesthood is authority given to man to act in the stead of God. President Joseph F. Smith spoke of it as "nothing more nor less than the power of God delegated to man by which man can act in the earth for the salvation of the human family, in the name of the Father and the Son and the Holy Ghost...."[11] On another occasion President Smith spoke of the Priesthood as "that authority which God has delegated to man, by which he may speak the will of God as if the angels were here to speak it themselves...."[12] If each man came to the realization that, as a Priesthood bearer, he was literally representing Deity, he would probably guard his thoughts and actions more carefully. Joseph Fielding Smith spoke of the Priesthood as "the authority of God delegated to man, by which he is given power to officiate in all of the ordinances of the Gospel, speak in the name of the Lord, [and] perform all duties pertaining to the building up of the kingdom of God on the earth. . . ."[13] Reception of the Priesthood requires one to work so as to build the Kingdom of God on earth; it is delegated for this very purpose. One grand design is to bring about the will of God on earth, even as it is in heaven.

There is no exaltation in the Celestial Kingdom without the Higher Priesthood. President Joseph Fielding Smith thus explained that "every man who holds the Priesthood [should] understand that he cannot enter into exaltation without the Priesthood."[14] First of all, a man must *receive* the ordinances that proceed from the Priesthood (baptism, confirmation, washing, anointing, sealing) in order to become a candidate for eternal life. Secondly, the Priesthood holder must *perform* the ordinances (within his stewardship) and gain experience in the operations of God's power before he is worthy of greater endowments of light and power; Joseph Smith therefore spoke of the value of *experience* in coming to know and appreciate the deeper things of God.[15]

Finally, since the keys of the spiritual blessings of the Church are contained in the Melchizedek Priesthood,[16] it is only through this power that man is able to mature spiritually to the point where he can bless himself, his family, and the world. It is only through Priesthood that man may partake of the enlivening powers of the Gospel, and thus grow grace for grace into the fulness of the glory of Christ.

ETERNITY OF THE PRIESTHOOD

The scriptures clearly teach that the Melchizedek Priesthood never had a beginning; there never was a time when Priesthood powers were not operative.[17] The Prophet Joseph Smith thus taught that "the Priesthood is an everlasting principle, and existed with God from eternity, and will to eternity, without beginning of days or end of years."[18] In the same light, President George Q. Cannon spoke:

> It [the Priesthood] had no beginning; no end. It is eternal as our Father and God, and it extends into the eternities to come, and it is as endless as eternity is endless, and as our God is endless: for it is the power and authority by which our Father and God sits upon His throne and wields the power He does throughout the innumerable worlds over which he exercises dominion.[19]

Though it is impossible for the finite mind to comprehend the infinite fact of no beginning, yet the Lord through His prophets has made it extremely clear that such is the case. We cannot conceive of a time when the power of the Gods was not operative. Inasmuch as there is no God without Priesthood, and since there never was a beginning to creation and redemption, there is no beginning to Priesthood. This infinite principle is beautifully illustrated in W. W. Phelps' "If You Could Hie to Kolob:"

If you could hie to Kolob
In the twinkling of an eye.
And then continue onward
With that same speed to fly.
D'ye think that you could ever.
Through all eternity
Find out the generation
Where Gods began to be?

There is no end to virtue;
There is no end to might;
There is no end to wisdom;
There is no end to light.
There is no end to union;
There is no end to youth;
There is no end to priesthood;
There is no end to truth.[20]

President Brigham Young explained that "the priesthood of God that was given to the ancients and is given to men in the latter-days is co-equal in duration with eternity. . . ."[21]

The Prophet Joseph made it clear that the Priesthood "not only administers on earth, but also in eternity."[22] The operation of Priesthood powers on both sides of the veil was further stressed by John Taylor; he said that ". . . when we elect officers to fill positions in this Church we choose men whose authority through their faithfulness will hold good not only on this earth, but in the heavens, and not only now but hereafter."[23] Elder Orson Pratt amplified this point when he remarked that "the Priesthood is not given for a few years and then to cease; but all the servants of God who have ministered here below by the authority of the Priesthood will continue their work among immortal beings, and among those living who will not have been changed to the immortal state."[24] President Harold B. Lee related an experience which emphasized the fact that every position we hold on earth will have a direct bearing on our station in the next world:

. . . I had reorganized the presidency of the Ensign Stake. We had named the bishop of one of the wards as stake president. It was near the end of the year, and he elected to remain as bishop, along with his first counselor, who was a bishop, until they had closed the books at the end of the year.

Six weeks after they were sustained, the stake president suddenly passed away. Then I began to receive a barrage of letters. Where in the world was the inspiration for you to call a man whom the Lord was going to let die in six weeks? They invited me to talk at his services, and some seemed to be expecting me to try to explain why I had appointed a man that the Lord was going to take home in six weeks.

President Joseph Fielding Smith sat on the stand and heard my attempt to satisfy these people, and he said to me, "Don't you let that bother you. If you have called a man to a position in this church and he dies the next day, *that position would have a bearing on what he will be called to do when he leaves this earth.*"

I believe that, I believe that every President of this church, every apostle of this church, every bishop, every stake president, every presiding position will have a bearing on what one is called to do when he leaves this earth.[25]

It appears, therefore, that the work beyond the veil is closely aligned with that of the outer Church. Undoubtedly, men who leave mortality assume their rightful place in the next sphere, according to Priesthood, office, or quorum. President John Taylor spoke of David W. Patten, the first martyr of this dispensation:

> . . . David Patten, one of the first Twelve, what about him? Another was to be ordained in his place, but *he was not to have his* [David's] *Priesthood*; of David, we are told, his Priesthood no man taketh—he should stand in his proper position [see D&C 124:130]. Where? He was dead. . . . but he lives behind the veil and *occupies his proper place there in his own quorum.*[26]

President Taylor continued in the same vein concerning the Modern Seer, Joseph Smith, and asked: "Has Joseph Smith ceased to minister in his office because he has left the earth? No; *he administers in his office* in the eternal worlds under the direction of the Son of God, and a proper presiding Priesthood as it exists in the heavens. And so will we."[27] Parley P. Pratt explained simply that should "a man pass the veil with the everlasting Priesthood, having magnified it to the day of his death, . . . you cannot get it off him; it will remain with him in the world of spirits."[28]

That man who lives faithful to the gift of Priesthood will be added upon. That man who endures to the very end in Priesthood service will eventually receive a fulness of Priesthood, and will thus stand as a King and Priest in the resurrection, possessing exaltation and eternal lives;[29] only the exalted will hold and exercise these powers in the worlds to come. Orson Pratt remarked that if Priesthood holders are "clothed with power and authority in this life, they do not leave their Priesthood when they leave this body. . . . We perceive that the Priesthood does not die with their bodies, the *kingly authority* does not cease with the mortal bodies; it is an office that continues forever, that continues in the spirit world, as well as after the resurrection."[30]

EARTHLY AND HEAVENLY POWERS

The Priesthood has two areas of operation, the heavens and the earth, but "they are governed by the same principle."[31] The will of God is conveyed from the perfect Priesthood organization in the heavens to the living Priesthood on the earth.[32] Those powers which are evident on earth are only the visible portion of a large iceberg, or as Orson Pratt explained, "This is only a little branch of a great tree of the Priesthood, merely a small branch receiving authority from heaven, so that the inhabitants of the earth may be benefited as well as the inhabitants of the eternal world; but the great trunk of the tree of the Priesthood is in heaven."[33] The purpose of the Dispensation of the Fulness of Times is to provide a time when all things might be gathered together in Christ, both things in heaven and things on earth. This latter dispensation is thus a time when this heavenly-earthly interaction is accentuated to bring about the will of God. John Taylor thus explained: "God has organized a priesthood, and that priesthood bears rule in all things pertaining to the earth and the heavens; one part of it exists in the heavens, another part on the earth; they both cooperate together for the building up of Zion, the redemption of the dead and the living, and the bringing to pass the 'times of the restitution of all things."[34] This process of co-functioning and communication between heaven and earth is the means by which things are sealed jointly on earth and in heaven. Daniel H. Wells thus stated that "Through the authority of the everlasting Priesthood, channels have been opened up between the heavens and the earth, by which we may seal upon earth, and it is sealed in heaven."[35] The Prophets have therefore made it clear that "... the Priesthood on the earth should operate and co-operate with the Priesthood of heaven in the accomplishment of the purposes of God."[36] An understanding of this principle places even greater responsibility upon the individual Priesthood bearer to insure that his motives are pure, and that his eye is single to the Divine Glory. Only as the Latter-day Saints as a united body begin to see eye to eye with themselves and God may the true cooperation between the work above and that below be realized; only as the Saints learn the principle of revelation, thus ensuring an open communication between the two Priesthoods, will the purposes of God be brought to pass.

As was pointed out earlier in this section, there is some evidence to indicate a continuation of the councils and quorums of the Priesthood beyond the veil. In speaking of his feelings toward the sudden passing of many brethren, President Wilford Woodruff said: "I have felt of late as if our brethren on the other side of the veil had held a *council*, and that they had said to this one, and that one, 'cease thy work on earth, come hence, we need help', and they have called this man and that man."[37] The Prophet Joseph taught that "men held *keys* first on earth, and then in heaven."[38] President John Taylor spoke further concerning a complete Priesthood organization in the heavens:

> Are the Priesthood operating behind the veil? Yes, and we are operating here. And we have a Priesthood here, and they have one there. Have we a Presidency? They have one there. Have we a Twelve? So they have there. Have we Seventies here? They have there. Have we High Priests here? They have there. Have we various quorums? Yes, and we operate in them; and when we get through we join our quorums above.[39]

ORDERS OF THE PRIESTHOOD

Joseph Smith taught that the "Melchizedek Priesthood ... is the grand head, and holds the highest authority which pertains to the Priesthood, and the keys of the Kingdom of God in all ages of the world.... All other Priesthoods are only parts, ramifications, powers and blessings belonging to the same, and are held, controlled, and directed by it."[40] The Melchizedek Priesthood thus comprehends all orders or aspects of the Lord's system of government. The Prophet said simply, "All Priesthood is Melchizedek, but there are different portions or degrees of it."[41] Concerning the different orders of the Priesthood, Joseph Smith stated:

> The Melchizedek Priesthood holds the right from the eternal God and not by descent from father and mother; and that priesthood is as eternal as God Himself, having neither beginning of days nor end of life.
>
> The Second Priesthood is Patriarchal authority. Go to and finish the temple, and God will fill it with power, and you will then receive more knowledge concerning this priesthood.
>
> The third is what is called the Levitical Priesthood, consisting of priests to administer in outward ordinance ... [42]

It might be well at this point to discuss the different orders of the priest-hood, all of which are comprehended within the Melchizedek Priesthood. The Church organization (under which we now live and operate) is composed of offices, councils, and quorums. It is that assemblage of positions (apostles, prophets, evangelists, pastors, teachers, etc.) of which the Apostle Paul spoke as necessary to bring the Saints to a point of union with one another and Christ.[43] The Church provides the means whereby the saving ordinances of the Everlast-ing Gospel may be performed for the living and the dead. It is the program

7

by which the people of the Lord might mature spiritually to the point where they may partake of the divine powers centered in Jesus Christ. In the Church program there exists a definite line of authority, by which the recipient of the Priesthood may trace his particular authority to its source, even Jesus Christ, the Head of the Church. The keys of the Kingdom of God are vested in one man—the senior Apostle on earth. It is through the delegation of these keys (right of presidency) to every officer in the Church that the organization is able to function effectively and efficiently. Each officer in a presiding position may thus have delegated to him the keys necessary to receive instruction and revelation for those over whom he has responsibility. Through a program of correlation and coordination, each officer is responsible to learn his own duty, and "act in the office in which he is appointed, in all diligence."[44] The Lord instructed the Church in a great revelation on Priesthood to "*let* every man stand in his own office, and labor in his own calling; and let not the head say unto the feet it hath no need of the feet . . ."[45] Every person is to be *allowed* to perform his own duty; for another to usurp his responsibilities and stewardship is as the head saying to the feet, "I have no need of thee." The ultimate role of the Church (and thus the Melchizedek Order of the Priesthood) is to build and exalt the family, whereby all government and organization will be centered in the righteous father in eternity. This is Patriarchal authority, by which "every family is a kingdom, a nation, a government, within itself. . . . and the head of the family is the legislator, the judge, the governor."[46]

The Patriarchal Order of Priesthood is "the Melchizedek Priesthood under patriarchal organization."[47] From the beginning, the Lord intended that the Priesthood powers be centered in the righteous father. President Joseph F. Smith stated that the "Priesthood was originally exercised in the patriarchal order; those who held it exercised their powers firstly by right of their fatherhood."[48] The descent of the Priesthood from Adam to Noah as given in the 107th Section of the *Doctrine and Covenants* is a descent of presiding patriarchs; this point is evident from verse 39 of this section which speaks of the calling of evangelical ministers or patriarchs.[49] Because of the slothfulness of the children of Israel at the time of Moses, the Higher Priesthood (which contains the keys necessary to establish the Patriarchal Order[50]) was taken from their midst. Joseph Fielding Smith described the situation as follows:

> The Priesthood which prevailed from Adam to Moses was the Patriarchal Order, yet it was only a part of the Melchizedek Priesthood. All of the ancient patriarchs were high priests, but the direction of the Church in those days was by patriarchs. After the time of Moses, when the Melchizedek Priesthood was taken from Israel, this order, as it is called, of Patriarchal Priesthood, did not continue.[51]

With the development of a temple-centered society among the Latter-day Saints have come the keys to re-establish the Divine Patriarchal Order. On April 3, 1836 the keys necessary to reorganize a true kingdom of Priests were restored to Joseph Smith and Oliver Cowdery. With the coming of Elias and Elijah to the Kirtland Temple, the Ancient Order was re-instituted. Elias, whose precise identity has not been revealed,[52] appeared and, in the words of Joseph Smith, "committed the dispensation of the gospel of Abraham, saying that in us and our seed *all generations after us should be blessed.*"[53] Elijah also appeared and "revealed" those powers in the Priesthood necessary to seal families unto eternal life, thus restoring the rights to set up again the perfected family order. This order centers in the House of the Lord, and its blessings are eventually given to every faithful father and mother.

The Aaronic Order of the Melchizedek Priesthood is that order by which the lessons of the Preparatory Gospel are given to the children of men.[54] The principles and ordinances of the Preparatory Gospel include faith, repentance, and baptism, and are the means by which man is justified before God. The Aaronic (which includes the Levitical) Order holds the keys to the ministering of angels,[55] but has not the power to sanctify man and bring him into the presence of God; these higher powers center in the Holy Priesthood. This order holds the keys necessary to administer in "outward ordinances" (temporal matters).[56]

> The Church has two characteristics—the temporal and the spiritual, and one is not without the other. We maintain that both are essential and that one without the other is incomplete and ineffectual. Hence, the Lord instituted in the government of the Church two priesthoods—the lesser or Aaronic, having special charge of the temporal, and the higher or Melchizedek, looking to the spiritual welfare of the people.[57]

Though the Aaronic Order is an appendage to the Higher, we are not to assume that the Lesser is of only a temporary nature. The Lord explained in a modern revelation that this Priesthood "continueth and *abideth forever* with the priesthood which is after the holiest order of God."[58] Elder Orson Pratt thus explained that "like unto the Melchizedek Priesthood, it [the Aaronic] is everlasting in its nature, not given for time alone, to be exercised here for a few years on the earth and then cease, but *it continues forever*, with the Priesthood after the holiest order of God."[59] President Joseph Fielding Smith spoke to this subject as follows:

> The Priesthood of Aaron, or the Levitical Priesthood, will not end when the sons of Levi make their offering in righteousness.... [D&C 13] We have need for this priesthood now and will *until the end of time* and as long as temporal matters are essential to the progress of the Church.[60]

PRIESTHOOD AS A
SOURCE OF REVELATION

Revelation, or the process by which heaven and earth are brought to a union, is made possible only through the Priesthood of God. The principle of revelation is a manifestation of the power of godliness, and without the Priesthood the power of godliness is not manifest unto man.[61] Joseph Smith spoke of the Priesthood as "the channel through which the Almighty commenced revealing His glory at the creation of this earth, and through which He has continued to reveal Himself to the children of men to the present time, and through which He will make known His purposes to the end of time."[62] Only after a man has received the ordinances of the Gospel, including truly *receiving* the Holy Ghost into his life, may he qualify for the guidance of the Spirit. After one has received the Priesthood and continues faithful, he stands in a new relationship to the Master; he is then more prepared than ever before to act as a vessel through which the Almighty may make known His mind and will. Elder John A. Widtsoe therefore declared that "*the first great gift of the Priesthood is revelation.*"[63] Similarly, the Prophet Joseph said that "it is also the privilege of any officer in this Church to obtain revelations, so far as relates to his particular calling and duty in the Church. . . . One great privilege of the Priesthood is to obtain revelations of the mind and will of God."[64] Inasmuch as the purpose of the Priesthood is to direct the lives of the Saints, the Prophet admonished the members on another occasion to "go on to perfection, and search deeper and deeper into the mysteries of godliness. A man can do nothing for himself unless God directs him in the right way; and *the Priesthood is for that purpose.*"[65]

The Priesthood not only enables man to find direction in his life, but also to come to know the things of God—the deeper things which are made known only to the pure in heart. Brigham Young thus declared that "it is the privilege of every person who is faithful to the priesthood . . . to . . . know, see, and understand, by revelation, the things of God just as naturally as we understand natural things that are around us."[66] President Young further pointed out that should the Priesthood bearer continue faithful, he "will secure to himself not only the privilege of receiving, but the knowledge of *how* to receive the things of God. . . ."[67] As the righteous man gradually learns the Spirit of God, he comes to know how to receive of God; this is a key to eventually coming into the presence of the Lord and receiving of greater endowments of power. Only as one learns how to worship Deity, as well as *who* he worships, may he grow in glory from grace to grace, until he is fully glorified in Christ.[68]

A final point to consider in this section is that men not only have the right to obtain revelation, but also are under obligation to do so. President Wilford Woodruff therefore stated boldly that "men who have held any portion of the Holy Priesthood, and have had its gifts, graces, and blessings bestowed upon them have been under the *necessity* of having communion with God."[69] President Woodruff asked on another occasion:

> What business have we with this priesthood, if we have not power to receive revelation? What is the priesthood given for? If we do not have revelation, it is because we do not live as we should live, because we do not magnify our priesthood as we ought to; if we did we would not be without revelation, none would be barren or unfruitful. . . . no man should undertake to act in positions affecting the interests of Zion, unless he lives so as to be guided and directed by the revelations of God. . . .[70]

Finally, Elder John A. Widtsoe said simply: "Priesthood *must* be in touch with the source of truth; its labors *must* be guided by revelation."[71]

PRIESTHOOD AS A SOURCE OF POWER

Priesthood is more than authority. Inherent in the Priesthood is a divine power, enabling the pure to have interaction and communion with the infinite. Priesthood is power to create. It is power to redeem, resurrect, and exalt. It is power over life and death. Speaking of the Priesthood holder, a revelation said: "Wherefore, he is possessor of all things; for all things are subject unto him, both in heaven and on the earth, the life and the light, the Spirit and the power, sent forth by the will of the Father through Jesus Christ, his Son."[72]

Priesthood is the right to penetrate the veil and enjoy the association of holy beings. Holders of the Aaronic Priesthood have the right, if they seriously seek for the things from above, to entertain angels. Orson Pratt emphasized this fact. He stated that "the privilege of the lesser Priesthood is to see angels. How should they seek after this blessing? . . . It is by giving heed to the teaching of this lesser Priesthood; and when this is done, we may claim the ministrations of holy angels."[73] The Higher Priesthood, holding the keys of the spiritual blessings of the Church, enables man to commune with the Church of the Firstborn, which is the grand assembly of celestial beings beyond the veil.[74] President David O. McKay therefore stated that "the veil is thin between those who hold the priesthood and those on the other side of the veil."[75] Elder Orson Pratt made the following remarks:

> The higher Priesthood after the order of the Son of God, we are told, in a modern revelation, holds the power to commune with the Church of the First-born that are in heaven, and that too *not in a spiritual sense alone,* . . . but in the literal sense, even the same as one man communes with another.[76]

The ultimate attainment is to be prepared to see the face of God, and thus be worthy to stand in His very presence. Elder Pratt continued his remarks on the rights of the Priesthood by stating that "it holds not only the power of the ministration of holy angels to be seen personally, but also the power of beholding the face of God the Father, that through the power and manifestations of the Spirit of God and of his angels we may be prepared to enter into the presence of God the Father in the world to come, and enjoy continual communion with him...."[77]

Needless to say, few men ever honor their Priesthood and covenants enough to rise to the state of power discussed in this section. Nevertheless, these rights and powers are very real, and do come to those who humble themselves before God, and become pure in heart. The promise is ever present that "inasmuch as you strip yourselves from jealousies and fears, and humble yourselves before me, ... the veil shall be rent and you shall see me and know that I am...."[78]

SUMMARY

1. The sacred and profound nature of the Holy Priesthood is to be understood only as one gives himself to much meditation, and prepares himself for true knowledge from above.

2. The Priesthood of God is many things. It is:

    A. A part of God's own power.

    B. The power by which the Gods direct the affairs of the innumerable creations.

    C. The power by which worlds are brought into being, redeemed, and glorified.

    D. Power delegated to man to act in the stead of God in blessing the world.

3. There is no exaltation in the Celestial Kingdom without the Priesthood.

4. Priesthood is everlasting and eternal: it has no beginning and no end.

5. The Priesthood has two areas of operation—the heavens and the earth. These are governed by the same principles, and co-operate to bring about the purposes of God.

6. The Church of Jesus Christ exists to build and exalt the family.

7. The Patriarchal Order of Priesthood is the Ancient Order of Priesthood, and is that arrangement which perfects the family order in eternity.

8. The Aaronic Order of Priesthood holds the keys of the ministering of angels, and administers in outward ordinances.

9. The first great gift of Priesthood is revelation; Priesthood bearers have the right and responsibility to receive revelations.

10. Priesthood is a divine power. It entitles the holder (upon righteousness) to enjoy the influence and companionship of holy beings, and to eventually enter the presence of the Father.

OATHS AND COVENANTS

THIS CHAPTER CONSISTS of a brief introduction to the Oath and Covenant which accompany the Melchizedek Priesthood. It is the intent of these pages to lay a foundation for the chapters to follow. Specifically, this chapter will discuss the place of oaths and covenants in the Gospel, and more directly, the nature of the promises between God and man in the Oath and Covenant of the Priesthood. In chapters three through ten each of the promises and blessings of the Covenant relationship will be treated in detail.

THE PURPOSE OF OATHS

In times past, men and women relied upon an oath as an outward evidence of the efficacy of some fact or matter. The oath represented a solemn attestation, and "to swear with an oath [was] the most solemn and binding form of speech known to the human tongue."[1] Elder Bruce R. McConkie made the following remarks concerning oaths:

> In ancient dispensations, particularly the Mosaic, the taking of oaths was an approved and formal part of the religious lives of the people. These oaths were solemn appeals to Deity, or to some sacred object or thing, in attestation of the truth of a statement or of a sworn determination to keep a promise. Those statements, usually made in the name of the Lord, by people who valued their religion and their word above their lives, could be and were relied upon with absolute assurance.[2]

God also makes oaths unto man. It was by an oath that God swore to Abraham, Isaac, and Jacob that their posterity should be as the sands of the seashore, and should continue into eternity. Note the words of the Lord to Isaac: "... *I will perform the oath which I sware unto Abraham thy father; And I will make thy seed to multiply as the stars of heaven* ... "[3] It was also by an oath that the Father declared that the Only Begotten should bear the Holy Priesthood. The Psalmist described the Father's words to the Son as follows: "*The Lord hath sworn, and will not repent, Thou art a priest for ever after the order of Melchizedek.*"[4] *The Book of Mormon* also evidences the frequent usage of oaths to bind persons by their words. We notice, for example, that Zoram, the slave of the wicked Laban, swore with an oath that he would continue with the party of Lehi.[5] The power with which that oath was received was described by Nephi's simple statement that "when Zoram had made an oath unto us, our fears did cease concerning him."[6]

The wicked utilization of the oath to bring about unholy ends began early in man's history. Cain swore unto Satan by an oath that he would not reveal the nature of the "great secret"—namely, that there was advantage to be gained in wanton murder.[7] From this inception have come the myriads of secret combinations, bound by unholy oaths, in which they have vowed to destroy the works of God. Among these groups, the Gadianton bands of ancient America were extremely powerful.[8]

In ancient times, men and women frequently swore by many things, including God, the heavens, parts of the body, etc. They might have said, "I swear by the heaven above," or, in the case of Cain, "I swear by my throat."[9] In the great Sermon on the Mount, Christ gave valuable instructions, as He set forth the fulfillment of the Mosaic code:

> Again, ye have heard that it hath been said by them of old time, Thou shalt not forswear thyself, but shalt perform unto the Lord thine oaths. [Leviticus 19:22]
>
> But I say unto you, *Swear not at all*; neither by heaven; for it is God's throne:
>
> Nor by the earth; for it is his footstool; neither by Jerusalem; for it is the city of the great King.
>
> Neither shalt thou swear by thy head, because thou canst not make one hair white or black.
>
> But let your communication be Yea, yea; Nay, nay; for whatsoever is more than these cometh of evil.[10]

Here was a call to a higher law. Man was no longer to swear by anything— his word was to be his bond; "Yes" or "No" was to be sufficient. Under the Law of Moses, there was always the possibility that a man might not keep his promises, except he sware by an oath (see Numbers 30:2). Under the Law of Christ, man was to be trustworthy enough so that oaths were not necessary.

THE PLACE OF COVENANTS IN THE GOSPEL

A covenant is a promise made between two or more persons. It is the highest form of human interaction. The Latter-day Saints are a covenant-making people, because the Society of Zion is based upon the principle of covenant. Only as the people of the Church enter into covenant relationships with themselves and God will they ever become truly pure in heart. Covenants are made not only to bring individuals to a *unity* of faith, but also to make people free and independent under God. The Prophet Joseph Smith therefore taught that it was his endeavor "to so organize the Church that the brethren might eventually be independent of every incumbrance beneath the celestial kingdom, by bonds and covenants of mutual friendship and love."[11] Elder ElRay L. Christiansen said in a similar vein:

> Why does the Lord make or require covenants and command-
> ments and obligations and laws? I have heard people ask, if he loves us
> why does he restrict us? Just as any father would restrict his child, if it is
> a blessing to that child, so our Father gives us these laws and ordinances
> and commandments and covenants, not that we should be burdened or
> restricted by them, but that *we may be lifted up and made free,* that our
> burdens may be light . . . [12]

Covenants are sacred, especially those in which man's promises involve God. They are not to be taken lightly, for God will not be mocked. Elder George A. Smith cautioned against making covenants without forethought, and explained further that "we should be careful to make our agreements so that we can fulfill them, and then do so, and if through some unforseen circumstances we are unable to do so, we should immediately make known the facts, and be honest."[13] Breaking covenants is most serious, and a man or woman does so at the peril of his or her eternal standing before God. President Heber C. Kimball gave his opinion of covenant-breakers; he said that "there are many who make covenants today and break them tomorrow. I would not give a dime for such persons, and God is going to send forth a test that will tumble them over the board, because there is not integrity in them. They are not honest, they will not fulfill the duties that are required of them. Justice will take her demands. . . ."[14] Just as in any other situation of transgression, those who violate covenants will have the Spirit of the Lord withdrawn from them to a noticeable degree. Wilford Woodruff therefore stated that "many have broken their covenants and turned away from the Lord, and the reason is that they stopped serving God and undertook to serve themselves, and that led them into darkness. They rejected the things of the kingdom of heaven, and *the Spirit of God was taken from them.* . . ."[15] The Lord said in the great revelation on eternal marriage: "For behold, I reveal unto you a new and everlasting covenant; and if ye abide not that covenant, then ye are damned; for no one can reject this covenant and be permitted to enter into my glory."[16] In referring specifically to this verse, President Joseph Fielding Smith said: "*That applies to any covenant.* It is not merely this one that the Lord is speaking of here that is going to bring upon us a condemnation if we violate it or refuse to receive it. That is true of every covenant that belongs to the gospel."[17] Latter-day Saints, and specifically Priesthood bearers, are thus under a strict charge to (1) understand the sacred nature of all covenants entered into, and (2) live so as to be in harmony with all promises and agreements made. Therein is safety.

COVENANTS WHICH LEAD
TO SALVATION

There is no salvation without the covenant relationship, for most (if not all) of the ordinances of the Gospel require that the participant make solemn promises to God and/or man. In reality, progress to eternal life consists in making and keeping a series of covenants; throughout man's existence, he has made one covenant after another, in attempting to reach the station of perfection.

That this covenant-making process antedates mortality is evident from many statements of Church leaders. President Lorenzo Snow stated that we often "forget we are working for God; we forget that we are here in order to carry out certain purposes that *we have promised the Lord that we would carry out*. It is a glorious work that we are engaged in. It is the work of the Almighty; and He has selected the men and the women whom He knows from past experience will carry out His purposes. . . ."[18] In speaking of life in the pre-earth existence, Elder Rulon S. Wells said: "The announcement was made and *a covenant made* with the children of God, even in that primeval day, when he revealed the gospel of the Lord Jesus to the children of God. Even then it was the power of God unto salvation, the new and the everlasting covenant that the Lord made with his children."[19] It seems clear, then, that even before entering mortality man made sacred promises with one another and God concerning the course to be followed on earth. The nature of some of these pre-earth covenants is discussed by Elder Orson Hyde as follows:

We all acknowledge that we had an existence before we were born into this world. How long before we took our departure from the realms of bliss to find tabernacles in flesh is unknown to us. Suffice it to say that we were sent here. We came willingly: the requirement of our Heavenly Father and our anxiety to take bodies brought us here.

Then if it be true that *we entered into a covenant with the powers celestial*, before we left our former homes, that we would come here and obey the voice of the Lord, through whomsoever he might speak, these powers are witnesses of the covenant into which we entered; and it is not impossible that we signed the articles thereof with our own hands—which articles may be retained in the archives above, to be presented to us when we rise from the dead, and be judged out of our own mouths, according to that which is written in the books.

What did we agree to before we came here? . . . The husband agreed to be a faithful servant of God, and to do his duty to all that were placed under his charge. The wife, on her part, covenants that she will be a faithful and devoted wife, and will obey her husband in the Lord in all things.

Children agreed to obey their parents, as parents agreed to obey their superiors in the kingdom of God; and parents were brought under obligation to train their children in the way they should go.[20]

The Gospel represents the "new and everlasting covenant." It is a covenant between man and God; man promises to obey laws and ordinances, while God promises that man may gain the "power of God unto salvation."[21] All other covenants and bonds and contracts are only parts of this comprehensive covenant. President Joseph Fielding Smith therefore asked: "What is the new and everlasting covenant? I regret to say that there are some members of the Church who are misled and misinformed in regard to what the new and everlasting covenant really is. The new and everlasting covenant is the sum total of all gospel covenants and obligations. . . ."[22] A modern revelation attested to this fact. The Lord said "blessed are you for receiving mine everlasting covenant, even *the fulness of my gospel*, sent forth unto the children of men, that they might have life and be made partakers of the glories which are to be revealed in the last days."[23] Inasmuch as the plan of salvation is called the Gospel of Jesus Christ, Jesus is known as the Mediator of the New Covenant,[24] or the one through whom the blessings of the Gospel are given to man. In serving as an instrument in restoring the true Church, Joseph Smith was therefore called to bring about a "renewal of the everlasting covenant."[25]

Baptism is the initial covenant one makes in mortality. This ordinance represents a spiritual rebirth and an entrance into the Church and Kingdom of God. The nature of the covenant relationship is best illustrated by Alma's words at the waters of Mormon:

> . . . Behold, here are the waters of Mormon (for thus were they called) and now, as ye are desirous to come into the fold of God, and to be called his people, and are willing to bear one another's burdens, that they may be light;
>
> Yea, and are willing to mourn with those that mourn; yea, and comfort those that stand in need of comfort, and to stand as witnesses of God at all times and in all things, and in all places that ye may be in, even until death, that ye may be redeemed of God, and be numbered with those of the first resurrection, that ye may have eternal life—
>
> Now I say unto you, if this be the desire of your hearts, what have you against being baptized in the name of the Lord, as a witness before him that *ye have entered into a covenant with him,* that ye will serve him and keep his commandments, that he may pour out his Spirit more abundantly upon you?[26]

One aspect of the covenant of baptism includes those things man promises as a new member of the Church. These include: (1) coming into the fold of God and being called His people, (2) bearing one another's burdens, (3) mourning with those that mourn, and offering comfort where needed. (4) standing as witnesses of God at all times, and (5) serving God and keeping His commandments. The Lord's part of the covenant includes the promised blessings to those who keep their end of the agreement: (1) man may be the redeemed of God, or, in other words, the powers of the Atonement may be applied in his behalf, (2) man may be raised in the first resurrection or the resurrection of the just, (3) man may eventually receive eternal life, the greatest of all the gifts of God, and (4) the Lord will pour out His Spirit abundantly upon the baptismal candidate, thus allowing him to walk in the light of the Lord. Baptism, one of the most far-reaching covenants, is the doorway to the path that leads to eternal life.

By far one of the most sacred yet ill-understood and little appreciated covenants is the Sacrament of the Lord's Supper. Latter-day Saints usually partake of the sacrament at least once each Sunday, and more often than not fail to grasp the solemn meaning and significance of this holy ordinance. Elder Melvin J. Ballard spoke to this subject as follows:

> I appreciate, I believe, my brethren and sisters, to some extent, the sacredness of the *covenant which we, as members of the Church, enter into when we partake of the sacred emblems*. I realize that each time we partake of these emblems, we manifest before the Father that we do remember his Son, and by the act of partaking of the bread and the cup, we make a solemn covenant that we do take upon us the name of our Redeemer, and that we do, further, make a pledge and an agreement by that act that we will keep his commandments.[27]

Though it is true that many Saints do try to ponder upon the life, mission, and Atonement of the Savior during the Sacrament Service, how many realize that by partaking they are, in very deed, covenanting with the Lord in a most holy manner? President McKay asked the question: "Do we always stop to think, on that sacred Sabbath day when we meet together to partake of the Sacrament, that we 'witness', promise, obligate ourselves, in the presence of one another, and in the presence of God, that we will do certain things?"[28] If seen in its true light, the sacrament becomes a time in which one may have a spiritual feast, a time when one may draw nearer the Almighty. For one thing, if approached properly, in the spirit of humility and meekness, this solemn occasion may be a time for remission of sins and spiritual enlightenment. Elder Ballard explained:

> If there is a feeling in our hearts that we are sorry for what we have done; if there is a feeling in our souls that we would like to be forgiven, then the method to obtain forgiveness is not through rebaptism, it is not to make confession to man, but it is to repent of our sins, go to those against whom we have sinned or transgressed and obtain their

forgiveness, and then repair to the Sacrament table where, if we have sincerely repented and put ourselves in proper condition, *we shall be forgiven, and spiritual healing will come to our souls.* It will really enter into our being.[29]

As man keeps his part of the agreement (as specified in the Sacramental prayers), God will bless him richly, such that he and the faithful "may always have his Spirit to be with them."[30]

The higher ordinances of the Priesthood received in the temples of God, including the endowment and eternal marriage ceremony, constitute the most beautiful and all-encompassing of covenants within the Gospel of Christ. The word "endowment" is almost onomatopoetic in its nature, suggesting in its very sound the process of enrichment and enlightenment. The endowment consists of a series of covenants and promises which, when complied with, enable the worthy son or daughter of Deity to "walk back to the presence of the Father, passing the angels who stand as sentinels, being enabled to give them the key words, the signs and tokens, pertaining to the Holy Priesthood, and gain ... eternal exaltation. ..."[31] The Prophet Joseph therefore taught the brethren that "you need an endowment ... in order that you may be prepared and able to overcome all things."[32] President Joseph F. Smith spoke generally concerning some of the covenants entered into in the House of the Lord:

> We entered into covenants with the Lord that we will keep ourselves pure and unspotted from the world. We have agreed before God, angels and witnesses, in sacred places, that we will not commit adultery, will not lie, that we will not steal or bear false witness against our neighbor, or take advantage of the weak, that we will help and sustain our fellow men in the right. ... We cannot neglect, slight, or depart from the spirit, meaning, intent and purpose of these covenants and agreements that we have entered into with our Father in heaven, without shearing ourselves of our glory, strength, right and title to His blessings and to the gifts and manifestations of His Spirit.[33]

Eternal marriage is a new and everlasting covenant, and is the basis of the Divine Patriarchal Order. The covenant relationship exists between husband, wife, and the Master. The woman agrees to abide by the law of her husband, or to respect his word as a definitive statement of truth, always keeping in mind that the Priesthood is authority to speak in the name of the Lord.[34] The man agrees to abide by the law of God, and to so live that the works of heaven might be readily manifest. Man and wife agree to multiply and replenish the earth, that the promises of Abraham might be fulfilled. They further consent to "raise up seed unto Christ," or to be the means by which spiritual powers and endowments may bless their posterity.[35] The Lord promises to the faithful couple the gift of *eternal lives* or the right to an innumerable posterity through eternity. In addition, all things are theirs, including kingdoms, thrones, principalities, powers and dominions.[36] President Brigham Young commented on the magnitude and infinite scope of eternal marriage:

> . . . the whole subject of the marriage relation is not in my reach, nor in any other man's reach on this earth. It is without beginning of days or end of years; it is a hard matter to reach. We can tell some things with regard to it; it lays the foundation for worlds, for angels, and for the Gods; for intelligent beings to be crowned with glory, immortality and eternal lives. In fact, it is the thread which runs from the beginning to the end of the holy Gospel of salvation—of the Gospel of the Son of God; it is from eternity to eternity.[37]

President Joseph Fielding Smith made the plea to all Latter-day Saint fathers and mothers to "impress upon their children that in no other way than by honoring the covenants of God, among which the covenant of eternal marriage is one of the greatest and most mandatory, can they obtain the blessings of eternal lives."[38]

Latter-day Saints are under the obligation to keep sacred and remember all of the covenants which lead to salvation. By pondering upon them and recommitting oneself to the path of obedience, it is possible periodically to *renew* these covenants. One important time to renew covenants is during the sacramental service; one should meditate carefully on the seriousness of all covenants, and should evaluate successes and failures. And, as Elder Ballard pointed out earlier, forgiveness for failures will come, if the heart is prepared properly for the reception of the sacred emblems. President David O. McKay states simply that "it is good to meet together and especially to renew our covenants with God in the sacrament of the Lord's Supper."[39] Similarly, Elder Ballard said: "I need the Sacrament. *I need to renew my covenant every week.* I need the blessing that comes with and through it."[40] The best way to renew covenants made in the House of the Lord is through regular temple attendance, where possible. Only as one enters the holy sanctuaries frequently (to perform vicarious work), and listens anew to the nature of the endowment ceremonies, may he come to appreciate and understand the mysteries of Godliness contained therein, and rekindle the flame of dedication to sacred principles.

THE OATH AND COVENANT
OF THE PRIESTHOOD

To this point we have discussed some of the covenants that must be made and entered into in order to attain salvation in the Celestial Kingdom. There is one final covenant to be discussed, one which involves all holders of the

Melchizedek Priesthood. The nature of this covenant is described in a great revelation on Priesthood given in September of 1832. After discussing some of the operations of the Aaronic and Melchizedek Orders of the Priesthood, the word of the Lord continues:

> For whoso is faithful unto the obtaining these two priesthoods of which I have spoken, and the magnifying their calling, are sanctified by the Spirit unto the renewing of their bodies.
>
> They become the sons of Moses and of Aaron and the seed of Abraham, and the church and kingdom, and the elect of God.
>
> And also all they who receive this priesthood receive me, saith the Lord; For he that receiveth my servants receiveth me;
>
> And he that receiveth my Father receiveth my Father's kingdom; therefore all that my Father hath shall be given unto him.
>
> And this is according to the oath and covenant which belongeth to the priesthood.
>
> Therefore, all those who receive the priesthood receive this oath and covenant of my Father, which he cannot break, neither can it be moved.
>
> But whoso breaketh this covenant after he hath received it, and altogether turneth therefrom, shall not have forgiveness of sins in this world nor in the world to come.
>
> And wo unto all those who come not unto this priesthood which ye have received, which I now confirm upon you who are present this day, by mine own voice out of the heavens; and even I have given the heavenly hosts and mine angels charge concerning you.
>
> And I now give unto you a commandment to beware concerning yourselves, to give diligent heed to the words of eternal life.
>
> For you shall live by every word that proceedeth forth from the mouth of God.[41]

The *Oath* which accompanies the reception of the Priesthood is an oath that God swears unto man. Just as the Father swore that the Beloved Son should be a priest forever (Psalms 110:4), so also does God swear with an oath that every Priesthood holder that keeps his end of the two-way promise (the covenant) shall receive incomprehensible blessings.[42] The *Covenant* which belongs to the Priesthood consists of (1) those things man promises to do, and (2) those blessings God promises to the faithful Priesthood bearer. Man covenants to: (1) obtain the Priesthood, (2) magnify callings in the Priesthood, (3) receive the Lord's servants, (4) beware concerning himself, (5) give diligent heed to the words of eternal life, and (6) live by every word of God. On the other hand, God promises that man may: (1) be sanctified, even to the renewing of his body, (2) become a son of Moses and of Aaron, (3) become the seed of Abraham, (4) be introduced into the church and kingdom of God, (5) become the elect of God, (6) receive the Lord Jesus Christ, (7) receive the Eternal Father, and (8) receive all that the Father hath.

Speaking of the Oath and Covenant of the Priesthood, Elder Ezra Taft Benson said: "Now this covenant is between our Heavenly Father and those of us who bear the priesthood. We promise when we receive it to be true and faithful, to honor the priesthood and magnify it. The Lord promises in return the richest blessings of eternity."[43] More specifically, Joseph Smith taught that only those who receive the Melchizedek Priesthood receive this powerful covenant. In speaking of the different orders of the Priesthood, the Prophet stated that the Levitical Order was *made without an oath; but the Priesthood of Melchizedek is by an oath and covenant.*"[44] Similarly, Paul, the Apostle stated that those who received the Higher Priesthood received "the oath," while the Lesser Order had no such oath accompanying its reception.[45] In essence, one purpose of the Aaronic Priesthood is to bring man to the point of maturity where he may comprehend and appreciate the seriousness of the Oath and Covenant.

Inasmuch as the Father is a God of truth and cannot lie, He cannot make covenants that He will not honor. President Nathan Eldon Tanner said simply "... that is the only thing I know the Lord cannot do, is break a covenant that he has made with his people; and when he says, 'All that I have is thine,' I would like to know, my brethren, what more we could ask for; and all we need to do is to keep the commandments and magnify our priesthood."[46] Although it is impossible for God to break His covenant, yet man may fail to keep his part of the agreement. The Lord therefore spoke of such by stating that those who fail to keep the covenant, and altogether turn from the Priesthood, shall not be granted repentance. President Wilford Woodruff spoke as follows: "Any man who receives this priesthood and tastes of the word of God, and of the powers of the world to come—any man that turns away from these things ... shall not, in accordance with the revelations of the Lord to Joseph Smith, 'have forgiveness of sins in this world nor in the world to come.'"[47] Speaking of the nature and severity of the punishment, Joseph Fielding Smith asked: "Is it not fair that the punishment for violation of that covenant, and the trampling of that priesthood under our feet, should bring a punishment, on the one hand, as severe as the reward will be glorious on the other?"[48]

Though the student of the scriptures must agree as to the seriousness of such an offense, yet one cannot help but notice the similarity of the promised punishment of the covenant-breaker to the awful fate of the Sons of Perdition.[49] The question therefore arises: Are those who do not honor the Priesthood liable to become Sons of Perdition? For an answer, we turn to a statement by Joseph Fielding Smith:

Now when a man makes a covenant that he will receive the priesthood and magnify it, and then he violates that covenant, "and altogether turneth therefrom"—there is a chance to repent if he does not altogether turn therefrom—then there is no "forgiveness of sins in this world nor in the world to come." This does *not* mean that man is going to become a son of perdition, but the meaning is that *he will never again have the opportunity of exercising the priesthood and receiving exaltation.* That is where his forgiveness ends. He will not again have the priesthood conferred upon him, because he has trampled it under his feet; but as far as other things are concerned, he may be forgiven.[50]

If one ponders carefully the nature of this covenant and especially the fate of those who do not keep their pledge, he is almost prone to say within himself, "If this matter is so serious, maybe I would be better off if I never received the Melchizedek Priesthood; at least I would not have as far to fall if I did not magnify my callings!"

Elder Marion G. Romney explained how he entertained similar feelings at one time:

> When I first began to seriously think about this statement [D&C 84:41], I wondered if it would not have been better for me never to have received the priesthood, if failing to magnify my callings in it would mean I would never receive forgiveness in this world nor in the world to come. As I pondered over this and the next verse, which reads, "And wo unto all those who come not unto this priesthood" (D&C 84:42), I finally came to the conclusion that I was on the horns of a dilemma—that my only hope was to receive the priesthood and magnify my callings in it.[51]

The promised blessings to those who abide this covenant are infinite in scope. Joseph Smith's Inspired Revision of Genesis gives some added insights as to the nature of these blessings, as understood by the ancients. Speaking of Melchizedek, the record states that "He was ordained an high priest after the order of the *covenant* which God made with Enoch. For God having sworn unto Enoch and unto his seed with an *oath* by himself; that every one being ordained after this order and calling should have power, by faith, to break mountains, to divide the seas, to dry up waters, to turn them out of their course; to put at defiance the armies of nations, to divide the earth, to break every band, to stand in the presence of God."[52] Referring to modern revelation and the few lines of the 84th Section of the *Doctrine and Covenants* which deal with the Oath and Covenant, Wilford Woodruff asked: "Who in the name of the Lord can apprehend such language as this? Who can comprehend that, by obeying the celestial law, all that our Father has shall be given unto us—exaltations, thrones, principalities, power, dominion—who can comprehend it? Nevertheless it is here stated."[53] President Woodruff said on a later occasion: "Now I sometimes ask myself the question, Do we comprehend these things? Do we comprehend that if we abide the laws of the priesthood we shall become the heirs of God and joint-heirs with Jesus Christ? I realize that our eyes have not seen, our ears have not heard, neither hath it entered into our hearts to conceive the glory that is in store for the faithful."[54] The splendor and beauty of such things are only to be approached through the mediation of the Holy Spirit, for only as the mind is renovated and enlivened may man even draw near to an understanding of such unspeakable things.

Can any human mind conceive of the immeasurable extent of the glory here promised—the immeasurable extent of exaltation here offered unto all those who receive the priesthood of the Son of God, and who magnify it? It is impossible for mortal man to have the least conception even when his mind is enlightened by the Spirit of God— that is, the least conception compared with the immeasurable extent of the glory that is here promised. *We can have some conception of it, we can have some fortaste of it, when we receive the Spirit of God, when it rests down upon us in power.*[55]

OATH AND COVENANT OF THE PRIESTHOOD

D&C 84:33–44

OATH: A solemn declaration by God that if man will abide by the Covenant of the Priesthood he shall eventually attain unto a fulness of Celestial glory.

COVENANT:

Man Promises
1. Obtain the Priesthood
2. Magnify callings in the Priesthood
3. Receive the Lord's servants
4. Beware concerning himself
5. Give diligent heed to the words of eternal life
6. Live by every word of God

God Promises
1. Sanctify man to the renewal of the body
2. Man to become son of Moses and Aaron
3. Man to become seed of Abraham
4. Man to be introduced into church and kingdom of God
5. Man to become the elect of God
6. Man to receive Jesus Christ
7. Man to receive the Eternal Father
8. Man to receive all the Father hath

The blessings promised to the faithful Priesthood bearer in the Oath and Covenant parallel those given in the 76th Section of the *Doctrine and Covenants* to the candidates for Celestial Glory. Marion G. Romney said in speaking of those who magnify their callings, "It is of such—that is, those who receive the priesthood and magnify it—so I believe, of whom the following was written: They are they unto whose hands the Father has given all things—They are they who are priests and kings, who have received of his fulness, and of his glory; And are priests of the Most High, after the order of . . . the Only Begotten Son. Wherefore, as it is written, they are gods, even the sons of God."[56] Finally, President Joseph Fielding Smith stated the following:

> In other revelations, you know, the Lord says: "And they who overcome by faith, and are sealed by the Holy Spirit of Promise. . . . They are they into whose hands the Father has given all things— . . . they are gods, even the sons of God."
>
> Here is a definite, positive statement that every man who receives the priesthood receives it with an oath and covenant that he will magnify his calling, that he will be faithful and true, and *his reward will be to become a son of God and joint-heir with Jesus Christ in having the fulness of the Father's kingdom.* No greater blessing could be offered.[57]

SUMMARY

1. In former dispensations, particularly the Mosaic, oaths served as solemn attestations of statements or promises.

2. In the Sermon on the Mount, Christ called for an end to the swearing of oaths by man; He declared that a man's word was to be his bond.

3. Covenants are sacred promises between two or more persons. Man is under obligation to (1) give much forethought to the nature of all covenants entered into, and (2) do all within his power to keep covenants made.

4. From the pre-mortal life to the resurrection, man is constantly in the process of making covenants with God and man.

5. The Gospel represents the New and Everlasting Covenant; all other covenants and bonds are only parts of this comprehensive covenant.

6. Each man that receives the Melchizedek Priesthood does so with an Oath and Covenant. The Oath is a solemn declaration on the part of Deity that if man will abide by the Covenant of the

Priesthood, he will eventually receive a fulness of Celestial glory. The Covenant consists of (1) those things man promises God, and (2) the blessings God promises the faithful Priesthood holder. Man promises to:

A. Obtain the Priesthood
B. Magnify callings in the Priesthood
C. Receive the Lord's servants
D. Beware concerning himself
E. Give diligent heed to the words of eternal life
F. Live by every word of God

God promises that man may:

A. Be sanctified, even to the renewing of his body
B. Become the son of Moses and of Aaron
C. Become the seed of Abraham
D. Be introduced into the church and kingdom of God
E. Become the elect of God
F. Receive the Lord Jesus Christ
G. Receive the Eternal Father
H. Receive all that the Father hath

7. Those who fail to magnify their callings in the Priesthood and altogether turn from it shall not have the privilege of exercising the Priesthood in the future; they cannot achieve exaltation.

8. Only as man has his mind enlightened by the Spirit of God may he even begin to comprehend the unspeakable blessings that await the true and faithful.

OBTAINING THE PRIESTHOOD

IN DISCUSSING MAN'S OBLIGATIONS to God in the Oath and Covenant, we frequently pass over lightly the fact that man must first *obtain* the Priesthood before he is able to magnify callings in it. Obtaining the Priesthood is no simple matter. As with most facets of the Restored Gospel, an understanding of how and why a particular man receives the Priesthood is beyond the comprehension of the student of the scriptures, if worthiness in mortality is the only consideration. To fully appreciate the reception of Priesthood powers in this life, we must turn our sights to the period of existence antedating the mortal sphere.

WORLDS WITHOUT END

As was pointed out in Chapter I, the Melchizedek Priesthood is everlasting and eternal; it had no beginning, nor will it have an end. For eons of time, glorified and perfected beings, have been the means of bringing life, redemption, and exaltation to myriads of souls. The work of the Gods is to "bring to pass the immortality and eternal life of man,"[1] and it has been so forever. Long before our world came rolling into existence, billions of similar creations had passed away and risen to the state of celestial orbs. Undoubtedly we were allowed to witness much of the creation and ultimate glorification of earths like that of our own—we longed and sighed for the day to come when our state of progression would be such as to merit mortality. President John Taylor, while writing to the sisters of the Church, spoke in poetic language: "Knowest thou not that eternities ago thy spirit, pure and holy, dwelt in thy Heavenly Father's bosom, and in His presence, and with thy mother, one of the queens of heaven, surrounded by thy brother and sister spirits in the spirit world, among the Gods? That as thy spirit beheld the scenes transpiring there, and thou grewest in intelligence, *thou sawest worlds upon worlds organized and peopled with thy kindred spirits who took upon them tabernacles, died, were resurrected, and received their exaltation on the redeemed worlds they once dwelt upon.*" President Taylor then reminded the sisters that they had been extremely "willing and anxious to imitate them, waiting and desirous to obtain a body, a resurrection and exaltation also ..."[2] All of these wonders were brought about through the fulness of Priesthood powers which center in God. George Q. Cannon remarked:

Shall I startle you when I say that our Father himself controls the universe and occupies His exalted station because of the Priesthood? Whether it is startling or not, it is nevertheless true. Our Eternal Father is the creator of all things through the power of the everlasting Priesthood—that Priesthood which has been bestowed upon and exercised by the servants of God in our day.[3]

Jehovah, the pre-earth Christ, while speaking in the name of the Father (by divine investiture of authority[4]), explained to Moses that "worlds without number have I created; and I also created them for mine own purpose; and *by the Son I created them, which is mine Only Begotten.*"[5] John the Beloved also spoke of Christ's powers before His (Christ's) entrance into mortality; "In the beginning was the Word, and the Word was with God, and *the Word was God. The same was in the beginning with God. All things were made by him:* and without him was not anything made that was made. He was in the world and *the world was made by him,* and the world knew him not."[6] The Apostle Paul gave a similar account of Christ's works when he spoke of the Master as having been "appointed heir of all things, *by whom he* [the Father] *made the worlds.*"[7] Finally, in this dispensation, Joseph Smith and Sidney Rigdon bore their testimonies of the living reality of Jesus, stating that "by him and through him, and of him, *the worlds are and were created.* . . ."[8] One question that arises at this point concerns the evident nature of Jesus Christ's power before His birth on the earth; specifically, how did He exercise Godhood while yet in a spirit state? Elder Orson Pratt gave a beautiful explanation :

Although Paul informs us that Jesus was called and made a High Priest centuries after the law was given, yet there is no doubt that *he was considered in the mind of his Father the same as a High Priest before the foundation of the world;* and that by *virtue of the Priesthood which he would, in a future age, receive, he could organize worlds and show forth almighty power.* God, by his foreknowledge, saw that his Son would keep all his commands, and determined, at a certain time, to call and consecrate him a High Priest; He determined, also that by virtue of that future consecration to the Priesthood, he should, thousands of years beforehand, have power to create worlds and govern them, the same as if he had already received the consecration. All his marvelous acts and doings, therefore, prior to his consecration, were just as much the results of the authority of the Priesthood as those performed by him since that time.[9]

THE COUNCILS IN HEAVEN

No man knows the endless ages that preceded our entrance into the world of flesh and bones. Without question, most of this time was spent in preparation for now, the period of mortality which is often abused. What a waste it is to barter away one's chances for eternal happiness by failing to master self in this short 70 or 80 years! Yet, such is the case too frequently.

The first glimpse we get into a specific preparation for earth-life is what is called in scripture "The Council of the Gods." It was at this council, held near unto the residence of Elohim, that plans were drawn up and final decisions made regarding the creation and redemption of this world and others. Joseph Smith said: "In the beginning, the head of the Gods called a *Council of the Gods;* and they came together and concocted a plan to create the world and people it:"[10] Regarding the circumstances of this meeting, Orson F. Whitney wrote:

> In solemn council sat the Gods;
>   From Kolob's height supreme,
> Celestial light blazed forth afar
>   O'er countless kokaubeam;
> And faintest tinge, the fiery fringe
>   Of that resplendent day.
> Luminated the dark abysmal realm
>   Where earth in chaos lay.[11]

Joseph Smith explained that "the grand councilors sat at the head in yonder heavens and contemplated the creation of the worlds which were created at the time."[12] We are uncertain as to specific names and/or personalities in attendance at this great planning session, though it is highly probable that Elohim and Jehovah were among those present. It was possibly this same body of Priesthood involved in the subsequent creation of the earth. Abraham records that God spoke and said: "Let us go down." The account continues: "And they went down at the beginning, and they, that is *the Gods,* organized and formed the heavens and the earth."[13]

Some time before coming to earth it appears from scripture that all of the spirit children of Elohim met in a great general conference to consider the plans to be followed in peopling the newly created earth(s), and providing a program whereby all could possibly return to the Celestial home as glorified and perfected souls. In Apostle Orson F. Whitney's "Elias: An Epic of the Ages," we gain many insights into the circumstances under which the Father's plan[14] was presented, and also the nature of the plan by which Lucifer plotted to rob man of his agency :

> "Father!" the voice like music fell,
>   Clear as the murmuring flow

Of mountain streamlet trickling down
From heights of virgin snow.
"Father," it said, "since one must die,
Thy children to redeem
From spheres all formless now and void.
Where pulsing life shall teem;

"And mighty Michael foremost fall
That mortal man may be;
And chosen savior Thou must send,
Lo, here am I—send me!
I ask, I seek no recompense,
Save that which then were mine;
Mine be the willing sacrifice,
The endless glory Thine!

"Give me to lead to this lorn world,
When wandered from the fold,
Twelve legions of the noble ones
That now Thy face behold;
Tried souls, 'mid untried spirits found,
That captained these may be,
And crowned the dispensations all
With powers of Deity.

"Who blameless bide the spirit state,
Clothe them in mortal clay,
The stepping-stone to glories all,
If man will God obey,
Believing where he cannot see,
Til he again shall know,
And answer give, reward receive,
For deeds done below.

"The love that hath redeemed all worlds
All worlds must still redeem;
But mercy cannot justice rob
Or where were Elohim?
Freedom—man's faith, man's work God's grace—
Must span the great gulf o'er,
Life death, the guerdon or to doom,

Rejoice we or deplore."

Still rang that voice, when sudden rose
Aloft a towering form,
Proudly erect as lowering peak
'Lumed by the gathering storm;
A presence bright and beautiful,
With eye of flashing fire
A lip whose haughty curl bespoke,
A sense of inward ire.
"Send me!"—coiled 'neath his courtly smile
A scarce concealed disdain
"And none shall hence from heaven to earth,
That shall not rise again.
My saving plan exception scorns.
Man's will?—Nay, mine alone.
As recompense, I claim the right
To sit on yonder Throne!"

Ceased Lucifer. The breathless hush
Resumed and denser grew.
All eyes were turned; the general gaze
One common magnet drew.
A moment there was solemn pause—
Listened eternity.
While rolled from lips omnipotent
The Father's firm decree:

"Jehovah, thou my Messenger!
Son Ahman, thee I send;
And one shall go thy face before,
While twelve thy steps attend.
And many more on that far shore
The pathway shall prepare,
That I, the first, the last may come,
And earth may glory share.

"After and ere thy going down.
An army shall descend
The host of God, and house of him
Whom I have named my friend.

Through him, upon Idumea
Shall come all life to leaven,
The guileless ones, the sovereign sons,
Throned on the heights of heaven.

"Go forth, thou chosen of the Gods,
Whose strength shall in thee dwell!
Go down betime and rescue earth.
Dethroning death and hell.
On thee alone man's fate depends,
The fate of beings all.
Thou shalt not fail, though thou art free
Free, but too great to fall.

"By arm divine, both mine and thine,
The lost thou shalt restore,
And man redeemed, with God shall be,
As God forevermore.
Return, and to the parent fold
This wandering planet bring
And earth shall hail thee conqueror,
And heaven proclaim thee King."
'Twas done. From congregation vast,
Tumultuous murmurs rose;
Waves of conflicting sound, as when
Two meeting seas oppose.
'Twas finished. But the heavens wept,
And still their annals tell
How one was choice of Elohim
O'er one who fighting fell.[15]

It was following this great conference and subsequent War in Heaven that much specific organization and planning were undertaken relative to mortality; the Prophet Joseph thus spoke of a "first organization" in heaven.[16] It was possibly at this stage of the pre-mortal existence that covenants were made and entered into regarding future roles on earth. Lorenzo Snow spoke of the covenants made to God: "We are here in order to carry out certain purposes that we have promised the Lord that we would carry out."[17] John Taylor wrote of a sister making "a covenant with one of thy kindred spirits to be thy guardian angel while in mortality, and also with two others, male and female spirits, that thou wouldst come and take a tabernacle through their lineage, and become one of their offspring. You also chose a kindred spirit whom you loved in the spirit world (and who had permission to come to this planet and take a tabernacle), to be your head, stay, husband, and protector on the earth and to exalt you in eternal worlds. *All these were arranged, likewise the spirits who should tabernacle through your lineage.*"[18] There is some indication that arrangements were made as to *when*, as well as *where* men and women would tabernacle the flesh.

> God that made the world and all things therein, seeing that he is Lord of heaven and earth, dwelleth not in temples made with hands;
>
> Neither is worshipped with men's hands, as though he needed any thing, seeing he giveth to all life, and breath, and all things;
>
> And hath made of one blood all nations of men for to dwell on the face of the earth, and *hath determined the times before appointed, and the bounds of their habitation. . . .*[19]

President Wilford Woodruff spoke of the Saints as "a handful of people chosen out of some twelve or fourteen hundred millions of people; and my faith in regard to this matter is that *before we were born . . . we were chosen to come forth in this day and generation* and do the work which God has designed should be done."[20]

ELECTION

The doctrine of election has its basis in the organizational councils in the pre-earth existence. Brigham Young and Willard Richards taught that "God has chosen or elected certain individuals to certain blessings, or to the performance of certain works. . . ."[21] There is much evidence, for example, to indicate that certain individuals were called or elected to come to earth through certain blood lines, as a consequence of faithfulness in pre-mortal life. Elder Parley P. Pratt explained:

> We read much in the Bible in relation to a choice or *election*, on the part of Deity, towards intelligences in His government on earth, whereby some were chosen to fill stations very different from others. And this election not only affected the individuals thus chosen, but their posterity for long generations, or even forever.
>
> It may be enquired where this election first originated, and upon what principle a just and impartial God exercises the elective franchise. We will go back to the earliest knowledge we have of the existence of intelligences.
>
> Among the intelligences that existed in the beginning, some were more intelligent than others, or, in other words, more noble; and God said to Abraham, "These I will make my rulers!" God said unto Abraham, "Thou art one of them; thou wast chosen before thou wast born."

... when He [God] speaks of nobility, He simply means an election made, and an office or a title conferred, on the principle of superiority of intellect, or nobleness of action, or of capacity to act. And *when this election, with its titles, dignities, and estates, includes the unborn posterity of a chosen man,* as in the case of Abraham, Isaac, and Jacob, *it is with a view of the noble spirits of the eternal world coming through their lineage,* and being taught in the commandments of God. Hence the Prophets, Kings, Priests, Patriarchs, Apostles, and even Jesus Christ, were included in the election of Abraham, and of his seed, as manifested to him in an eternal covenant.[22]

President Harold B. Lee also spoke concerning this election of grace: "It would seem very clear ... that those born to the lineage of Jacob ... were born into the most illustrious lineage of any of those who came upon the earth as mortal beings. All these rewards were seemingly promised, or foreordained before the world was. Surely these matters must have been determined by the kind of lives we had lived in the premortal spirit world."[23] In continuing his remarks, President Lee said:

... may I ask each of you again the question, "Who are you?" You are all the sons and daughters of God. Your spirits were created and lived as organized intelligences before the world was. You have been blessed to have a physical body because of your obedience to certain commandments in that premortal state. You are now born into a family to which you have come, into the nations through which you have come, as a reward for the kind of lives you lived before you came here.[24]

It is clear, then, that those who came through the Abrahamic lineage were called and elected to do so, and will be the means of blessing the world. This concept was taught to the Saints in the early history of the Church; they were informed that "God elected or chose the children of Israel to be His peculiar people, and to them belong the covenants and promises, and the blessings received by the Gentiles come through the covenants to Abraham and his seed ... and thus the house of Israel became the ministers of salvation to the Gentiles; and this is what the house of Israel was elected unto, not only their own salvation, but through them salvation to all others...."[25]

It is through those called and elected in the organizational councils that the Priesthood is to be given, should they prove worthy on earth. One of the great promises of God to Abraham was that the Priesthood would continue in his seed throughout eternity.[26] Parley P. Pratt continued his discourse on the doctrine of election in the flesh:

In this peculiar lineage, and in no other, should all the nations be blessed. From the days of Abraham until now, if the people of any country, age or nation, have been blessed with the blessings peculiar to the everlasting covenant of the Gospel, its sealing powers, Priesthood, and ordinances, it has been through the ministry of that lineage, and the keys of Priesthood held by the lawful heirs according to the flesh . . . no man can hold the keys of Priesthood or of Apostleship, to bless or administer salvation to the nations, unless he is a literal descendant of Abraham, Isaac, and Jacob.

Knowing of the covenants and promises made to the fathers, as I now know them, and the rights of heirship to the Priesthood, as manifested in the election of God, I would never receive any man as an Apostle or a Priest, holding the keys of restoration, to bless the nations, while he claimed to be any other lineage than Israel.[27]

In a revelation given in December of 1832 to Joseph Smith the Seer, the Lord said: "Therefore, thus saith the Lord unto you, with whom the priesthood hath continued through the lineage of your fathers—For *ye are lawful heirs, according to the flesh*, and have been hid from the world with Christ in God—Therefore your life and the priesthood have remained, and must needs remain through you and your lineage. . . ."[28] Brigham Young spoke in tribute to the Prophet Joseph, and touched upon Joseph's election: "The Lord had his eye upon him and upon his father, and upon his father's father, and upon their progenitors clear back to Abraham, and from Abraham to the flood, and from the flood to Enoch, and from Enoch to Adam. *He has watched that family and that blood as it has circulated from its fountain to the birth of that man.*"[29]

Many individuals were thus called and elected to positions of prominence and authority, and many were elected to receive eternal life. But, contrary to many prevailing doctrines of unconditional election, those persons called in eternity were required to pass the tests in mortality in order to receive the promised blessings—all elections were based upon righteousness. Elder Orson Pratt, in speaking of Paul's words to Titus, said: ". . . the Apostle says 'In hope of eternal life, which God, that cannot lie, promised before the world began.' To whom did he make that promise? I contend that he made the promise of eternal life before the world began *on certain conditions*—if we would comply with the gospel of the Son of God by repenting of our sins and being faithful in keeping the commandments of God."[30] Joseph Smith said simply that "unconditional election of individuals to eternal life was not taught by the Apostles. God did elect or predestinate, that all those who would be saved, should be saved in Christ Jesus, and through obedience to the Gospel. . . ."[31]

FOREORDINATION

Whereas the doctrine of election has reference to the fact that all persons (men and women) who perform timely works and missions were chosen to perform those works in the organizational councils. Joseph Smith taught that "every *man* who has a calling to minister to the inhabitants of the world was *ordained* to that very purpose in the Grand Council of heaven before the world was."[32] Foreordination thus consists of a more specific aspect of the principle of election, in which certain men were set apart and ordained to perform various roles in the Priesthood. The scriptures plainly teach of the fore-ordination of great Priesthood leaders. Peter referred to Christ as "a lamb without blemish and without spot: who verily was *foreordained before the foundation of the world.* . . ."[33] Wilford Woodruff spoke in a similar vein of other Prophets: "The Prophet Joseph taught us that father Adam was the first man on the earth to whom God gave the keys of the everlasting priesthood. He held the keys of the presidency, and was the first man who did hold them. Noah stood next to him, he being the father of all living in his day, as Adam was in his day. *These two men were the first who received the priesthood in the eternal worlds, before the worlds were formed.*"[34] In speaking of the council of the noble and great ones. Abraham said: "And God saw these souls that they were good, and he stood in the midst of them, and he said: These I will make my rulers; for he stood among those that were spirits, and he saw that they were good; and he said unto me: Abraham, thou art one of them; *thou wast chosen before thou wast born.*"[35] To the Prophet Jeremiah the word of the Lord came: "*Before I formed thee in the belly I knew thee; and before thou camest forth out of the womb I sanctified thee, and I ordained thee a prophet unto the nations.*"[36] Joseph Smith, the Latter-day Seer, was unquestionably among the noble and great foreordained to a mighty mission in mortality. In speaking of Joseph, President George Q. Cannon said: "He, therefore, was a Prophet, Seer and Revelator before he was ordained in the flesh. Did you ever think of it? Brother Joseph Smith was a Prophet, Seer and Revelator before he ever received any Priesthood in the flesh—"[37]

Foreordination to Priesthood offices and callings is not limited to the Prophets of God. All who receive Priesthood in mortality were called to that position before the earth was formed. Joseph Fielding Smith said: "In regard to the holding of the priesthood in pre-existence, I will say that there was an organization there just as well as an organization here, and men there held authority. Men chosen to positions of trust in the spirit world held priesthood."[38] Similarly, Wilford Woodruff encouraged us to "magnify our callings, and honor this priesthood which we received before we came here. . . ."[39]

> Joseph Smith was ordained before he came here, the same as Jeremiah was. Said the Lord unto him. "Before you were begotten I knew you," etc.

So do I believe with regard to this people, so do I believe with regard to the apostles, the high priests, seventies and the elders of Israel bearing the Holy Priesthood. *I believe they were ordained before they came here*; and I believe the God of Israel has raised them up and has watched over them from their youth, has carried them through all the scenes of life both seen and unseen, and has prepared them as instruments in His hands to take this kingdom and bear it off.[40]

Perhaps the most beautiful and detailed description of the fore-ordination of Priesthood bearers was given by a *Book of Mormon* Prophet. After preaching a great discourse to the people concerning the plan of salvation and the role of the Savior in that plan, Alma continued :

And again, my brethren, I would cite your minds forward to the time when the Lord God gave these commandments unto his children; and I would that ye should remember that the Lord God ordained priests, after his holy order, which was after the order of his Son, to teach these things to the people.

And those priests were ordained after the order of his Son, in a manner that thereby the people might know in what manner to look forward to his Son for redemption.

And this is the manner after which they were ordained—being called and prepared from the foundation of the world according to the foreknowledge of God, on account of their exceeding faith and good works; in the first place being left to choose good or evil; therefore they having chosen good, and exercising exceeding great faith, are called with a holy calling, yea, with that holy calling which was prepared with, and according to, a preparatory redemption for such.

And thus they have been called to this holy calling on account of their faith, while others would reject the Spirit of God on account of the hardness of their hearts and blindness of their minds, while, if it had not been for this they might have had as great privilege as their brethren.

Or in fine, in the first place they were on the same standing with their brethren; thus this holy calling being prepared from the foundation of the world for such as would not harden their hearts, being in and through the atonement of the Only Begotten Son, who was prepared—

And thus being called by this holy calling, and ordained unto the high priesthood of the holy order of God, to teach his commandments unto the children of men, that they also might enter into his rest—

This high priesthood being after the order of his Son, which order was from the foundation of the world; or in other words, being without beginning of days or end of years, being prepared from eternity to all eternity, according to his foreknowledge of all things—

Now they were ordained after this manner—being called with a holy calling, and ordained with a holy ordinance, and taking upon them the high priesthood of the holy order, which calling, and ordinance, and high priesthood, is without beginning or end—

Thus they become high priests forever, after the order of the Son, the Only Begotten of the Father, who is without beginning of days or end of years, who is full of grace, equity and truth. And thus it is. Amen.[41]

After studying these nine verses carefully, the following points seem to take on great meaning: First, God has chosen men, and ordained them to the Priesthood after the order of His Son, to teach the people concerning the Atonement and the path back into the presence of God. These men were ordained after the order of the Son of God, because it is only to Christ that man may look for redemption and eternal life. Second, these men were called, prepared, and ordained in the pre-earth councils, according to the foreknowledge of God. This calling and ordination came because of their exceeding faith and good works in the ages preceding mortality; that is to say, these brethren indicated a faithful and valiant spirit in following the path of greatest truth, and thus exercised their agency so as to be added upon. Third, these men, called and ordained before the foundations of the earth, came to earth and were left to themselves, either to choose good or evil; they had the right to exercise agency once again. Having chosen good, and once more shown great faith, they are ordained on earth to a holy calling in the High Priesthood. Fourth, others of their brethren who were called, elected, and ordained with them in the organizational councils have come to earth, rejected the promptings of the Holy Spirit, and therefore turned away from the light of the Gospel and subsequent calling and ordination to the Priesthood in mortality. In the beginning (in the world of spirits), all of these men were on the same standing, and thus had the same opportunity for advancement and progression. But because of the power of the flesh, many did not live worthy of Priesthood and its rights. Finally, these men are ordained priests after the order of the Son of God, which calling (to the Melchizedek Priesthood) and ordinance (the laying on of hands) are eternal and most holy. They are given these rights in order that they might bless the world, and ultimately bring all the pure in heart into the rest of God, or the fulness of His glory.[42]

THE WORD OF PROPHECY

Latter-day Saints state as a policy of belief : "We believe that a man must be called of God by prophecy...."[43] The gifts of prophecy and revelation are exercised daily in the True Church, and are the means by which men and women are called to positions of responsibility in the Church; through prophecy and revelation, Priesthood leaders, Bishops, Stake Presidents, and General Authorities receive the sure knowledge as to the exact persons to be called and set apart to particular offices and positions.

The word of prophecy actually had its beginnings in the grand councils in heaven. It was here that many of the sons of God were prophesied to receive specific offices and attendant blessings in the mortal state. President John Taylor said: "There are thousands of men upon the earth today, among the Saints of God, of whom it was *decreed* before they came that they should occupy the positions they have occupied and do occupy...."[44] An important principle to realize in a consideration of the word of prophecy is that prophecy does not predestinate. The fact that many were prophesied to attain unto life eternal does not preclude the possibility that these may fall from grace in mortality; Alma testified to this particular point (Alma 13:4–5). In reality, the word of prophecy represented a glimpse of things as they *could* be, if the particular person continued in the present state of righteousness.

RECEIVING THE PRIESTHOOD IN MORTALITY

Exceeding faith and good works before coming here are not enough to enable man to act in the name of God on earth. Though it may have been decreed (prophesied) that certain men *may* attain unto transcendant blessings and rights, yet all things are dependent upon man's sensitivity to the things of the Spirit on earth. President George Q. Cannon made a most interesting observation concerning the Prophet Joseph and his foreordination: "He was ordained a Prophet, doubtless, before he came here; but that ordination did not give him the right to immerse men and women in the waters of baptism, neither did it give him the power to lay on hands for the gift of the Holy Ghost. *He had to await the authority from on high.*"[45] In speaking of man's worthiness to receive the Priesthood in mortality, Elder John A. Widtsoe explained:

> Men should be fit to receive the Priesthood. Men must prove themselves worthy by their lives to receive the Priesthood; and their advancement in the Priesthood should be determined by their lives within the Gospel fold. Fitness to receive the Priesthood is defined by the Priest Jethro, who, when advising Moses to secure helpers to administer the affairs of Israel, said, "Moreover, thou shalt provide out of all the people able men, such as fear God, men of truth, hating covetousness." That is, to receive the Priesthood, men must be able and God-fearing men of truth, hating covetousness.[46]

In addition to personal worthiness, the individual must be *willing* to serve in the Priesthood and its offices, and must be *sustained* by a vote of the people.[47] Having met these qualifications, man is ready to act in the offices to which he is called, and to represent Deity in an acceptable manner.

SUMMARY

1. Man's ordination to the Priesthood is not fully appreciated without a careful consideration of his calling and ordination in the pre-earth existence.

2. During the organizational councils before the foundations of the earth, covenants and promises and arrangements were made; it was decided as to time, place, and lineage through which men and women would come to earth.

3. The doctrine of election has reference to the fact that God has called and chosen certain individuals to the performance of certain works and the reception of certain rights and blessings.

4. According to the election in the flesh, the lineage of Abraham is the chosen of God, and is the means whereby the people of the world are blessed. It is only through Israel that the keys of the Priesthood descend.

5. In the organizational councils men were ordained to specific offices and blessings in the Priesthood.

6. Before men came to earth, the word of prophecy was exercised, insomuch that it was prophesied that certain men and women would attain unto certain callings and blessings.

7. Prophecy does not predestinate, and men may fall from grace, and from the possibilities decreed in the pre-mortal existence.

8. To be worthy and prepared to receive the Priesthood in mortality, men must be God-fearing, and should despise covetousness. In addition, they must be willing to serve in the Priesthood, and be sustained by a vote of the Church.

MAGNIFYING CALLINGS IN
THE PRIESTHOOD

UPON OBTAINING THE PRIESTHOOD, one has the responsibility to "receive" it. The word "receive" is significant here. In the case of confirmation following baptism, the new candidate for the Kingdom is instructed to "receive the Holy Ghost." This is *not* a command for the Holy Ghost to enter and dwell in the individual, but is a statement of instruction for the person to open the heart, purge the mind and body, and be sensitive enough to invite and entertain this Spirit and its influences. So it is with the Priesthood. We are nowhere given to understand that mere ordination to the Priesthood entitles one automatically to the working of miracles, the manifestations of the Spirit, or the presence of God the Father; such gifts and blessings only come as one opens his heart and mind to *receive* the Priesthood, and continues faithful in the performance of his duties.

Part of man's covenant with God regarding the Priesthood is that he will *magnify* his callings. Inasmuch as every calling that a person has or will receive is by the word of prophecy through the appointed channels, Priesthood bearers will be judged according to how they perform in every specific office and position; in a real sense, man may magnify the Priesthood only through magnifying the specific callings within it.

MEANING OF "MAGNIFY"

In one sense, to magnify is to enlarge upon or to make something grow to have greater dimensions. In the context of this discussion, to magnify a calling is to enlarge upon it, and make it become more important. For example, to magnify the calling one has as a home teacher is to make this calling one of the most important things he has under his charge; it is to treat this calling the same way, and with the same respect, that one would treat the calling of Bishop or Apostle.

To magnify is also to emphasize and accentuate details. Anyone who has looked through a magnifying instrument will note that one of the products of the magnification process is the way in which minute details of the object become more visible and apparent. One who magnifies his calling in the Priesthood will begin to understand that even a small, seemingly insignificant job to which he may have been appointed is multi-faceted and requires more time and effort to perform it effectively than previously anticipated. The Elder's Quorum President who magnifies his calling begins to realize that this responsibility goes beyond the physical and spiritual well-being of the members. He recognizes that the Elders in his quorum are beings of many needs—social, emotional, and intellectual—all of which must be met if true happiness and fulfilment is to follow.

Finally, to magnify means to hold in greater esteem or respect, and to praise highly. While serving in the Eastern part of the United States as a missionary, this writer came into direct contact with a stake president in one of the New England stakes. This man was one of the most dynamic Church leaders that I had ever met; he commanded the respect of all, simply because of his dignified and spiritual manner. He worked professionally with one of the larger insurance companies in the nation, and was extremely successful in his business dealings. After returning home from the East, I found that this man had moved with his family to the Salt Lake City area, and continued his regular employment through the Utah office. It was at a missionary reunion that I was able to renew contact with this ex-president, for the mission president asked that he speak to us concerning our spiritual lives since returning from a mission. His discourse was most inspiring, but above all things I recall one section of his remarks most vividly. He said, in essence, "Since moving to Salt Lake, my family and I have become very involved in the ward of which we are members. I have been called to serve as the Advisor to the Priests. I love my calling. It is the most important and challenging calling I have ever received. I pray that the Lord will help me to rise to the occasion, that I might perform in this appointment as He would have me." Here was a man, who only months before had served in the "prestigious" position of president of a stake. Here was a man, who a short time before had made decisions which directly influenced the lives of thousands. And here was a man who was now being asked (in the natural eyes) to condescend to the seemingly menial task of struggling with a group of head-strong teenagers. But this noble soul knew the value of truly magnifying his new calling, and the importance of treating this appointment with the greatest of respect.

Men who learn to magnify their callings in the Priesthood stand out from the crowd. President Charles W. Penrose said: "I know that men holding the Priesthood, and who magnify it and receive the spirit and power of it, are different from other men, their influence and motives are different, their feelings are different and the spirit and influences they carry with them are different."[1] According to President Penrose, then, these men are different because of (1) the purity of their motives, and (2) the spirit and influence they radiate. Men who magnify their callings are pure in their hearts, and their motives are therefore clean. Strictly speaking, they do things for the right reasons, and are less concerned with pleasing man than God. Such persons are right with themselves and right with God—there is no veneer to cover improper motivation. The Lord's promise to those who magnify their callings is that they are "sanctified by the Spirit unto the renewing of their bodies."[2] It is no wonder that this quality of person would have a positive aura and radiate the Spirit of God; persons whose eyes are single to God's glory (and none other) may receive the great blessing of being filled with the Spirit, such that eventually their "whole bodies shall be filled with light."[3]

It is through the Holy Spirit that one comes to understand the seriousness of his calling, for by the Spirit man may "know the truth of all things."[4] The Holy Ghost is a revealer, an enlightener, a teacher, a prompter, and a sanctifier. Only as the Priesthood bearer gains the companionship of this holy being will he ever be capable of magnifying callings. Simply stated, without the aid of the Holy Ghost, man cannot understand *how* to magnify his calling. President John Taylor taught that

> ... all men holding the Priesthood, who are humble and faithful and diligent and honest and true to the principles of our religion, if they seek unto God with that faith that he requires of us, he will give them wisdom under all circumstances and on all occasions, and the Holy Spirit will never fail to indicate the path they should pursue. This is the order of God in relation to these matters, that every man holding any position in the Church, through his faithfulness, shall have his Spirit commensurate to the duties devolving upon them, *to enable them to magnify their calling* to the acceptance of God and their brethren.[5]

As the humble man attempts to perform his task as the Master would have it done, this man will be added upon. Though it is true that God uses the weak and simple to bring about His purposes, yet it is also true that the Almighty will so endow men that they may perform commensurate with their righteous desires. George Q. Cannon made a statement in this regard: "God has shown that however weak and imperfect a man may be, if he will seek to magnify that Priesthood, God will honor and sustain him."[6] Similarly, Heber C. Kimball taught that the "Priesthood is a gift from the Almighty, and He has placed a portion of it upon me to honor, and *if I honor that calling, that Priesthood will honor me, it will magnify me before God, and before the world*."[7] President Kimball made it clear that man may be magnified or endowed with greater spiritual powers, if he will but honor and magnify his callings in the Priesthood. Here again, the man's heart must be in the right place. He must not acquire a particular office in order to be elevated in the eyes of men, for such is sin. John Taylor warned very simply that "we must seek to magnify our offices, and not expect our offices to magnify us."[8] Often this is a difficult lesson to learn, for man's eye is not always single to the proper glory. It is because of this type of spiritual myopia that many fall. Man must honor the Priesthood, or instead of being the means of exalting him, this power will be the means by which he will be damned. A modern revelation therefore declared: "For of him unto whom much is given much is required; and he who sins against the greater light shall receive the greater condemnation."[9]

LEARNING THE DUTY

Every person called to a position in the Church is under the obligation to learn of every facet of that particular office, and to be diligent in the performance of the duty. A revelation on Priesthood given in 1835 ended with the following significant verses:

Wherefore, now *let every man learn his duty,* and act in the office in which he is appointed, in all diligence.

He that is slothful shall not be counted worthy to stand, and *he that learns not his duty and shows himself not approved shall not be counted worthy to stand.*[10]

The Lord's instructions are clear: every man is to learn his duty, and act in the office to which he has been appointed. Each man is to "stand in his own office, and labor in his own calling."[11] and not attempt to labor in another's office. He who performs his work in a slothful manner, or he who learns not his duty well enough to perform effectively, shall not have the privilege of standing hereafter among those who exercise Priesthood. In speaking specifically of these verses, President Joseph Fielding Smith said:

This means that the man who accepts the priesthood also accepts the responsibilities that go with it. He promises that he will give service and make himself approved. If he breaks this covenant—for it is a covenant—then he will have to stand among those who do not exercise priesthood: *he cannot stand among those who are approved.* Let every man who holds the priesthood understand that he cannot enter into exaltation without the priesthood. If he refuses to use that priesthood when it is conferred upon him, he will not be found worthy to hold it in that day when men are rewarded according to their works.[12]

No man is capable of magnifying his calling unless he fully understands his calling. Certainly this places responsibility upon the Priesthood leader who calls one to an office or position to explain (1) what the job is, (2) what is expected of the one called, (3) how to best perform the task, and (4) where the individual may learn the details of the calling. The person then has the responsibility to go to and learn all that he can *before* he goes about doing the job; as the old adage goes, a little bit of knowledge is dangerous. John Taylor spoke of the importance of every Saint understanding his true role in the Church: "The growth of the

Church and the changes continually taking place render it necessary that this work to which we have been called be attended to. It is very desirable and necessary, too, that *every man should understand his true position in the Church;* that he may the better magnify his calling, and attend to every duty devolving upon him."[13]

Many times Priesthood bearers get bogged down in the mechanical role of their offices, and lose the vision necessary to maintain effectiveness. Often men cannot understand how their simple tasks can possibly aid in the establishment of Zion, or in building the Kingdom of God on earth. To such persons, the word of the Lord in modem revelation is especially meaningful: "Wherefore, be not weary in well-doing, for ye are laying the foundation of a great work. And *out of small things proceedeth that which is great.*"[14] One who magnifies his calling and seeks to learn his duty will receive the comforting assurance that no work is small in the sight of God; miracles can be wrought by the steady and faithful performance of simple tasks. This is perhaps what it means to gain the spirit of one's calling. Charles W. Penrose made the following remarks:

> . . . every man called to occupy any position can, if he seeks aright, obtain the *spirit of that calling,* and in that there is peace and joy and satisfaction, so that he is paid in his labors in any office which he may be called to fill. Every man . . . can find something to do for the exercise of the powers with which he is endowed, magnifying his office or calling in the priesthood—for we nearly all have some portion of the priesthood. If we seek for the spirit of that calling, we shall find plenty of opportunity for the exercise of its duties.[15]

To have the spirit of one's calling is to be in the frame of mind whereby God may reveal the gifts and powers necessary to be effective in the particular office. Elder Cannon thus taught that the Lord "is ready to bless every man in His Church who will magnify his office and calling. He is ready to bestow the *gifts and qualifications* of that office upon every man according to his diligence and faithfulness. . . ."[16]

Finally, to have the spirit of a calling is to find peace and contentment in performing the tasks required. George Q. Cannon thus taught that "It is not in occupying this or the other honorable and prominent station that the Elders should find gratification alone. . . . it is in knowing, whatever their station or calling may be, that they are in the position which the Lord, through His servants, wishes them to occupy and that they have His approval and His sweet and precious Spirit imparting unto them happiness and peace."[17]

POWER IN THE PRIESTHOOD

The man who magnifies his callings gains *power* in the Priesthood. There is a difference between having the authority, as a result of ordination, and having the power which comes to those few who learn to operate in the Priesthood as they should. Elder John A. Widtsoe explained:

> The Priesthood conferred on man carries with it real power to do effective work in behalf of the plan of salvation. Under the normal organization of the Church, when things are moving on in the ordained way, there is no insistent extraordinary evidence of the power possessed by those who have the Priesthood, and who, therefore, can act for God in matters pertaining to the Church. Under such a condition there is a quiet, steady use of *authority* in behalf of the daily work of the Church—each man performing the labor that has been assigned to him, in addition to which each man may use his authority in his own behalf as seems him fitting. Yet, *power* is with the Priesthood, and when need arises [and the Priesthood holder is a fit vessel], it becomes recognized as the voice of God, which all must hear.[18]

One great lesson of Section 121 of the *Doctrine and Covenants* is that power in the Priesthood is based upon the principle of righteousness. John Taylor therefore taught that "any manifestation of power through the priesthood on the earth is simply a delegated power from the priesthood in the heavens, and the more *the priesthood on the earth becomes assimilated with and subject to the priesthood in the heavens the more of this power shall we possess.*"[19] Two points from President Taylor's statement are most interesting: First, all power that man receives on earth is simply delegated from the perfect organization in heaven. Thus Orson Pratt spoke of the Priesthood on earth as "a small branch receiving authority from heaven. . . ."[20] Second, the more that man brings himself in strict harmony with the will of the Almighty (or the powers of heaven), the greater will be the display of Priesthood power on the earth. David O. McKay said: "We can conceive of the power of the priesthood as being potentially existent as an impounded reservoir of water. Such power becomes dynamic and productive of good only when the liberated force becomes active. . . . So *the priesthood, as related to humanity, is a principle of power only as it becomes active in the lives of men,* turning their hearts and desires toward God and prompting service to their fellow men."[21]

What are some characteristics of those who have power in the Priesthood? First of all, men powerful in the Priesthood are dynamic, and capable of leading others. The Holy Spirit acts upon a man to give him an energetic approach to life, a charismatic way with people, and an impelling sense of independence. (His is the quiet confidence and a sensitive aggressiveness when it comes to inspiring and leading others: he is bold and fearless when it comes to declaring his witness but ever attuned to the humanity and frailties of the children of God. Those who enjoy power in the priesthood are leaders, though not necessarily leaders in the formal Church organization. They are effective leaders because they are supportive followers. But theirs is an independent witness of the truth, a testimony planted and nourished by the Spirit.) The Holy Ghost acts to enliven, enlighten, and regenerate. President Brigham Young said:

> Those men . . . who know no more about the power of God, and the influence of the Holy Spirit, than to be led entirely by another person, suspending their own understanding, and pinning their faith upon another's sleeve, will never be capable of entering into the celestial glory, to be crowned as they anticipate; they will never be capable of becoming Gods. They cannot rule themselves, to say nothing of ruling others. . . . They never can hold sceptors of glory, majesty, and power in the celestial kingdom. Who will? Those who are valiant and inspired with the true independence of heaven, who will go forth boldly in the service of their God. . . .[22]

Power in the Priesthood is also characterized by one possessing the gifts of the Spirit, and thus being capable of working miracles.[23] The angel that appeared to John the Beloved on Patmos explained that *the testimony of Jesus is the spirit of prophecy.*[24] After pondering these words, one cannot avoid the tendency to evaluate himself: "Do I really have the testimony of Jesus, as I say I do? If so, do I then have the spirit of prophecy?" Likewise, Joseph Smith explained that "no man can receive the Holy Ghost without receiving revelations. The Holy Ghost is a revelator."[25] Again, one is forced to ask: "Do I really have the Holy Ghost and its gifts?" Orson Pratt said boldly: "A person who is without a spiritual gift has not the Spirit of God dwelling in him, in a sufficient degree, to save him. . . ."[26] Moroni also made it clear that "if the day cometh that the power and gifts of God shall be done away among you, it shall be because of unbelief."[27] Men endowed with power in the Priesthood are those who have sought after and obtained the abilities and rights needed to partake of the spiritual gifts enumerated in the scriptures.

As was discussed earlier, the quantity and quality of power delegated to man is a function of righteousness. President Wilford Woodruff stated that "we have no right to break any law that God has given unto us. The more we do so the less power we have before God, before heaven and before the earth, and *the nearer we live to God, . . . the more power we will have.*"[28] Power in the Priesthood is thus an accurate standard by which one may judge his degree of personal worthiness and uprightness.

So many times Priesthood holders perform sacred ordinances without having the true power to make such ordinances efficacious. Thus, little good is done. Elder Parley P. Pratt assisted the Prophet Joseph in numerous healings in the Montrose, Iowa area in 1839. Of one such occasion, Elder Pratt made the following interesting observation:

> Brother Joseph, while in the Spirit, rebuked the Elders who would continue to lay hands on the sick from day to day *without the power to heal them.* Said he: "It is time that such things ended. *Let the Elders either obtain the power of God to heal the sick, or let them cease to minister the forms without the power.*"[29]

President Brigham Young attempted to explain why Priesthood bearers are often unable to exercise power in the performance of Priesthood functions:

> How often have we sealed blessings of health and life upon our children and companions in the name of Jesus Christ and by the authority of the Holy Priesthood of the Son of God, and yet our faith and prayers did not succeed in accomplishing the desires of our hearts. Why is this? In many instances our anxiety is so great that we do not pause to know the spirit of revelation and its operations upon the human mind. We have anxiety instead of faith. . . . *It is in consequence of not being completely moulded to the will of God.*[30]

LATTER-DAY EXAMPLES OF POWER IN THE PRIESTHOOD

The Dispensation of the Fulness of Times is a dispensation of miracles and the manifestation of Priesthood power. William F. Cahoon made this report of the Prophet Joseph's power:

> I have seen the sick healed under his administrations in many instances. I have seen cripples healed immediately, and leap for joy after being administered to. I was present and well remember a case of healing at Montrose, Iowa. One day about two o'clock in the afternoon, I was down at Brother [Elijah] Fordham's to see if he was still alive, (he being very low,) and as I was going home I saw Brother Joseph, the Prophet, coming up from the river. He went immediately to the house of Brother Fordham, opened the door and went in. I then, with two or three of the brethren, went back to Fordham's immediately. The Prophet went to Brother Fordham's bedside and said, "Are you very sick Brother Fordham?" But he could not speak; he made a little motion with his head. The Prophet then laid his hands upon the sick man's head, and said, "Brother Fordham, in the name of the Son of God, and the Holy Priesthood which I hold, be thou made well from this very moment.

In a few minutes the Prophet said, "Brother Fordham, get up, put on your clothes, and go with me to visit some more sick people. And all saw the Prophet and Brother Fordham, going off to another house together. I am willing to testify to this before God, and angels, and all men at any time.[31]

Lorenzo Dow Young told of a miraculous healing that took place in January of 1836:

I was so low and nervous that I could scarcely bear any noise in the room. The next morning after the visit of the doctors, my father came to the door of the room to see how I was, and I recall his gazing earnestly at me with tears in his eyes. As I afterwards learned he went from there to the Prophet Joseph and said to him: "My son, Lorenzo, is dying; can there not be something done for him?" The Prophet studied for a few moments and replied, "Yes; of necessity I must go away to fill an appointment which I cannot put off. But you go and get my brother Hyrum, and with him get together twelve or fifteen good faithful brethren; go to the home of Brother Lorenzo and all join in prayer; one by mouth and the others repeat after him in unison. After prayer divide into quorums of three. Let the first quorum who administer annoint Brother Young with oil, then lay hands on him, one being mouth, and the other two repeating in unison with him. When all the quorums have, in succession, laid their hands on Brother Young and prayed for him, begin again with the first quorum by anointing, continuing the administration in this way until you receive a testimony that he will be restored."

My father came with fifteen of the brethren and these instructions were strictly followed. The administrations were continued until it came the turn of the first quorum the third time. Brother Hyrum Smith led. The Spirit rested mightily upon him and he was full of blessing and prophecy. He said that I should regain my health, live to go with the Saints into the bosom of the Rocky Mountains to build up a place there, and that my cellar should overflow with wine and fatness.

At that time I had not heard about the Saints going to the Rocky Mountains; possibly Brother Smith had. After he was through the administration he seemed surprised at some things he had said, and wondered at the manifestations of the spirit. I coughed no more and rapidly recovered. I had been pronounced by the best physicians in the country past all human aid. I am now a living witness of the power of God through the Administrations of the Elders.[32]

Obviously, Priesthood power consists of more than miraculous healing. Speaking of the first miracle of this dispensation, the Prophet Joseph Smith wrote:

During the month of April [1831] I (Joseph Smith) went on a visit to the residence of Mr. Joseph Knight, of Colesville, Broom County, N.Y.... We held several meetings in the neighborhood; we had many friends and some enemies. Our meetings were well attended, and many began to pray fervently to Almighty God that He would give them wisdom to understand the truth. Among those who attended our meetings regularly was Newel Knight, son of Joseph Knight. He and I had many serious conversations on the important subject of man's eternal salvation. We were in the habit of praying much at our meetings, and Newel had said that he would try and take up his cross and pray vocally during meeting; but when we again met together he rather excused himself. I tried to prevail upon him, making use of the figure, supposing that he should get into a mud hole would he not try to help himself out? And that we were willing now to help him out of the mud hole. He replied, "that provided he had got into a mud hole through carelessness, he would rather wait and get out himself than have others to help him, and so he would wait until he should get into the woods by himself and there he would pray." Accordingly he deferred praying until next morning, when he retired into the woods, where, according to his own account afterwards, he made several attempts to pray, but could scarcely do so—feeling that he had not done his duty, but that he should have prayed in the presence of others. He began to feel uneasy, and continued to feel worse in mind and body until, upon reaching his own house, his appearance was such as to alarm his wife very much. He requested her to go and bring me to him. I went and found him suffering very much in his mind, and his body acted upon in a very strange manner. His visage and limbs distorted and twisted in every shape and appearance possible to imagine; and finally, he was caught up off the floor of the apartment and tossed about most fearfully.... After he had thus suffered for a time, I succeeded in getting hold of him by the hand, when almost immediately he spoke to me, and with very great earnestness requested of me that I should cast the devil out of him; saying, "that he knew that he was in him, and that he also knew that I could cast him out." I replied, "if you know that I can it shall be done," and then, almost unconsciously, I rebuked the devil, and commanded him in the name of Jesus Christ to depart from him; when immediately Newel spoke out and said, "that he saw the devil leave him and vanish from his sight."

The scene was now entirely changed; for as soon as the devil had departed from our friend his countenance became natural; his distortions of body ceased and almost immediately the Spirit of the Lord descended upon him, and the visions of eternity were open to his view. He afterwards related his experience as follows:

"I now began to feel a most pleasing sensation resting upon me, and immediately the visions of heaven were opened to my view. I felt myself attracted upward, and remained for some time enrapt in contemplation, insomuch that I knew not what was going on in the room. By-and-by I felt some weight pressing upon my shoulder and the side of my head, which served to recall me to a sense of my situation, and I found that the Spirit of the Lord had actually caught me up off the floor, and that my shoulder and head were pressing against the beams."

All this was witnessed by many, to their great astonishment and satisfaction, when they saw the devil thus cast out and the power of God and His Holy Spirit thus made manifest. . . . As may be expected, such a scene as this contributed much to make believers of those who witnessed it; and, finally, the greater part of them became members of the Church.[33]

One of the classic examples of Joseph Smith's power occurred while serving as a prisoner in November of 1838. Though not directly an example of Priesthood functioning, this incident demonstrates the Modern Seer's profound power in rebuking the powers of evil. Elder Parley P. Pratt wrote:

In one of those tedious nights we had lain as if in sleep till the hour of midnight had passed, and our ears and hearts had been pained, while we had listened for hours to the obscene jests, the horrid oaths, the dreadful blasphemies and filthy language of our guards, . . . as they recounted to each other their deeds of rapine, murder, robbery, etc., which they committed among the "Mormons" while at Far West and vicinity. They even boasted of defiling by force wives, daughters and virgins, and of shooting or dashing out the brains of men, women, and children.

I had listened till I became so disgusted, shocked, horrified, and so filled with the spirit of indignant justice that I could scarcely refrain from rising upon my feet and rebuking the guards; but had said nothing to Joseph, or any one else, although I lay next to him and knew he was awake. On a sudden he arose to his feet, and spoke in a voice of thunder, or as the roaring lion, uttering, as near as I can recollect, the following words: "*Silence, ye fiends of the infernal pit. In the name of Jesus Christ I rebuke you, and command you to be still; I will not live another minute and hear such language; Cease such talk, or you or I die THIS INSTANT!"*

He ceased to speak. He stood erect in terrible majesty. Chained, and without a weapon; calm, unruffled and dignified as an angel, he looked upon the quailing guards, whose weapons were lowered or dropped to the ground; whose knees smote together, and who, shrinking into a corner, or crouching at his feet, begged his pardon, and remained quiet till a change of guards.

I have seen the ministers of justice, clothed in magesterial robes, and criminals arraigned before them, while life was suspended on a breath, in courts of England; I have witnessed a Congress in solemn session to give laws to nations; I have tried to conceive of Kings, of royal courts, of thrones and crowns; and of emperors assembled to decide the fate of kingdoms; but dignity and majesty have I seen but *once*, as it stood in chains, at midnight, in a dungeon in an obscure village of Missouri.[34]

BLESSING THE FAMILY

Though the programs of the Church are extremely demanding on the time of the Priesthood bearers, yet their most important responsibility is to their families. President Harold B. Lee said repeatedly: "The greatest of the Lord's work you brethren will ever do as fathers will be within the walls of your own home."[35] One might be the most effective bishop in the Church, so far as meeting the needs of the ward, and yet, through neglecting his own family, fall short of the exalted state. President McKay's classic statement that "no other success can compensate for failure in the home,"[36] is most appropriate in this light.

Successes in business, education, human relations, or the Church do not cover the sin of omitting to care properly for the family. Elder John H. Vandenberg said: "There is no calling in this Church that supersedes that of being a father. No assignment in the Church should ever be considered as an excuse to neglect the home."[37] Elder Vandenberg said in the same discourse that "There is no need of searching out your genealogy if you do not know where your children were last night."[38] That is powerful! What good would a completed genealogical line back to Adam be if a father had not been able to save his *own* children? Such a one would be left without posterity at the coming of Christ. If all families were to be in such a state at the coming of the Lord, then the earth would literally be "an utter waste."[39] Priesthood bearers are therefore under strict obligation to set their priorities in the proper perspective.

This writer has often thought of the meaning of the word "bless" as it pertains to the blessing of families. Too often we limit the true connotation of the word, and think only of administrations in times of illness. In reality, to bless the family is to be the means whereby they may receive of the full blessing of the Gospel of Christ, and grow into life eternal. If our sole means of blessing the family is through administrations, then there will be few ways to bless them in the millennium; *there is no sickness or death then.*

How, then, may families be blessed each day by a righteous father? *First* of all, families will be blessed as the man honors his Priesthood; the Holy Ghost dwells in such a home. President McKay said simply: "A home is transformed because a man holds and honors the priesthood."[40] *Second,* a man may bless his family by training and teaching of the value and importance of spiritual things—knowledge of the things of God should be prized far more than things of the world. President Spencer W. Kimball therefore taught that "in the divine scheme every soul has been given a father whose responsibility is not only to sire and provide the necessities of life, but also *to train for mortality and life eternal.*"[41] Because many heads of families fail to disseminate things holy to the family members, Joseph Smith stated that "there are many teachers, but, perhaps, *not many fathers.*"[42] *Third,* fathers should give periodic patriarchal blessings to family members for purposes of comfort, instruction, and inspiration.

Concerning the great Patriarch Adam, a modern revelation explained that three years previous to his death he called all of his righteous posterity together in the valley of Adam-ondi-Ahman, there to bestow his "last" blessing. The account continues: "And Adam stood up in the midst of the congregation; and ... predicted whatsoever should befall his posterity unto the latest generation."[43] In speaking of this great council, President John Taylor explained:

> Adam, before he left the earth, gathered his people together in the Valley of Adam-ondi-Ahman, and the curtain of eternity was unfolded before him, and he gazed upon all events pertaining to his descendants, which should transpire in every subsequent period of time, and he prophesied to them ... *Many other men have possessed a portion of the same power, influence, knowledge and intelligence,* and they have obtained it from the same source.[44]

This type of blessing, accompanied with the spirit of prophecy and revelation, should become one of the sacred traditions that father and family may share. Eliza R. Snow said that with the restoration of the keys of Priesthood has come also "the ancient order of patriarchal blessings." This noble sister continued: "Each father, holding the priesthood, stands as a patriarch, at the head of his family, with invested right and power to bless his household, and to predict concerning the future, on the heads of his children, as did Jacob of old."[45] Every father, after he has received his own patriarchal blessing,[46] may therefore confer this type of blessing upon his family.

A faithful father who holds the Melchizedek Priesthood may bless his own children, and that would be a patriarchal (father's) blessing. Such a blessing could be recorded in the family records, but it would not be preserved in the archives of the Church. Every father who is true to this priesthood is a patriarch over his own house. In addition, children may receive a blessing by an ordained patriarch. A father blessing his own child could, if he received the inspiration to do so, declare the lineage of the child.[47]

Finally, Priesthood bearers may bless the family through living so as to transmit the powers of the Spirit to succeeding generations. President Brigham Young taught that "the father should be full of kindness, and endeavor to happify and cheer the mother, . . . that her love for God and righteousness may vibrate throughout her whole being, that she may bear and bring forth offspring impressed and endowed with all the qualities necessary to a being designed to reign king of kings and lord of lords."[48] Heber C. Kimball, counselor to Brigham Young, spoke in a similar manner:

Jesus Christ proceeded from his Father. He is called "His only begotten Son," and inherited germs of his Father's perfections and the attributes of his Father's nature, so that he sinned not. So with us; *if the attributes of our nature become refined and regenerated by the truth, our offspring must inherit those perfections,* more or less. Then, how essential it is that parents should, by living their religion, improve themselves for the improvement of their race.[49]

BLESSING THE WORLD

That man who magnifies his calling in the Priesthood is desirous of blessing all mankind. Joseph F. Smith thus spoke of the Priesthood as the power by which man "can act in the earth for the *salvation of the human family.*"[50] The faithful man of the Priesthood finds his prayers turning to those far and near, friend and foe. He is filled with an overflowing disposition to light the lives of all the children of the Eternal Father, and his heart is expanded ten fold as he gradually comes to love and forgive every soul that walks the earth. F. D. Richards taught that "every officer in the Church, from the Deacon unto the Apostle, should realize that it is his duty to endeavor to administer blessings by the virtue of the calling of God which is upon him." Elder Richards then continued: "Every one in all the Church should be filled with a spirit of blessing. *The authority of the Priesthood should cause a gushing forth from the fountain of the heart, a bubbling forth of streams of blessing. . . .*"[51]

Elder Orson Hyde said that "inasmuch as the salvation of the world is to a great extent dependent upon our integrity and the faithful performance of our duties in this Priesthood, do you not see that we are required to work not only for our own salvation, but for the welfare and salvation of others?"[52] President Joseph F. Smith gave instructions as to how Priesthood bearers are to bless the world:

> It is the duty of this vast body of men holding the holy Priesthood, which is after the order of the Son of God, to exert their influence and exercise their power for good among the people of Israel and the people of the world. It is their bounded duty to *preach and to work righteousness,* both at home and abroad.[53]

Men of the Priesthood are to *preach* and to *work* righteousness; the world is blessed through their preaching of Gospel truths, both by precept and example. By so doing, the Priesthood will become a powerful force for good, and will ultimately be the means of salvation for all who will abide by the principles of perfection as found in the Church of Jesus Christ. By this means, men of the Priesthood may become the "saviors of mankind."[54]

SUMMARY

1. After obtaining the Priesthood, one has the responsibility to "receive" the powers and rights that accompany it, through righteous actions and thoughts.

2. To "magnify" a calling in the Priesthood is to:
    A.   Enlarge upon it, and concentrate upon its importance.
    B.   Accentuate the details of it, and attempt to learn and perform all facets.
    C.   Honor and respect it.

3. Men who magnify their callings are different from the norm in the spirit and influence they radiate.

4. Only through the Holy Spirit may one come to appreciate the sacred nature of his calling in the Priesthood.

5. If a man will magnify his calling, the Priesthood will magnify that man.

6. Every man who receives responsibilities in the Priesthood is under strict obligation to learn every facet of the duty. Those who prove slothful, and learn not their duty, will not be permitted to stand hereafter among men who exercise Priesthood.

7. There is a difference between having authority of the Priesthood and having *power* in the Priesthood. Power, which is a delegated force from the heavens, comes only to the faithful.

8. Through honoring their Priesthood, fathers may bless their families:
    A. By training and teaching of the importance of spiritual and holy things.
    B. By giving periodic patriarchal blessings for comfort, instruction, and inspiration.
    C. By being powerful in the Spirit, so as to transmit spiritual powers to succeeding generations.

9. Those who magnify their callings are filled with a spirit of blessing, and strive earnestly to uplift and save the whole of mankind.

BEWARE CONCERNING
YOURSELVES

A VITAL PART OF THE COVENANT pertaining to the Melchizedek Priesthood is man's promise to "beware concerning himself." This is the Lord's plea for man to watch carefully his personal thoughts and behavior, for, as the Prophet Joseph Smith taught, "the power, glory and blessings of the Priesthood could not continue with those who received ordination only as their righteousness continued."[1] In a revelation given in 1831, the Master gave instructions that each Priesthood holder "beware lest he do that which is not in truth and righteousness before me."[2] As was pointed out in the preceding chapter, true power in the Priesthood is a delegated force from the heavens, and only comes as a result of personal cleanliness and overall worthiness.

Though a man may appear to fulfill every requirement necessary in magnifying his calling, he may yet dam the resource of power from himself, by cutting himself off from the great reservoir of Priesthood in the heavens; this is often done through lack of personal purity. Only as a man comes to honor himself will he ever be able to honor the Priesthood. In a very real sense, man shows an utter disrespect for the power of the Gods whenever he fails to keep his soul clean. Heber C. Kimball spoke to this subject: "We all have a Priesthood to honor, which it is impossible for us to do unless we honor ourselves; and all who hold the Priesthood and honor themselves, are worthy of honor; and *it is impossible to honor the Priesthood in that man and not honor the vessel that holds it.*"[3]

BE YE CLEAN

The command of the Almighty has always been to forsake the things of the world and "go ye out from Babylon." To those called to receive the Priesthood, the word of the Lord is explicit: "Be ye clean that bear the vessels of the Lord."[4] Having spoken of the faithful Priesthood holder as the "possessor of all things," such that "all things are subject unto him," a revelation stated: "But *no man is possessor of all things except he be purified and cleansed from all sin.*"[5] Simply stated, the Priesthood is not a source of power to those tainted with serious transgression; only those who apply the atoning blood of Christ in their behalf, such that they obtain and retain a remission of sins from day to day[6] are on the path to eternal life and to becoming possessor of all things. One cannot have all things subject unto him if he has not learned to place his own flesh in subjection to his spirit. George A. Smith taught that "if we would inherit the blessings of the Priesthood—if we would stand in the presence of the Almighty—stand upon Mount Zion and inherit the blessings of a glorious celestial dominion, we have got to be clean: we must cleanse ourselves, put away our follies, and be prepared to stand united."[7]

The quality and quantity of the power possessed by the Priesthood bearer is a direct function of his ability to commune with God and partake of the sacred powers available to the pure. Communion with the infinite forces depends almost completely upon one's ability to overcome the flesh and yield to the Holy Spirit. President Wilford Woodruff made the following declaration:

> Let us lay aside all evil practices—all those habits which will prevent our communing with God. We have not yet got power to occupy a throne and to govern according to the laws of heaven. Of this we are all sensible. Then if these little things have a tendency to hinder our enjoyments and debase us in the eyes of the Lord, we ought to lay them aside, and manifest a determination to do the will of our Father in Heaven, and to accomplish that work which is laid upon us to perform.[8]

Only by putting aside evil practices and habits may man grow in spirituality, and in power with the Priesthood. President David O. McKay gave us to understand that spirituality is "consciousness of victory over self, and communion with the Infinite." President McKay continued: "Spirituality impells one to conquer difficulties and acquire more and more strength. To feel one's faculties unfolding and truth expanding the soul is one of life's sublimest experiences."[9]

Men given solemn authority to act for God must avoid any acts of uncleanness. Obviously, all men of the Priesthood are under strict obligation to observe and keep the Word of Wisdom, for the Spirit will not continue in a tabernacle which has been defiled by those things which the Lord has forbidden. Men holding the power of God must not be guilty of pride, for such was the state of many nations which fell. Priesthood holders must avoid all loud laughter and lightmindedness, for the Latter-day Saints must learn to smile. Men of the Priesthood must be neat and comely in their appearance, and thus convey an image of cleanliness. The Spirit of God prompts man to be at his very best, both inside and out.

Of all the means by which the powers of the Priesthood may be withheld and the spirituality of a man drained, sexual sin is among the most serious. Illicit sexual relations have proven to be contributive to the moral degeneration and ultimate downfall of many cultures. Inasmuch as the sexual union is the path to the fountain of life, tampering with such powers illicitly is most heinous, for in so doing one prostitutes the most sacred of all God-given rights. President Joseph F. Smith boldly stated: "No more loathsome cancer disfigures the body and soul of society today than the frightful affliction of sexual sin. It vitiates the very fountains of life and bequeaths its foul effects to the yet unborn as a legacy of death."[10] It is no wonder, therefore, that adultery or sexual fornication are classed as second only in seriousness to the crime of murder.[11] In a revelation known as the Law of the Church, the Lord said: "Thou shalt not commit adultery; and he that committeth adultery, and repenteth not, shall be cast out."[12] In a most stirring address to the Priesthood of the Church, President Harold B. Lee preached against the growing mass of immorality:

> *I want to warn this great body of priesthood against that great sin of Sodom and Gommorah,* which has been labeled as a sin second only in seriousness to the sin of murder. *I speak of the sin of adultery,* which, as you know, was the name used by the Master as he referred to unlicensed sexual sins of fornication as well as adultery; *and besides this, the equally grievous sin of homosexuality,* which seems to be gaining momentum with social acceptance in the Babylon of the world, of which Church members must not be a part.
>
> The common judges of Israel, our bishops and stake presidents, must not stand by and fail to apply disciplinary measures within their jurisdiction, as set forth plainly in the laws of the Lord and procedures as set forth in plain and simple instructions that cannot be misunderstood. Never must we allow supposed mercy to the unrepentant sinner to rob the justice upon which true repentance from sinful practices is predicated.[13]

President McKay gave a similar warning:

> *To the man of the priesthood I give this caution. Your weakest point will be the point at which Satan tries to tempt you and will try to win you,* and if you have made it weak yourself before you have undertaken to serve the Lord, he will add to that weakness. Resist him and you will gain strength.
>
> Now, I mention this because there are too many broken hearts in our Church because men, some of whom hold the priesthood and prominent positions, are tempted right where they are weak. They forget that they have made covenants with the Lord, and step aside from the path of virtue and discretion. . . .[14]

Though sexual transgression is most serious, the Lord has provided that the guilty party may return to fellowship and regain the powers of the Priesthood through confession to the legal administrator and Godly repentance.

GUARDING THE THOUGHTS

Not only must holders of Priesthood guard against sinful acts, but they must also discipline the *thought* patterns. The powerful message in the latter part of Matthew 5 is that the Law of Christ is a system of proper attitudes and thoughts, as well as proper actions. Jesus therefore spoke: "Ye have heard that it was said by them of old time, Thou shalt not commit adultery: But I say unto you, That *whosoever looketh on a woman to lust after her hath committed adultery with her already in his heart.*"[15] Here the heart is emphasized, and irreverent and unholy thoughts are condemned alongside the abominable act. The instructions to "*Let thine heart keep my commandments*"[16] are thus very applicable here. In a modern revelation the Master explained that "he that looketh upon a woman to lust after her shall deny the faith, and *shall not have the Spirit; and if he repents not he shall be cast out.*"[17] This statement makes clear the fact that an immediate consequence of harboring evil and degrading thoughts is a withdrawal of a portion of the Spirit of God; such a withdrawal will lead one away from the path of virtue and into the chains of hell, until eventually he is cast out, or cut off from the Church.

The men of the Priesthood must also be active enough to avoid *idleness* in thought. Letting the mind wander is dangerous business; the old adage that "an idle mind is the devil's workshop" is more true than most people would want to believe. Man cannot remain a passive agent and yet maintain complete control over mind and body, for as man relaxes, Satan begins his labors. There is no such thing as being idle and remaining neutral; if man does not have charge of his thinking process, then someone else is directing it. And that someone is almost always the Father of Lies.

President McKay gave a great discourse on the value of controlling thoughts and actions. Part of this discourse was as follows:

Man is responsible not only for every deed, but also for every idle word and thought. Said the Savior: ". . . every idle word that men shall speak, they shall give account thereof in the day of judgment." (Matthew 12:36)

As a boy I questioned that truth when I first heard it expressed by my father. I remember saying to myself, "Not even the Lord knows what I am thinking now." I was very much surprised, therefore, when later as a student in the university, I read the following in William James' *Psychology* about the effect of thought and action on human character: "*We are spinning our own fates good or evil, and never to be undone. Every smallest stroke of virtue or of vice leaves its ever so little scar. Down among [the] nerve cells and fibers the molecules are counting it, registering it up to be used against him [man] when the next temptation comes. Nothing we ever do is, in strict scientific literalness, wiped out.* Of course, this has its good side as well as its bad one. Let no youth have any anxiety about the upshot of his education, whatever the line of it may be. If he keeps faithfully busy each hour of the working day, he may safely leave the final result to itself. He can with perfect certainty count on waking up some fine morning, to find himself one of the competent ones of his generation, in whatever pursuit he may have singled out."[18]

The key to success in this area is thus to strive to keep one's thoughts clean by constantly pondering upon noble and worthwhile things. Thought is the father of action. It is true that "what a man continually thinks about determines his actions in times of opportunity and stress."[19] After all is said and done, man will be judged according to the purity and goodness of his heart, and the heart is a composite of man's thoughts and desires. In reality, as a man thinketh *in his heart*, so is he.[20] The quality of thought that takes place when man is not forced by the situation into serious contemplation or concentration is an accurate indicator of the quality of the man. President McKay said simply: *"I will know what you are if you tell me what you think about when you don't have to think."*[21] It should be remembered at this point that there is no sin in having an impure thought enter the mind, for even the Savior was tempted. The sin lies in harboring such a thought. Analogously, there is nothing wrong with having a bird light in your hair, but things are a bit out of hand if the bird is permitted to build a nest there! As Priesthood bearers practice faithfully to become masters of their own minds, they will find themselves becoming masters of their bodies. This is the process by which one gradually overcomes all things, and becomes possessor "of all things; for all things are subject unto him."[22]

MANY CALLED, FEW CHOSEN

In making an important distinction between two groups of people, the Lord said: "Behold, there are many called, but few are chosen."[23] Specifically, who are those called? And who are the chosen? President Harold B. Lee explained:

> Despite that calling which is spoken of in the scriptures as "fore-ordination," we have another inspired declaration: "Behold, there are many called, but few are chosen. . . ." (D&C 121:34)
>
> This suggests that even though we have our free agency here, *there are many who were foreordained before the world was, to a greater state than they have prepared themselves for here.* Even though they might have been among the noble and great, from among whom the Father declared that he would make his *chosen leaders,* they may fail of that calling here in mortality.[24]

According to President Lee, then, many individuals *called* and elected and foreordained in the pre-earth councils come to earth, only to fail to be sensitive to spiritual things, such that they never become the *chosen* of the Lord—they never attain unto the positions and blessings it was decreed that they should receive. In the words of Alma, those called but not chosen "reject the Spirit of God on account of the hardness of their hearts and blindness of their minds, while, if it had not been for this they might have had as great privilege as their brethren."[25] Many are called to receive the Priesthood in mortality, but few live so as to merit the transcendent blessings that accompany this sacred power, blessings that were promised (on a contingent basis) years before.

A most revealing statement is given in modern scripture as to why many are called but few chosen: "But behold, verily I say unto you, that there are many who have been ordained among you, whom I have called but few of them are chosen. They who are not chosen have sinned a very grievous sin, in that *they are walking in darkness at noon-day*."[26] To walk in darkness at noon-day would be impossible, unless one had closed his eyes to the brilliant sunlight or been shielded in some way from its rays. In the Gospel context, one walks in darkness at noon-day when he (1) has closed his spiritual faculties to the powers and influences of the Holy Ghost and is thus oblivious to sacred things, or (2) has shielded himself from spiritual light through the processes of corruption and unrepentant sin. There are some in the Church who are active-attenders and tithe-payers, and yet have not developed their spiritual faculties to things holy. There are Priesthood holders who, likewise, are spiritually blind to the rights, privileges, and blessings of the sacred power they possess. It is, perhaps, of such that the Lord spoke as being called but not chosen.

THE THINGS OF THIS WORLD

What causes a man to reject the Spirit of God and harden his heart? The Lord explained in modern revelation: "And why are they not chosen?" First of all, "Because *their hearts are set so much upon the things of this world. . . .*"[27] A classic example of one whose heart was set upon the things of this world was the Rich Fool. Jesus spoke in parable:

And he spake a parable unto them, saying, The ground of a certain rich man brought forth plentifully:

And he thought within himself, saying, What shall I do, because I have no room where to bestow my fruits?

And he said, This will I do: I will pull down my barns, and build greater; and there will I bestow all my fruits and my goods.

And I will say to my soul, Soul, thou hast much goods laid up for many years; take thine ease, eat, drink and be merry.

But God said unto him, Thou fool, this night thy soul shall be required of thee: then whose shall those things be, which thou has provided?

So is he that layeth up treasure for himself and is not rich toward God.[28]

In the opening chapters of the Book of Acts, the tragic story is related of a man named Ananias and his wife Sapphira. At this point in the history of the early Christian Church (some time following the Ascension of the Savior), the Saints had experienced a marvelous spiritual reawakening, such that each man loved his neighbor as himself. They began to covenant with one another and God, and soon began to abide by an economic order in which all properties and funds were channeled into a common treasury.[29] The people were of one heart and one mind, and there were no poor among them. The powers of the Spirit were very evident, and the Saints experienced great joy in serving one another and praising God. Ananias and Sapphira were, undoubtedly, members of the Church. They looked upon the Saints from a distance, and desired in their hearts to partake of the pure love manifest among their fellow brethren and sisters. And so this couple sold their possessions, with the intention of laying all of the money at the feet of the Apostles, who were in charge of collecting the consecrations. Just prior to their encounter with the Apostles, however, Ananias and Sapphira decided to retain a small portion of the money, fearing, perhaps, that their inheritance or stewardship would not be great enough to meet their wants. As Ananias approached Peter, Sapphira waited outside the gate for her husband to transact the business involved. As the money was laid at the feet of Peter, the selfish desires of the couple were made known by revelation. Peter spoke: "Ananias, why hast Satan filled thine heart to lie to the Holy Ghost, and to keep back part of the price of the land?" Then came the piercing words: "Thou hast not lied unto men, but unto God." The account explains that Ananias, hearing these words and being tormented in his own guilt, dropped to the ground and gave up the ghost. After three hours, Sapphira came to the Apostles in search of her husband. Peter approached her and asked: "How is it that ye have agreed together to tempt the Spirit of the Lord? behold, the feet of them which have buried thy husband are at the door, and shall carry thee out." Sapphira then dropped dead, and was buried near her husband.

Needless to say, very seldom do the judgments of God come as speedily as they came to the Rich Fool and to the New Testament couple. Yet, it is important to realize that such judgments do come, eventually, to every person who sets his heart upon the things of the world. Too often Priesthood bearers attempt to put one foot in the Celestial Kingdom while leaving the other foot in Babylon. Such is impossible to do, for man cannot serve God and mammon.[30]

Joseph Smith taught that in order for man to be able to exercise saving faith in the Lord Jesus Christ, he must be willing to sacrifice all worldly things:

> ... from the first existence of man, *the faith necessary unto the enjoyment of life and salvation never could be obtained without the sacrifice of all earthly things.*
>
> Those, then, who make the sacrifice, will have the testimony that their course is pleasing in the sight of God; and those who have this testimony will have faith to lay hold on eternal life, and will be enabled, through faith, to endure unto the end, and receive the crown that is laid up for them that love the appearing of our Lord Jesus Christ. But those who do not make the sacrifice cannot enjoy this faith, because men are dependent upon this sacrifice in order to obtain this faith: therefore, they cannot lay hold upon eternal life, because the revelations of God do not guarantee unto them the authority so to do, and without this guarantee faith could not exist.[31]

President Wilford Woodruff pleaded with the Priesthood: *"Brethren, for God's sake do not let us set our hearts on the things of this world to the neglect of the things of eternal life."*[32] In a similar way Joseph Fielding Smith explained that "few find the strait and narrow way which leadeth to the exaltation and the eternal lives, which is the family order, because their minds are set upon the things of this world, and they refuse to accept the things which pertain to the celestial world."[33] We see, therefore, that many are called to high and holy stations, but few are chosen to receive the full blessings of such positions; their hearts and minds are aimed at the wrong goal—they are spiritually nearsighted. Christ's instructions in the Sermon on the Mount are most appropriate here:

> Lay not up for yourselves treasures upon earth, where moth and rust doth corrupt, and where thieves break through and steal:
>
> But lay up for yourselves treasures in heaven, where neither moth nor rust doth corrupt, and where thieves do not break through nor steal:
>
> For where your treasure is, there will your heart be also.[34]

ASPIRING TO THE HONORS OF MEN

In continuing His explanation as to why many are called but few chosen, the Lord stated that many persons "aspire to the honors of men...."[35] There is no sin in aspiring or hoping for greater things. Nor is one guilty of sin who is honored and held in high esteem by other men. *The sin lies in seeking for greater things in order to obtain the praises and honors of others.* In speaking of those who have subtly gained the public acclaim, the Lord said simply: "They have their reward."[36] The Gospel of Christ consists of more than a system for control of actions; it also entails a disciplined approach to thoughts and desires. In this context, the Gospel teaches that man should do good, *but for the right reasons.* The Master taught that to do righteous deeds in order to be seen of men is hypocrisy. To pray in order that others might hear the majestic phrases and be impressed with the eloquent Gospel vocabulary is to pray in vain. To fast from food or drink and then make known openly the nature and duration of the fast is to fast in vain. Such practices will eventually canker the soul, for the Spirit of the Lord cannot continue with one whose heart is turned from virtue.

The Prophet Joseph once reproved a man for the praise-seeking nature of his blessing on the food: "Brother Joshua, don't let me hear you ever ask another such blessing."[37] In describing the simple yet pure quality of a prayer offered by the Prophet, Daniel Tyler said: "There was no ostentation, no raising of the voice by enthusiasm, but a plain conversational tone, as a man would address a present friend." Brother Tyler then added: "That prayer, I say, to my humble mind, partook of the learning and eloquence of heaven...."[38]

To aspire to the honors of men is also to place the learning of the world or theories of men on a higher plane than the powers of revelation and the words of the prophets. It is sad that many Priesthood bearers who are "learned" feel the need to push aside Gospel truths in favor of knowledge gained through the worldly disciplines. Obviously, to gain secular knowledge is important in mortality, but such an acquisition should never preclude the learning of the things of God. The Nephite Prophet Jacob gave a timely and enduring warning:

> O that cunning plan of the evil one! O the vainness, and the frailties, and the foolishness of men! *When they are learned they think they are wise, and they hearken not unto the counsel of God, for they set it aside, supposing they know of themselves,* wherefore, their wisdom is foolishness and it profiteth them not. And they shall perish.
> *But to be learned is good if they hearken unto the counsels of God.*[39]

As the children of God seek for righteousness and truth out of sanctified motives they will become those whom the Lord designates as "the chosen."

GRATIFYING PRIDE AND VAIN AMBITION

The rights of the Priesthood are conferred on many men. However, some men misuse these rights by attempting to cover their sins or gratify pride and vain ambition.[40] One of the gravest sins that such persons attempt to cover is a selfish desire for esteem and public recognition. President John Taylor said simply: "Men holding the Priesthood should not be governed by personal ambition, but feel full of the love of God...."[41] Those persons which have the true love of God, or, in other words, the pure love of Christ (charity[42]), are not concerned with vaunting themselves. Paul the Apostle taught that the charitable person is one who lives outside himself, and is devoted to serving others; this person does not elevate self, and is not puffed up.[43] George Q. Cannon therefore explained that "the man who receives it [the Priesthood] should not do so to gratify some feeling that he may have that he would like to hold authority that would give him some dignity or place him in a position above others of his brethren and sisters...."[44] President Cannon said on another occasion: "*No man should seek to hold a position to gratify a vain ambition to excel.* And whatever the position that may be assigned him, he should therewith be content." He continued his discourse with the following powerful lesson: "If an Elder's happiness be affected by the prominence or obscurity of his station, it is an evidence that *he is dependent upon something beside the Spirit of God for happiness...*"[45] President Cannon then explained that true happiness comes "not in occupying this or the other honorable and prominent station ... [but] in knowing, whatever their station or calling may be, that they are in the position which the Lord, through His servants, wishes them to occupy...."[46]

EXERCISING UNRIGHTEOUS DOMINION

In the 121st Section of the book of *Doctrine and Covenants*, Christ explained further why many are called but few chosen: "We have learned by sad experience that it is the nature and disposition of almost all men, as soon as they get a little authority, as they suppose, they will immediately begin to exercise unrighteous dominion. Hence many are called, but few are chosen."[47] To exercise unrighteous dominion is to coerce or control others in unholy ways or for less than noble reasons. In many cases, it consists of lifting self at the expense of others. Joseph Smith the Prophet taught that "it is a false principle for a man to aggrandize himself at the expense of another."[48] It is contrary to the order of heaven for anyone to be coerced in the Priesthood government of the Kingdom of God. George Q. Cannon stressed the difference between priest craft and Priesthood. Said he: "Priestcraft builds up itself, it is not authorized of God. Priestcraft oppresses the people; but the Priesthood of God emancipates men and women and makes them free."[49] The Priesthood is given to bless, lift, and exalt mankind, and there is no provision within this sacred power for binding the souls of others:

> Does this authority give men any power to bind the souls of men? Not in the least. Does it give men authority to coerce anybody in any shape, form or manner? Not in the least. On the contrary, we are told in revelations of God, that the power of this Priesthood must not be used to coerce, not to bind the souls of men.[50]

AMEN TO THE PRIESTHOOD

What are the fateful results that follow those who attempt to use the rights of the Priesthood to cover sins, gratify pride and vain ambition, or to exercise unrighteous dominion? The Lord gives the answer: *"The heavens withdraw themselves; the Spirit of the Lord is grieved; and when it is withdrawn, Amen to the priesthood or the authority of that man.* Behold, ere he is aware, he is left unto himself, to kick against the pricks, to persecute the saints, and to fight against God."[51] First, the heavens withdraw themselves, and the link between heavenly and earthly powers is broken, thus removing the source of power from the man on earth. Wilford Woodruff taught that "if we attempt to use it [the Priesthood] for unrighteous purposes, like lightning from heaven, our power, sooner or later, falls, and we fail to accomplish the designs of God."[52] When the Spirit of the Lord is withdrawn (as a result of transgression), the powers of the Priesthood are also taken.[53] Thus, Amen to the Priesthood or the authority of that man. One who continues in this wayward path, unless he takes time to re-evaluate himself, will lay a strong foundation for a permanent apostasy. Joseph Smith therefore said: "The moment you permit yourselves to lay aside any duty that God calls you to perform, to gratify your own desires, that moment you permit yourselves to become careless, you lay a foundation for apostasy."[54] Wilford Woodruff also taught: "Let that man use that priesthood for any other purpose than the building up of the kingdom of God ... and the heavens withdraw themselves, *the power of the priesthood departs,* and he is left to walk in darkness and not in light. . . ."[55] Any man who has lost the Spirit and is "left unto himself" will eventually begin to "kick against the pricks," or to fight against God and His chosen servants. He becomes an enemy to the Church and to the work of salvation.

> When a man begins to be an enemy to this work, he hunts me, he seeks to kill me, and never ceases to thirst for my blood. *He gets the spirit of the devil—the same spirit that they had who crucified the Lord of Life—*the same spirit that sins against the Holy Ghost. You cannot save such persons; you cannot bring them to repentance; they make open war, like the devil, and awful is the consequence.[56]

Every man should examine carefully his motives, attitudes, and desires. If he finds that much of his motivation for doing good is to aggrandize self and gain the acclaim of his fellow men, then his heart is wrong. If he finds that he frequently desires to dominate or control others through the use of Priesthood rights, then he may rest assured that apostasy is not far away.

GOVERNING THE SAINTS:
THE LORD'S WAY

The Lord's tools for working with people in the Church are given in scripture.[57]

1. *Persuasion* entails reasoning, urging, and righteous provocation. In speaking of the Master's approach in dealing with men, the hymn says:

     He'll call, persuade, direct aright,
        and bless with wisdom, love, and light,
     In nameless ways be good and kind,
        but never force the human mind.[58]

2. *Long-suffering* is a Saintly virtue, and consists of patience while (possibly) enduring trying times in the process of working with another.

3. *Gentleness* is a characteristic implying moderation and consideration in dealing with others. *Meekness* is a quality in which a person has garnered control over the impulses of the flesh. The meek person is free from pride and haughtiness; he is submissive and teachable, even as a little child.

   Of such the Lord said: "And blessed are the meek, for they shall inherit the earth."[59]

4. *Unfeigned love* is Christlike love. It is unconditional, is not ostentatious, and is, above all, sincere. Priesthood bearers will have success in working with individuals and groups only as they are endowed with a divine love for those over whom they have responsibilities.

5. *Kindness* is a tool requiring an empathetic heart, a benevolent manner, and a cordial concern.

6. *Pure knowledge* is knowledge from a pure source; it is knowledge by revelation, received by means of the Holy Ghost. It is also called "pure intelligence,"[60] and serves to enlarge the soul and aid man in becoming perfect in Christ Jesus.

7. *Sharp reproof* is to be used betimes (quickly), *when the bearer of the Priesthood is moved upon by the Holy Ghost.* If and when reproof is used, it is to be followed by a subsequent display of love toward the one reprimanded.

8. *Charity* is defined as the "pure love of Christ."[61] This definition of charity may be viewed in two separate but related ways. First, it is to *love Christ* purely. Second, it is to *love purely*, even as Christ does.

9. *Virtue* is moral excellence, and is required by the Lord of all Priest-hood bearers, in order that they may be confident in the working of spiritual matters.

When asked once how he was able to govern such a large body of people, Joseph the Prophet replied simply, "I teach them correct principles and they govern themselves."[62] As to the nature of the correct principles, Brigham Young said: "Teach the people *true knowledge*, and they will govern themselves."[63] Lead-ing the Saints of God is thus dependent upon the reception of knowledge from on high. John Taylor explained that "the Holy Ghost, which has been given to all who have obeyed the Gospel, and have lived faithful to its precepts, takes of the things of God and shows them forth through a living Priesthood to a people enlightened and instructed by the Spirit of revelation from God." President Taylor then continued by stating that *"the people thus enlightened, instructed and blessed by the Spirit of light, voluntarily and gladly sustain the Priesthood and minister unto them."*[64] It is clear, then, that through accepting correct principles the Saints become agents unto themselves, and are able to "do many things of their own free will, and bring to pass much righteousness. For the power is in them...."[65] Priesthood holders should thus understand that only through the teaching and application of Gospel principles will they ever be able to lead and govern the Lord's people, for such is the way ordained.

The Priesthood of God are also to lead through serving. A revelation there-fore explained: "He that is ordained of God and sent forth, the same is appointed to be the greatest, notwithstanding he is the least and the servant of all."[66] Every man ordained of God to lead the souls of men must look upon himself with humility; it is not necessarily true that he is the "least," but he should see himself as such. As long as such an attitude of meekness burns within the heart of the leader, the followers need never be concerned with the leader's vain ambitions or unrighteous dominion. One filled with a spirit of humility will seek to raise others, rather than oppress them. Joseph Smith therefore taught that *"if you will elevate others, the very work will exalt you."*[67]

Among the most challenging yet essential requirements for leading and governing the Saints is the ability to unite them in the bonds of brotherhood and love. The Lord said simply, "if ye are not one ye are not mine."[68] Such a union has its source in the powers and influences of the Holy Spirit; try as man may, "it is impossible to produce a true and correct union without the Spirit of the living God...."[69] No man can lead a people unless they are united, and such a union comes only as the Comforter works upon the hearts of the people, to refine and regenerate their motives and desires. The Prophet Joseph explained that "union flows from the Spirit, through the Priesthood; which Spirit, and power, and Priesthood, can only exist with the humble and meek of the earth."[70] George Q. Cannon expressed concisely one role of the Holy Ghost. He said that this Spirit exists to "unite the hearts of those who receive it and make them one."[71] With the powers of the Spirit active in the lives of the people, governing the Saints is a simple matter. Brigham Young queried: "Who gives me power, that 'at the pointing of my finger,' the hosts of Israel move, and at my request the inhabitants of this great territory are dispersed; at my command they are here? Who gives me that power? Let the world inquire." President Young then answered his own question: "It is the God of heaven; it is the Spirit of the Holy Gospel; it is not of myself; it is the Lord Jesus Christ, trying to save the inhabitants of the earth."[72] President Young said on another occasion:

> Is there any particular art in making this people obedient? There is just one. *If you Elders of Israel can get the art of preaching the Holy Ghost into the hearts of the people, you will have an obedient people.* This is the only art required. *Teach the people truth, teach them correct principles;* show them what is for their best good and don't you think they will follow in that path? They will.[73]

AN EYE SINGLE TO THE GLORY OF GOD

The scriptures plainly teach that those pure in their hearts have "an eye single to the glory of God." What does this mean? Christ explained to Moses: "For behold, this is my work and my glory—to bring to pass the immortality and eternal life of man."[74] If our eye or mind is single to God's glory, then all we do must be an attempt to meet this end: the bringing to pass the immortality and eternal life of ourself, our family, and others. This is the Divine Standard by which all actions, programs, and organizational developments may be judged; namely, will what is to be done actually assist God in the working out of the plan of salvation, and in the redemption of mankind? If it does not, then it has no place in the Church!

In speaking to the brethren of the Church, President David O. McKay explained: "Whenever the priesthood is delegated to man, it is conferred upon him not as a personal distinction, although it becomes such as he honors it, but as authority to represent Deity and *an obligation to assist the Lord in bringing to pass the immortality and eternal life of man.*"[75] As the man of the Priesthood attempts to center his eye on God's glory, he will find that all aspects of his life—vocation, avocation, education, etc.—will gradually come to be in harmony with the Divine Standard mentioned above.

The process by which man's eye is made single to God is a difficult one, but is most rewarding. *First*, man must be willing to set aside personal wishes and ambitions, and accept the will of the Almighty. A revelation to Emma Smith thus instructed her to "*lay aside the things of this world, and seek for the things of a better.*"[76] President Joseph F. Smith taught that "men must set aside their own prejudices, and pay deference to the great cause of truth that is spreading abroad in the world."[77] To accept the will of the Almighty requires that one first *know* the will of the Almighty. This may necessitate many hours of sincere, humble prayer, in order that the Lord might (1) purge the soul of selfish desires, and (2) teach the Divine Will. As long as man's mind is colored by personal ambitions, he is less amenable to holy promptings. Brigham Young thus made it clear that "until a selfish, individual interest is banished from our minds, and we become interested in the general welfare, we shall never be able to magnify our Holy Priesthood as we should."[78] As a man overcomes personal ambitions, he comes to appreciate his role in the Kingdom-building process; he learns that the Kingdom should come first. John Taylor said: "If we understand ourselves and our position, it ought to be with us, *the kingdom of God first and ourselves afterwards.*"[79]

Second, the Priesthood holder makes his eye single to the glory of God as he learns to counsel with the Lord in all matters of existence, and to acknowledge the hand of God in all outcomes. The wise Solomon instructed man to "*trust in the Lord with all thine heart; and lean not unto thine own understanding. In all thy ways acknowledge him, and he shall direct thy paths.*"[80] Alma also gave wise instructions:

> Yea, and cry unto God for all thy support; yea, *let all thy doings be unto the Lord,* and whithersoever thou goest let it be in the Lord; yea, *let thy thoughts be directed unto the Lord;* yea, *let the affections of thy heart be placed upon the Lord forever.*
>
> *Counsel with the Lord in all thy doings,* and he will direct thee for good; yea, when thou liest down at night lie down unto the Lord, that he may watch over you in your sleep; and when thou risest in the morning let thy heart be full of thanks unto God; and if ye do these things, ye shall be lifted up at the last day.[81]

The blessings that come to one whose eye is single to the glory of God are evident in the Holy Scriptures. The Master taught in Jerusalem: "The light of the body is the eye: if therefore thine eye be single, thy whole body shall be full of light."[82] A beautiful elaboration of this promise was given in modern revelation on December 27, 1832: "And if your eye be single to my glory, your whole bodies shall be filled with light, and there shall be no darkness in you; and that body which is filled with light comprehendeth all things."[83] That man whose eye (mind[84]) is single will thus be filled with the light and truth that emanate from God.[85] Darkness has no place in such an one, for any darkness is repelled by the powerful influences of the Holy Spirit. If that man maintains such a state of being, he will grow grace for grace, increasing daily in favor with the Lord. Christ explained: "That which is of God is light; and he that receiveth light, and continueth in God, receiveth more light; and *that light groweth brighter and brighter until the perfect day.*"[86] We read in another place: "He that keepeth his [God's] commandments receiveth truth and light, *until he is glorified in truth and knoweth all things.*"[87] As one matures in the powers and attributes of the Spirit, he increases in wisdom and knowledge, both of which have their source in God. John Taylor said: "There is no officer in the Church, who acts with a single eye to the glory of God but what will have wisdom given him according to his capacity."[88] As man grows in light and truth, he eventually reaches the point where in the resurrection (the "perfect day"), filled completely with the glory of God, he is able to comprehend all things.

God has promised that those who channel their minds into proper glory shall eventually receive the fulness of the earth. The words of Jesus are most inspiring: "But seek ye first the kingdom of God, and his righteousness; and all these things [comforts of the world] shall be added unto you."[89] Brigham Young amplified this point in a great discourse:

> I say again, "seek ye first the kingdom of God and His righteousness," and in due time, no matter when, whether in this year or the next, in this life or in the life to come, "all these things" (that appear so necessary to have in the world) "shall be added unto you." Everything that is in heaven, on the earth, and in the earth, everything the most fruitful mind can imagine, shall be yours, sooner or later.[90]

Those who seek first the Kingdom of God, that is, who place their spiritual priorities in the proper perspective, shall receive more than enough of the comforts necessary in mortality. Such persons may become rich to the things of the world, simply because they seek for the riches to care for the well-being of others. Unlike the Rich Fool, such persons are able to maintain much in store, because they are also rich toward God. The *Book of Mormon* Prophet Jacob taught a great principle in the following words:

> Think of your brethren like unto yourselves, and be familiar with all and free with your substance, that they may be rich like unto you.
> But *before ye seek for riches, seek ye for the kingdom of God.*
> *And after ye have obtained a hope in Christ ye shall obtain riches, if ye seek them; and ye will seek them for the intent to do good*—to clothe the naked, and to feed the hungry, and to liberate the captive, and administer relief to the sick and the afflicted.[91]

SUMMARY

1. The power and blessings of the Priesthood only continue with those who forsake the things of the world, and are clean from the stain of Babylon.

2. Priesthood holders are under covenant to abide by the Lord's moral code, including the commission to maintain purity of thought.

3. Many men were *called* in the pre-earth councils, but few on earth become the *chosen* of the Lord. Some prime characteristics of those called and not chosen include:
    A. Their hearts are set upon the things of the world.
    B. They aspire to the honors of men.
    C. They attempt to gratify their pride and vain ambition through the Priesthood.
    D. They attempt to exercise unrighteous dominion through the Priesthood.
    E. They are walking in darkness at noon-day.

4. Those persons who do not learn that the rights of the Priesthood are inseparably connected with the powers of heaven, and continue to use the rights of the Priesthood in unholy ways, are laying a strong foundation for apostasy.

5. Divine tools in leading the Saints include:
    A. Persuasion
    B. Long-suffering
    C. Gentleness and meekness
    D. Unfeigned love
    E. Kindness
    F. Pure knowledge
    G. Sharp reproof, when moved upon by the Holy Ghost
    H. Charity
    I. Virtue

6. Through teaching correct principles (true knowledge), Priesthood leaders are able to guide the Saints in an effectual manner.

7. One whose eye is single to the glory of God works so as to aid God in bringing to pass the immortality and eternal life of man.

8. In making his eye (mind) single to God's glory, man must:
    A. Be willing to set aside personal wishes and ambitions.
    B. Learn and accept the will of the Almighty.

    C.   Counsel with the Lord in all matters, and acknowledge His hand in all things.

9.   Blessings that come to those who bring their hearts in tune with God and seek first His righteousness include:

    A.   They shall receive light and truth.

    B.   They shall grow in intelligence (light and truth) until, at the perfect day, they are able to comprehend all things.

    C.   They receive the comforts and righteous pleasures of the world, inasmuch as they seek them so as to do good and aid others.

THE WORDS OF
ETERNAL LIFE

THOSE CALLED TO HOLD and exercise the Melchizedek Priesthood covenant to "give diligent heed to the words of eternal life."[1] The words of eternal life are the words which, when abided by, lead one to the ultimate state of glorification in the presence of God the Father. Though it is impossible for man to receive the fullness of eternal life (glory of the Celestial Kingdom[2]) while yet in mortality, he may receive the "words of eternal life," or added endowments of the Spirit as they center in Jesus Christ, and are given by the Holy Ghost.[3] Jehovah thus explained to Father Adam that those who apply the atoning blood of Christ and become "born again" are "sanctified from all sin, and *enjoy the words of eternal life in this world, and eternal life in the world to come, even immortal glory.*"[4]

The words of eternal life come from different sources, but all contribute to the spiritual growth and enrichment of the individual, as he prepares to meet God. First, sacred powers and truths are transmitted to the soul as one studies carefully the Holy Scriptures, and attempts to apply the lessons learned by valiant men and women, as recorded in holy writ. Second, through accepting and internalizing the counsel of the living prophets man may learn the will of God, as it applies to a modern world, and thus mature in the vital principle of obedience.[5] Third, as man analyzes himself, he will eventually learn the procedures necessary to break down the barriers that prevent true communication with self; self-revelation comes as the Priesthood bearer gives much time to pondering and meditation. Fourth, as the Priesthood becomes a source of power, the principle of prayer will take on greater significance, and this mode of communication will become a prime source of pure intelligence. Finally, through the diligent application of each of the above sources of truth, the pure man may grow in the principle of revelation, and reach the point of spiritual readiness so as to "learn by faith."

It was to the Temptor that Jesus explained: "Man shall not live by bread alone, but by every word that proceedeth out of the mouth of God."[6] To live by every word of God is to strive for excellence in the whole law of the gospel. It is to avoid extremes, fanaticism, and gospel hobbies. Of gospel hobbies, for example, President Joseph F. Smith warned:

> Brethren and sisters, don't have hobbies. Hobbies are dangerous
> in the Church of Christ. They are dangerous because they give undue

prominence to certain principles or ideas to the detriment or dwarfing of others just as important, just as binding, just as saving as the favored doctrines or commandments.

Hobbies give to those who encourage them a false aspect of the gospel of the Redeemer; they distort and place out of harmony its principles and teachings. The point of view is unnatural. Every principle and practice revealed from God is essential to man's salvation, and to place any one of them unduly in front, hiding and dimming all others is unwise and dangerous; it jeopardizes our salvation, for it darkens our minds and beclouds our understandings.[8]

Similarly, Elder Bruce R. McConkie noted that it was his experience that "people who ride gospel hobbies, who try to qualify themselves as experts in some specialized field, who try to make the whole plan of salvation revolve around some field of particular interest to them—it is my experience that such persons are usually spiritually immature and spiritually unstable. . . . We would do well to have a sane, rounded, and balanced approach to the whole gospel and all of its doctrines."[9]

SEARCHING THE SCRIPTURES

The Standard Works of the Church, as canonized scriptures, are among the most effective means of building the Holy Spirit in one's life. Wilford Woodruff stated that "the Bible, the Book of Mormon, the Doctrine and Covenants [and the Pearl of Great Price] *contain the words of eternal life unto this generation*, and they will rise in judgement against those who reject them."[10] President Marion G. Romney explained that he could "think of no surer way to seek instruction and inspiration for daily living than to daily read and prayerfully contemplate a chapter or so in these sacred works which contain the *law of heaven*. To do so has ever been the counsel of the Lord."[11] It is interesting that President Romney speaks of the Standard Works as containing the "law of heaven." Within these four volumes are contained the patterns of living, as given from the heavens to living oracles on earth. They are *standard* works, because they are the standard measure by which all should be done, and the standard of all that is and should be taught in the Church.[12]

In speaking of scripture in general, Paul explained to Timothy that it is given "by inspiration of God, and is profitable *for doctrine, for reproof, for correction, for instruction in righteousness: That the man of God may be perfect, thoroughly furnished unto all good works.*"[13] First of all, then, the scriptures are given to establish truthfulness or falseness of points of doctrine. Through a careful search of the holy words, man may come to distinguish the power of truth from the philosophy of men. Second, scriptures are given for reproof. As one reads the scriptures, he is often chastened by the Holy Ghost for those things in his personal life not in strict harmony with the written word of God. Third, the scriptures not only reprove, but teach the principles necessary to correct the misdeeds. Fourth, the words and spirit of the scriptures serve to instruct the reader in righteousness. Finally, the scriptures exist to bring man to a state of perfection, wherein he enjoys a spiritual union with Christ forever and ever.

Joseph Smith taught the brethren that "the Book of Mormon was the most correct of any book on earth, and the keystone of our religion, and a man would get nearer to God by abiding by its precepts than by any other book."[14] In speaking of the *Book of Mormon*, a revelation explained that this record contained "the fulness of the gospel of Jesus Christ."[15] Some in the Church have asked: "How is it that the *Book of Mormon* can contain a fulness of the Gospel of Christ, if there is no mention of baptism for the dead, or the degrees of glory within its pages?" The key in resolving this question is to realize that the *Book of Mormon* does not contain the fulness of *Gospel doctrine*, but contains the principles and teachings necessary to bring one to the point where he can ultimately partake of the fulness of the glory of the Celestial Kingdom. The First Principles and Ordinances, if adhered to strictly, are the means whereby man may enter the presence of God. Faith, repentance, baptism, and the gift of the Holy Ghost, if comprehended in their infinite and eternal context, contain a fulness of the Gospel. Joseph Fielding Smith stated: "By fulness of the gospel is meant all the ordinances and principles that pertain to the exaltation in the celestial kingdom. . . ."[16] In giving instructions to the Priesthood of the Church, the Lord thus explained in 1831: "And again, the elders, priests and teachers of this church shall teach the principles of my gospel, which are in the Bible and the Book of Mormon, *in the which is the fulness of the gospel.*"[17] In giving tribute to another of the Lord's book of scriptures, Wilford Woodruff said: "I consider that the Doctrine and Covenants, *our testament*, contains a code of the most solemn, the most Godlike proclamations ever made to the human family."[18] In speaking of the set of Standard Works then in print President Brigham Young taught:

> The Old and New Testaments, the Book of Mormon, and the Book of Doctrine and Covenants . . . are like a lighthouse in the ocean or a fingerpost which points out the road we should travel. *Where do they point? To the fountain of light. . . . That is what these books are for. They are of God;* they are valuable and necessary; *by them we can establish the doctrine of Christ.*[19]

Priesthood bearers, as well as all members of the Church, are under obligation to search and contemplate the scriptures. Marion G. Romney explained:

> . . . ancient Israel was to be judged by their compliance or noncompliance with the content of the Book of the Law [see Deut. 31:24–26]. By

the same token, *modern Israel will be judged by their compliance or non-compliance with the law of heaven contained in our standard works.*[20]

If modern Israel is to be judged by the things written in our Standard Works, then it behooves all Saints to study carefully the code of ethics and plan of salvation as given in scripture. Priesthood bearers must study the scriptures in order to magnify their callings in the Priesthood.[21] President Joseph F. Smith spoke of the value of men studying specifically the revelations on Priesthood:

> I now say to the brethren holding the Priesthood . . . *magnify your callings; study the scriptures;* read the 107th Section of the Doctrine and Covenants on Priesthood; learn that revelation, which was given to the Prophet Joseph Smith, and live by its precepts and doctrine, and you will gain power and intelligence to straighten out many kinks that have heretofore existed in your minds, and to clear up many doubts and uncertainties in relation to the rights of the Priesthood.[22]

George Albert Smith, in speaking of the responsibility of parents to teach the scriptures to their children, said:

> *Will our Father hold us guiltless when we go home, if we have failed to teach our children the importance of these sacred records? I think not.* He called his sons, one by one, and they gave their lives that we might have the Old Testament. He sent His only Begotten Son into the world, and His life was sacrificed in order that we might have the teachings of the New Testament. The prophets of God recorded in the Book of Mormon laid down their lives and sealed their testimonies with their blood, in order that the children of men might know what the Father desired of them. He sent the Prophet Joseph Smith, and he gave his life, together with his brother Hyrum, in order that we might have the truths contained in the sacred record known as the Doctrine and Covenants. Do you suppose that after the Lord has done all this for us, has given to this world the choicest and sweetest of men and women, whose lives have been dedicated to the blessing of mankind, many of them sealing their testimony with their blood, has placed within our reach the excellent teachings contained in these holy records, that He will consider us appreciative if we fail to teach them to our families and to impress them upon those with whom we come in contact?[23]

As important as the *words* contained in scripture is the *spirit* of enlightenment which accompanies their reception. Perhaps the most important result of studying the words of the prophets, then, is not necessarily the intellectual understanding one gains, but the spirit of peace and comfort that flow from these holy pages. Joseph F. Smith made it clear that "that which characterizes above all else the inspiration and divinity of the Scriptures is the spirit in which they are written and the spiritual wealth they convey to those who faithfully and conscientiously read them." President Smith continued his remarks: "*They are intended to enlarge man's spiritual endowments and to reveal and intensify the bond of relationship between him and his God.*"[24]

PONDERING AND MEDITATION

In today's busy world, man spends too little time alone with himself. Caught up in a world which demands practically every minute of the waking day, man seldom sets aside time to ponder and meditate upon things of substance. It is only through meditation and constant self-analysis that the Priesthood holder will ever be capable of giving an honest answer to the query: "Who am I?" In addition to a veil of forgetfulness which separates man from eternity, there is a constant barrier being established and fortified between reality and appearances. This barrier, composed of layers of self-deceit and personal dishonesty, must be dissolved if man is ever to know God and understand the divine will.

The powers of the Gospel of Jesus Christ exist to bring man to the point of spiritual, emotional and intellectual honesty and sincerity, so that every man might know who he is and what his possibilities and potentials are. Dr. Truman G. Madsen expressed the nature of this particular quest in life in the following words: "One begins mortality with the veil drawn, but slowly he is moved to penetrate *the veil within himself. He is, in time, led to seek the holy of holies within his own being.*"[25] To remove such a veil requires diligent evaluation, meaningful interpretation, and intense concentration.

As one spends valuable time in concentration, evaluates carefully his thoughts and actions, and interprets them in light of Divine and personal standards, he is on the path which leads to self-revelation. Few men have reached the point where they could proclaim as did Joseph Smith, "*Would to God, brethren, I could tell you who I am! Would to God I could tell you what I know.*"[26] Even more profound are the words of Jehovah to Moses: "I AM THAT I AM."[27] (Those closest to the source of truth—those who hold communion with the Infinite—know of the perfections and power of their Father and God, and, at the same time, of their own familial tie to Deity. Occasionally the Lord thins the veil of forgetfulness and provides those "spirit memories" which whisper that we are but strangers here, seekers after that holy home from whence we came and those sublime associations which once were ours.)

Try as they may, people of the world may search and search into the Eastern philosophies and religions, but *they will never become one with themselves until they accept the Gospel and come to know God.* This great truth is heralded in one of the most sobering yet inspiring statements that Joseph Smith ever made. In the great funeral sermon of King Follett, he said: "*If men do not comprehend the character of God, they do not comprehend themselves.*"[28] Only the pure man, the man devoted to the cause of Christ, is capable of understanding the character of God; only this type will be discerning enough to come to recognize and analyze the inner man. Interestingly enough, President Brigham Young taught that these two processes (knowing self, knowing God) are interrelated, and that one is strictly dependent upon the other. President Young stated in April of 1870 that "to know and understand ourselves and our own being is to know and understand God and His being."[29] He spoke on another occasion and made clear the fact that "there is no man that can know himself unless he knows God, and he cannot know God unless he knows himself."[30] If it is life eternal to know God and Christ (John 17:3), then it must also be life eternal to know self.

Through pondering and meditation, the Priesthood bearer may come to understand the deeper things of God. The Prophet thus explained that "the things of God are of deep import; and time, and experience, and *careful and ponderous and solemn thoughts can only find them out*."[31] President David O. McKay spoke frequently of the value of meditation in building spirituality among the Saints.

> I think we pay too little attention to the value of meditation, *a principle of devotion*. In our worship there are two elements: one is spiritual communion arising from our own meditation; the other, instruction from others, particularly from those who have authority to guide and instruct us. Of the two, the more profitable introspectively is the meditation. *Meditation is the language of the soul.* It is defined as "a form of private devotion, or spiritual exercise, consisting in deep, continued reflection on some religious theme." Meditation is a form of prayer. . . . *Meditation is one of the most secret, most sacred doors through which we pass into the presence of the Lord.*[32]

President McKay further explained that these inspirational moments come as man is alone with himself and God. He continued: "These secret prayers, these conscientious moments in meditation, these yearnings of the soul to reach out to feel the presence of God—*such is the privilege of those who hold the Melchizedek Priesthood.*"[33]

Harold B. Lee spoke of President McKay's admonitions:

> President McKay sometime ago in talking to the Presidency and the Twelve, urged us *to give more time for meditation so that we could tune in with spiritual forces* that we had a right to and should expect to direct us in our work. He said, "The best time for me is early in the morning when my mind and body are rested. But when the inspiration comes . . . you have to have the courage to do what he instructs you."[34]

There is great power in taking the time necessary to ponder upon the written scriptures. President Marion G. Romney indicated in a conference address that one way to magnify Priesthood callings is through pondering these particular words of eternal life. Said he: "*Pondering is, in my feeling, a form of prayer. It has, at least, been an approach to the Spirit of the Lord on many occasions.*"[35] The mighty seer in the *Book of Mormon*, Nephi, wrote:

> And upon these [the plates] I write the things of my soul, and many of the scriptures which are engraven upon the plates of brass. For *my soul delighteth in the scriptures, and my heart pondereth them....*
>
> Behold, my soul delighteth in the things of the Lord; and my heart pondereth continually upon the things which I have seen and heard.[36]

Great revelations have come as men of God have applied the powers of concentration with regard to the Holy Scriptures. Joseph Smith and Sidney Rigdon wrote:

> For while we were doing the work of translation, which the Lord had appointed unto us [an inspired translation of the Bible], we came to the twenty-ninth verse of the fifth chapter of John....
>
> And while we meditated upon these things, the Lord touched the eyes of our understandings and they were opened, and the glory of the Lord shone round about.[37]

In the minutes and hours that followed, there was revealed to man one of the most glorious of all theophanies, for these two brethren were given a "Vision of the Glories." President Joseph F. Smith wrote:

> On the third of October, in the year nineteen hundred and eighteen, I sat in my room *pondering over the scriptures* and reflecting upon the great atoning sacrifice that was made by the Son of God for the redemption of the world....
>
> As I pondered over these things which are written [1 Peter 3:18–20; 4:6], the eyes of my understanding were opened, and the Spirit of the Lord rested upon me, and I saw the hosts of the dead, both small and great.[38]

President Smith then went on to describe a great "Vision of the Redemption of the Dead," in which many marvelous truths were revealed regarding the organized missionary efforts in the spirit world. These and numerous other accounts bear testimony of the fact that as men of the Priesthood treasure in their hearts the words of life, and let the solemnities of eternity rest upon their minds, the powers of truth and light will bring knowledge to their spirit, and whisper peace to their soul.[39]

PRAYING IN SPIRIT

Searching the scriptures and pondering cannot be completely effective without the aid of prayer. Prayer is the primary tool which opens the door to a meaningful relationship with Deity; twenty-four hours a day of scripture study and/or meditation will not bring a man to a point of spiritual union with Christ where effective prayer is lacking. Too often we forget that prayer is a form of *communication*. Communication requires three things in order to bring about a positive end: *a sender, a receiver, and feedback*. The first two items of the communicative process are almost always present in the situation of prayer. That is, man speaks to God, and, usually, God listens. But true communication between heaven and earth is not established without feedback. More often than not, man ignores the feedback that the heavenly powers might give—in plain words, man does not take the time to *listen* for any answer to prayer, whether through the spoken word or impressions. If Priesthood bearers expect to gain power in the Priesthood, and thus be capable of blessing the lives of others, then they must learn to wait on the Lord, and expect answers to prayer. The Psalmist declared: "I wait for the Lord, my soul doth wait, and in his word do I hope."[40]

Men of the Priesthood must also learn perseverance in prayer. A classic example of one who continued in prayer and fasting until an answer to prayer was given was President Lorenzo Snow. President Woodruff's health had been failing for some time. Lorenzo Snow, as President of the Council of the Twelve, feared greatly lest the tremendous burden of Church leadership should fall upon his shoulders. In addition to the fact that the church was suffering under financial strain, President Snow was an aged man, at that point in time (1898) being in his eighty-sixth year. Upon receiving word from the doctors that President Woodruff would not remain much longer, Brother Snow went to his room in the Salt Lake Temple, where he was residing at the time. He adorned himself in the robes of the Priesthood and, kneeling in the Holy of Holies, poured out his soul to Almighty God. He pleaded with the Lord to preserve the life of Wilford Woodruff, begging that the present prophet leader might be permitted to outlive him. Yet the humble Brother Snow promised that he would perform any task required of him. President Woodruff's passing occurred in California on the morning of September 2nd, and the solemn word was forwarded to the brethren in Utah. Brother Snow retired again to the altar in the sacred House of the Lord, whereupon he pleaded so as to know the will of God.

He presented himself and asked that he be instructed and guided in the matters necessary to maintain a spirit of continuity in the Kingdom on earth. After finishing his prayer, he waited for the reply of the Lord. But none came. For hours and hours he waited, continuing in prayer before God. Brother Snow received no voice, no visitation, no manifestation. He left the holy room, greatly disappointed at having received no instructions. He passed through the Celestial room and out into the large corridor leading to his room. It was at this point in the temple where a most glorious manifestation was given to President Snow.

The following account is told by his granddaughter, Alice Young Pond, who was with President Snow on a later occasion in the temple:

> After we left his room and while we were still in the large corridor, leading into the Celestial room, I was walking several steps ahead of Grandpa when he stopped me, saying: "Wait a moment, Allie, I want to tell you something. *It was right here that the Lord Jesus Christ appeared to me at the time of the death of President Woodruff.* He instructed me to go right ahead and reorganize the First Presidency of the church at once and not wait as he had done after the death of the previous presidents, and that I was to succeed President Woodruff."
>
> Then Grandpa came a step nearer and held out his left hand and said: "He stood right here, about three feet above the floor. It looked as though he stood on a plate of solid gold."
>
> Grandpa told me what a glorious personage the Savior is and described His hands, feet, countenance and beautiful White Robes, all of which were of such a glory of whiteness and brightness that he could hardly gaze upon Him.
>
> Then Grandpa came another step nearer me and put his right hand on my head and said: "Now, granddaughter, I want you to remember that this is the testimony of your grandfather, that he told you with his own lips that he actually saw the Savior here in the Temple and talked with Him face to face."[41]

Often men of the Priesthood are required to persevere in their prayers in order to obtain the blessings of revelation and divine teaching. The American Prophet Enos, while still a youth, prayed day and night before obtaining the word of the Lord and a subsequent remission of his sins.[42] In our own day, President Spencer W. Kimball reported that as Jacob of old wrestled all night until the breaking of day for a blessing, so he also went through that experience for 85 nights, "praying to the Lord to help me and strengthen me and make me equal to this great responsibility that has come to me [as a member of the Twelve."[43] There is a great lesson to be learned from these noble and great men of God. Those who receive the Priesthood with full purpose of heart will honor it, and will seek the Lord continually in prayer, in order to receive His comforting and enlightening influence.

Prayer is the most powerful means of obtaining the Holy Spirit. Joseph Smith said: "*I urge the necessity of prayer, that the Spirit might be given,* that the things of the Spirit might be judged thereby. . . ."[44]

A modern revelation also declared that "the Spirit shall be given unto you by the prayer of faith. . . ."[45] Acquiring the powers of the Holy Ghost is essential to a genuine communion with Deity, for it is by the Spirit that one receives the peace and joy that come to the faithful seeker. Some valuable instructions as to the role of the Holy Ghost in prayer were given by Nephi:

> And now, my beloved brethren, I perceive that ye ponder still in your hearts; and it grieveth me that I must speak concerning this thing. *For if ye would harken unto the Spirit which teacheth a man to pray ye would know that ye must pray; for the evil spirit teacheth not a man to pray, but teacheth him that he must not pray.*[46]

In those few words are some powerful lessons. *First,* the Holy Ghost will always teach a man of the importance of prayer. Thus the necessity for gaining the Spirit in the process of prayer. This testimony of prayer will come as one is faithful in kneeling before God morning and night. Man must initiate the process by kneeling and sincerely seeking after God; after doing so, the Spirit, with its comforting influences will be given. President Brigham Young taught of the importance of man making the first move. "It matters not whether you or I feel like praying, when the time comes to pray, *pray. If we do not feel like it, we should pray till we do* [that is, until the Spirit enters].... You will find that those who wait till the Spirit bids them pray will never pray much on this earth."[47] *Second,* there is another way to view Nephi's words. Not only does the Holy Ghost teach one that he should pray, but the Spirit also teaches man *HOW* to pray. This includes (1) the words to be spoken, (2) the things for which to pray, and (3) the way in which God is to be approached. In this context, President Wilford Woodruff said: "*Many of you have learned how to pray;* then fail not to let your prayers ascend up into the ears of the God of Sabaoth; and He will hear you. I think sometimes that we do not fully comprehend the power that we have with God in knowing *how to approach Him acceptably.*"[48] The Prophet Joseph also said: "*Having a knowledge of God, we begin to know how to approach him, and how to ask so as to receive an answer.* When we understand the character of God, and to know how to come to him, he begins to unfold the heavens to us...."[49]

The Saints of God have ever been commanded to *pray in the Spirit.*[50] What does this mean? It means that man's prayer is literally given to him from above. One who prays in the Spirit finds that his words reach beyond his thoughts, namely because the words are not his own. A modern revelation explained: "*He that asketh in the Spirit asketh according to the will of God; wherefore it is done even as he asketh. And ye must give thanks unto God in the Spirit for whatsoever blessing you are blessed with.*"[51] Because such prayers are of divine origin, they are often most instructive and enlightening. Brigham Young stated: "When you have labored faithfully for years, you will learn the simple fact—that if your hearts are aright and you still continue to be obedient, continue to serve God, *continue to pray, the Spirit of revelation will be in you like a well of water springing up to everlasting life.*"[52] President Young was even more specific on another occasion: "*Let all persons be fervent in prayer, until they know the things of God for themselves. . . ."*[53] Prayer in the Spirit is therefore an important avenue in the reception of the words of eternal life.

GROWING IN THE PRINCIPLE
OF REVELATION

Though every member of the church is entitled to the promptings and directions that come from divine sources, those ordained to the Melchizedek Priesthood hold the keys necessary to unlock heavenly powers to a greater degree, for "the first great gift of the Priesthood is revelation."[54] There is only one man on the earth at a time who may receive revelations for the entire Church, but every Elder, Seventy, and High Priest has the right to inspiration and *personal revelation.* Joseph Smith taught that "it is . . . the privilege of any officer in this Church to obtain revelations so far as relates to his particular calling and duty in the Church.[55] Every man, then, may receive revelations to aid him in his positions in the Church, whether as secretary, advisor, president or father. The revelation may come in the form of instruction, so that the officer may be given to understand how best to perform the task. Or it may come in the form of pure inspiration, wherein the recipient is uplifted or comforted or assured in his particular duty. President Brigham Young referred to the principles learned through revelation as "true knowledge," and stated that this quality of knowledge "flows through the Priesthood, to enable us to know how to order our lives, to overcome every principle that tends to the death, and to embrace every principle that tends to the life. . . ."[56] Similarly, Elder John A. Widtsoe explained that "those who hold the Priesthood are entitled, if their lives are pure, to revelation from God to guide them in their private affairs and official actions within the Church. . . ."[57]

The Prophet Joseph gave a beautiful description of the workings of the spirit of revelation in man. Said he:

> A person may profit by noticing the first intimation of the spirit of revelation; for instance, when you feel pure intelligence flowing into you, it may give you sudden strokes of ideas, so that by noticing it, you may find it fulfilled the same day or soon; (i.e.) those things that were presented unto your minds by the Spirit of God will come to pass; *and thus by learning the Spirit of God and understanding it, you may grow into the principle of revelation, until you become perfect in Christ Jesus.*[58]

There are two points here of particular interest. First, the Prophet teaches that one way to recognize the spirit of revelation is by sudden flashes of knowledge. Pure intelligence, or intelligence (light and truth[59]) from the pure source, when it comes upon man, has the property of causing a rush of ideas to the mind. The author has, on many occasions, been blessed with similar experiences. After having prayed intently for the purpose of receiving added enlightenment in teaching a difficult lesson to the Priesthood quorum, I have often found myself flooded with ideas concerning doctrinal principles and practices while going about my daily activities. And often I have asked that my wife bring a paper and pencil, so that the ideas could be written down and not be forgotten. Joseph the Prophet spoke specifically about sudden strokes of ideas concerning things that would shortly come to pass; this is *the spirit of prophecy and revelation.*

Second, as man learns the Spirit of God, or learns how to recognize the onset of such manifestations, he begins to grow into the principle of revelation. The gift of revelation is not something that is acquired overnight, but is actually something into which man must grow (spiritually); it is acquired in degrees, ranging from simple impressions to a life in which man relies wholly upon revelation as a source of knowledge. As one matures in this great principle, he is eventually made perfect in Christ. This approach to revelation (flashes of ideas) is only one means by which the Lord may reveal His mind and will. A revelation to Oliver Cowdery explained how a knowledge of the translation process would come:

> Yea, behold, *I will tell you in your mind and in your heart,* by the Holy Ghost, which shall come upon you and which shall dwell in your heart.
>
> Now, behold, *this is the spirit of revelation. . . .*[60]

Man may know things by the Holy Ghost, and these may be revealed to the mind and/or the heart. In a revelation given in the same month, Oliver was instructed that after studying a matter over in his mind, to then ask God if it be right. He was informed that should his decision be of God, then the Almighty would "cause that your bosom shall burn within you; therefore, you shall feel that it is right." On the other hand, "if it be not right you shall have no such feelings, but you shall have a stupor of thought. . . ."[61] The warm sense of peace and tranquility serves as an affectional assurance that the decision is of God, while the state of mental and emotional dissonance indicates that the thing is not right in the sight of God. Revelation may also come in the form of a "still small voice,"[62] an audible voice,[63] a vision,[64] or a dream.[65]

Although reception of the Priesthood entitles one to the gifts of revelation, these gifts are only operative upon the principle of individual worthiness. President Marion G. Romney said simply: "Since revelation is by nature spiritual, man, to receive it, must be spiritually born again."[66] To be "born again" is to be made clean and innocent through the blood of Christ and to be even as a newborn infant.[67] Brigham Young also explained: "A really pure person is very scarce: but *when the heart is truly pure, the Lord can write upon it,* and the truth is received without argument, or doubt, or disputation."[68] Those who are pure have hearts that are as *spiritual tabula rasas,* in the sense that the Lord writes the words of eternal life upon those souls.

UNFOLDING THE MYSTERIES

In a revelation given in 1832 the Lord explained, in speaking of the Melchizedek Priesthood: "And this greater priesthood administereth the gospel and *holdeth the key of the mysteries of the kingdom,* even the key of the knowledge of God."[69] A later revelation made the same declaration: "The power and authority of the higher, or Melchizedek Priesthood, is to hold the keys of all the spiritual blessings of the church—*To have the privilege of receiving the mysteries of the kingdom of heaven. . . .*"[70] What are the mysteries? In one sense, they are those principles and doctrines which bring one to a knowledge of God (see above). In another sense, mysteries are principles unknown to most men. Elder Bruce R. McConkie said:

> A mystery is something which cannot be explained, either because it is beyond human comprehension in general, or because some particular man has not learned enough to understand it. Accordingly, some matters of doctrine, philosophy, or science *may be a mystery to one person and not to another.* When a thing is understood it is no longer a mystery. In the eternal sense there are no mysteries; all things are known to and understood by Deity. . . .[71]

President Brigham Young also said:

> There is no mystery to me in what God has revealed to me, or in what I have learned, whether it has been through Joseph, an angel, the voice of the Spirit, the Holy Ghost, or the Spirit of the Lord; no matter how I have learned a thing, *if I understand it perfectly it is no mystery to me.*[72]

The Priesthood of God entitles one to the reception of the mysteries of Godliness, or those things which are not made known to every man. One may receive his own "vision of the glories" or "vision of the redemption of the dead," and these matters would no longer be classified as mysteries to him, though they might be mysterious to others in the Church who have not received the same manifestations. The only barriers to the reception of such sacred knowledge are (1) man's lack of spiritual readiness and (2) God's will so far as how much one man may be given. Joseph Smith made it clear that "God hath not revealed anything to Joseph, but what He will make known to the Twelve, and even *the least Saint may know all things as fast as he is able to bear them. . . .*"[73] It is the will of the Lord that man seek for an understanding of holy things, for as Christ explained: "*I delight in those who seek diligently to know my precepts,* and abide by the law of my kingdom; for *all things shall be made known unto them* in mine own due time, and in the end they shall have joy."[74] In explaining the value of receiving the mysteries, the Lord said in 1831: "But unto him that keepeth my command-ments I will give the mysteries of my kingdom, and the same shall be in him *a well of living water, springing up unto everlasting life.*"[75] According to these words, the mysteries of Godliness, when received and utilized by the proper individual, become a powerful source of spiritual strength, and the impetus needed to usher one into the presence of the Gods. Again the Master spoke: "If thou shalt ask, thou shalt receive revelation upon revelation, knowledge upon knowledge, that *thou mayest know the mysteries and peaceable things—that which bringeth joy, that which bringeth life eternal.*"[76]

There is much evidence that Joseph Smith, the modern Prophet, desired greatly to teach the Saints many of the mysteries which he had acquired, but they would not receive them. Joseph explained on one occasion that "the moment you teach them some of the mysteries that are retained in the heavens and are to be revealed to the children of men when they are prepared for them, they will be the first to stone you and put you to death. . . ."[77] Wilford Woodruff, in speaking of Joseph's trial in this regard, said: "His mind was opened by the visions of the Almighty, and the Lord taught him many things by vision and revelation that were never taught publicly in his days; for the people could not bear the flood of intelligence which God poured into his mind."[78] Another of the early brethren spoke of the way in which Joseph was restricted in his teachings: "What he had to communicate was so much more comprehensive, enlightened and dignified than that which the people generally knew and comprehended, it was difficult for him to speak; he felt fettered and bound, so to speak, in every move he made."[79] Finally, Joseph described the "stiffneckedness" of the Saints of his day in these most descriptive terms:

> . . . there has been a great difficulty in getting anything into the heads of this generation. It has been like splitting hemlock knots with a corn-dodger for a wedge, and a pumpkin for a beetle. *Even the Saints are slow to understand.* I have tried for a number of years to get the minds of the Saints prepared to receive the things of God; but we frequently see some of them after suffering all they have for the work of God, will fly to pieces like glass as soon as anything comes that is contrary to their traditions; they cannot stand the fire at all.[80]

The question arises: Why would the Latter-day Saints reject many of the beautiful truths that Joseph had to offer? Likewise, why do many today not attempt to learn the things of God that are available through the blessings of the Priesthood? The *Book of Mormon* prophet, Alma, made these profound remarks:

> *It is given unto many to know the mysteries of God;* nevertheless they
> are laid under a strict command that they shall not impart only accord-
> ing to the portion of his word which he doth grant unto the children of
> men, according to the heed and diligence which they give unto him.
>
> And therefore, he that will harden his heart, the same receiveth
> the lesser portion of the word; and *he that will not harden his heart, to
> him is given the greater portion of the word,* until it is given unto him to
> know the mysteries of God until he know them in full.
>
> And *they that will harden their hearts, to them is given the lesser por-
> tion of the word until they know nothing concerning his mysteries;* and then
> they are taken captive by the devil, and led by his will down to destruc-
> tion. Now this is what is meant by the chains of hell.[81]

According to Alma, those who will not harden their hearts or reject the Spirit
of God, will receive a greater portion of the words of eternal life; they entitle
themselves to the mysteries of God. Those who refuse to seek after the things
from above are becoming hardened in their approach to the Gospel, and, if they
continue on the same course, will lay a foundation for apostasy from the truth.
Their minds and hearts will be bound by Satan.

One should exercise some cautions in seeking for the mysteries of the
Kingdom. *First,* holders of the Priesthood must remember that it is not wise to
seek for "meat" when the spiritual digestive system can only tolerate "milk." (One
neither seeks to rush into divine experience nor to dissipate his energies on
unresolved doctrinal difficulties.) *Second,* the manner in which one seeks for the
deeper things is most important. Instead of "bless me, O Lord, that I may have
a vision," one's prayer should be "bless me, O Lord, that I may prepare myself
for what thou wouldst give me. I desire only what thou knowest I am ready for.
May thy will be done."

Just three months before his sudden death, President Harold B. Lee gave a
moving address to the students at Brigham Young University, in which he made
the following statements:

> As I pray for the guidance of the Spirit, and seek to rise to the
> responsibility which has been given me, *I don't ask for any special endow-
> ment. I only ask to go where the Lord would have me go, and only to receive
> what the Lord would have me receive,* knowing that more important
> than sight is the witness that one may have by the witness of the Holy
> Ghost to his soul that things are so and that Jesus is the Christ, a living
> personage. It is that which guides me through many of the experiences
> of life.[82]

Finally, man is to be discerning in discussing with others sacred things
received in the spirit of revelation. As Alma explained, the mysteries are to be

imparted to others only as the Spirit may dictate, for they must be prepared to receive such things; to do otherwise is to risk "casting pearls before swine." The Lord's words are most direct: "Remember that *that which cometh from above is sacred, and must be spoken with care, and by constraint of the Spirit;* and in this there is no condemnation. . . ."[83] Most important, however, is the fact that although one may receive marvelous manifestations, instructions, or doctrinal clarifications, he is not to teach such things as doctrine and policy of the Church. The right to interpret and declare doctrine rests with one man only, and that is the President of the High Priesthood, the Prophet of God. Priesthood bearers thus have the responsibility to cherish and keep sacred all things received of God for their own personal enlightenment. Elder John A. Widtsoe instructed:

> Divine manifestations for individual comfort may be received by every worthy member of the Church. In that respect all faithful members of the Church are equal. Such manifestations most commonly guide the recipients to the solution of personal problems; though, frequently, they also open the mind to a clearer comprehension of the Lord's vast plan of salvation. *They are cherished possessions, and should be so valued by those who receive them.*[84]

KNOWLEDGE BY FAITH

As man grows in the principle of revelation on the path to perfection, he will soon gain the keen assurance that the greatest and most precious of all truth is to be gained by the Holy Ghost. Knowledge gained by the senses and human intellect, though essential in mortality, take a back seat in eternal value to that truth gained by revelation. In 1832 the Lord gave wise counsel to the Elders of the Church:

> And *as all have not faith,* seek ye diligently and teach one another words of wisdom; yea, seek ye out of the best books words of wisdom; *seek learning, even by study and also by faith.*[85]

It is interesting that these directions are prefaced by the negative clause, "And as all have not faith. . . ." The Master's instructions are, in essence: since all do not have the faith necessary to learn by any other means, then seek learning by study and the use of the intellectual processes. In other words, if all *did* have the requisite faith, then learning by studying from the best books would not be necessary. This was a call for man to undertake "learning by faith." President John Taylor pleaded with the Priesthood: "Let me speak . . . to all men holding authority, to seek to God, seek for wisdom, *seek for faith,* and learn to approach God, that we may draw down blessings from heaven and *partake of that faith* which was once delivered to the Saints."[86]

The Prophet Joseph taught:

We consider that God has created man with a mind capable of instruction, and a faculty which may be enlarged in proportion to the heed and diligence given to the light communicated from heaven to the intellect; and that the nearer a man approaches perfection, the clearer are his views, and the greater his enjoyments, till he has overcome the evils of his life and lost every desire for sin; and like the ancients, *arrives at that point of faith where he is wrapped in the power and glory of his Maker, and is caught up to dwell with Him.*[87]

It becomes clear from the statements above that faith in Jesus Christ is obviously more than a strong belief or conviction in the Master, but is actually a principle of power. The Prophet thus taught that those who continue in seeking after God shall "like Enoch, the brother of Jared, and Moses, ... *obtain faith in God, and power with him to behold him face to face.*"[88]

The transcendent level of faith and commensurate spirituality of men like Enoch, the brother of Jared, and Moses was such as to allow them to receive eternal truths more often and more completely than most men. As to the price that must be paid to receive knowledge in this divine manner, President Harold B. Lee said: "The acquiring of knowledge by faith is no easy road to learning. It will demand strenuous effort and continual striving by faith." Then, quoting Elder B. H. Roberts, President Lee continued:

Such a process requires the bending of the whole soul, the calling up from the depths of the human mind and linking the person with God. *The right connection must be formed; then only comes knowledge by faith,* a kind of knowledge that goes beyond secular learning, that reaches into the realms of the unknown and makes those who follow that course great in the sight of God.[89]

One who brings himself to this point of dedication will also be capable of receiving of other types of knowledge more effectively by the powers of the Holy Spirit. A Latter-day Saint writer stated in 1910:

Knowledge, then, is to be obtained by study and by faith, and *where faith is strong enough, knowledge may be more easily acquired.* The Lord has declared that nothing may be obtained unless a person strives for it; yet *to him who obeys the commandments of God, the Holy Spirit may be given in such great abundance that knowledge may come easily.* Therefore ... a righteous man may acquire knowledge more rapidly than an unrighteous man. It is through the comforter or the Spirit of God that the Latter-day Saints are to receive the gift of knowledge.[90]

As to the nature of the spiritual truths gained through the powerful exercise of faith, Joseph Smith often spoke of "*a superior intelligence* bestowed upon such as obey the Gospel with full purpose of heart."[91] Speaking of this "superior intelligence," President Marion G. Romney said:

> *Such truth is not to be had through man's ordinary learning processes.* His sensory powers are calculated and adapted to deal only with the things of this telestial earth. Without revelation, man's intellect is wholly inadequate for the discovery of the ultimate truth with which the gospel deals.
>
> *The spirit of revelation turns the key which opens the mind and spirit of man to an understanding of the gospel. There is no other approach to such knowledge.* Thinkers have philosophized, poets have dreamed, and scientists have experimented; but only God speaks with a sure knowledge of all truth.[92]

Speaking at the dedicatory services of the cornerstone of the Far West Temple, Sidney Rigdon explained:

> One part of the house [the proposed temple], shall be set apart for a place of worship, where we may invoke our God for revelations, *when we have gone as far as human skill can carry us,* that by revelations, visions, etc., we may fill the vacuum still left after science and philosophy have done all they can do. . . .
>
> *When science fails, revelation supplies its place,* and unfolds the secrets and mysteries of the unseen world, leads the mind into knowledge of the future existence of man, makes it acquainted with angels, principalities, and powers, in the eternal world . . . so that *when science fails and philosophy vanishes away, revelation, more extensive in its operations, begins where they end,* and feasts the mind with intelligence, pure and holy, from the presence of God. . . .[93]

Thus knowledge by faith consists of a pure manifestation of Godly intelligence, a manifestation which surpasses the known cognitive processes. Joseph the Seer therefore taught that "the best way to obtain truth and wisdom is not to ask it from books, but to go to God in prayer, and obtain *divine teaching.*"[94]

It is in this context that another of Joseph's popular yet little-understood statements finds meaning: "*Could you gaze into heaven five minutes, you would know more than you would by reading all that ever was written on the subject.*"[95] As the Spirit of the Lord works on the entire system of a being, the person is capable of receiving truth by means other than the five senses; this is the essence of having the "whole body filled with light." Moses was permitted to see in vision every *particle* of the earth,[96] and was so imbued with the glory of God that he saw by other means than his eyes; if he would not have been changed so as to view this scene through spiritual "eyes," he would still be looking today![97] Mrs.

Sarah N. Williams Reynolds of Salt Lake City made the following fascinating statement:

> I was a close neighbor of Philo Dibble who visited me often. He had been very familiar and intimately acquainted with the Prophet Joseph Smith, and took great delight in rehearsing his wealth of information concerning this acquaintance. Brother Dibble stated to me that the Prophet Joseph told him in connection with the others who were present in Father Johnson's home at the time the vision [D&C 76] was given to the Prophet Joseph and Sidney Rigdon, that (the Prophet speaking): "MY WHOLE BODY WAS FULL OF LIGHT AND I COULD SEE EVEN OUT AT THE ENDS OF MY FINGERS AND TOES."[98]

Such is the action of the Holy Ghost, as it seeks to purify man, and to bring him Godly knowledge through the exercise of faith.

SUMMARY

1. Those who receive the Melchizedek Priesthood covenant to give diligent heed to the words of eternal life.

2. Though the full blessings of eternal life are not attainable in mortality, the men of the Priesthood may receive the "words of eternal life," or endowments of the Spirit, in preparation for eternal life in the worlds to come.

3. Through searching the scriptures man may:
    A. gain from the lessons taught in the holy writ, and
    B. receive the spirit of life and enlightenment that accompany these holy words.

4. If a man does not comprehend the character of God, he does not comprehend himself; conversely, if a man does not come to know and truly evaluate self, he cannot know God. Pondering and meditation are forms of worship, and are essential in coming to an understanding of God and self.

5. Priesthood holders should learn the importance of praying in the Spirit, in order to gain the words of eternal life.

6. The gift of revelation is not acquired overnight, but is something into which man must grow.

7. The Priesthood of God entitles one to the mysteries of Godliness. The degree that such mysteries will be revealed is dependent upon:

    A.   individual worthiness, and

    B.   the will of God

8.   Men of the Priesthood should seek to acquire knowledge by faith. This type of knowledge is a superior intelligence, and leads one to the presence of God.

RECEIVING THE LORD'S SERVANTS

As was discussed in chapter six, Elders, Seventies, and High Priests are under covenant to give diligent heed to the words of eternal life. In this context, Priesthood bearers are responsible to give heed to the Spirit of truth as it is conveyed by the Lord's Anointed. By so doing, men of the Priesthood will prepare for the full rights and blessings of eternal life in the world to come. The message of the Master in the Oath and Covenant is simply: *"For he that receiveth my servants receiveth me."*[1] In commenting on this particular aspect of the covenant, President Marion G. Romney said: "The word *servants* as used in this statement includes the Lord's representatives in the various presiding offices of the priesthood—general, regional, priesthood quorum, stake, mission, ward, branch, etc. It behooves us to keep this in mind when we are tempted to disregard their counsel and direction."[2] The Lord explained in His preface to the revelations and commandments of this dispensation: "What I the Lord have spoken, I have spoken, and I excuse not myself; and though heavens and the earth pass away, my word shall not pass away, but shall all be fulfilled, *whether by mine own voice or by the voice of my servants, it is the same.*"[3] In a revelation given through John Taylor in 1882, the Master spoke in the same vein. Speaking of President Taylor, the Lord said: "I will honor him, and he shall speak forth the words that I will reveal unto him, . . . and *ye shall listen to his words as my words,* saith the Lord your God."[4] Holders of the Priesthood must reach the state of spiritual preparation wherein they see the mantle of authority resting upon the leaders of the church, and have the witness that these leaders speak the will of God, even as He would speak it.

> Wherefore, meaning the church, thou shalt give heed unto all his [Joseph Smith's] words and commandments which he shall give unto you as he receiveth them, walking in all holiness before me;
> For his word ye shall receive, as if from mine own mouth, in all patience and faith.
>
> For by doing these things the gates of hell shall not prevail against you; yea, and the Lord God will disperse the powers of darkness from before you, and cause the heavens to shake for your good, and his name's glory.[5]

A true standard by which man may judge his conversion to the Lord and the divine work is the degree to which he supports and sustains the leaders of the Church. President Brigham Young spoke in 1862:

> Without revelation direct from heaven it is impossible for any person to fully understand the plan of salvation. We often hear it said that the living oracles must be in the Church, in order that the kingdom of God may be established and prosper on the earth. I will give another version of this sentiment. I say that *the living oracles of God, or the Spirit of revelation, must be in each and every individual to know the plan of salvation and keep in the path that leads them to the presence of God.*[6]

President Harold B. Lee stated in a most powerful way that "the measure of your true conversion and whether or not you hold to those ideals, is whether or not you are so living that *you see the power of God resting upon the leaders of this Church and that testimony goes down into your heart like fire.*"[7]

THE LIVING ORACLES

Among the leaders of the Church which all of the Priesthood must sustain are the Prophets, Seers, and Revelators. Every man who has the testimony of Jesus is a *prophet,*[8] and is under obligation to guide those under his jurisdiction in the spirit of prophecy. A *revelator* is one who makes known or reveals the will of God to others. A *seer* is one who uses his spiritual eyes effectively to "see" and understand past, present, and future, and possesses qualities and gifts of both the prophet and the revelator. A passage from the Book of Mormon explains the power held by a seer:

> And the king said that *a seer is greater than a prophet.*
>
> And Ammon said that *a seer is a revelator and a prophet also;* and a gift which is greater can no man have, except he should possess the power of God, which no man can; yet a man may have great power given him from God.
>
> But a seer can know of things which are past, and also of things which are to come, and by them shall all things be revealed, or, rather have secret things be made manifest, and hidden things shall come to light, and things which are not known shall be made known by them, and also things shall be made known by them which otherwise could not be known.[9]

Though it is possible for every Priesthood holder to be a prophet, seer, and revelator to his own family, or to those in his group or quorum, yet such rights for the entire Church center only in those sustained as Prophets, Seers, and Revelators *to the Church* (the Council of the First Presidency and the Quorum of the Twelve Apostles stand in such positions), and are the Living Oracles, along with the other General Authorities of the Church of Jesus Christ.[10] In speaking of those who receive his promptings,[11] the Lord said in 1831:

> And *whatsoever they shall speak when moved upon by the Holy Ghost shall be scripture,* shall be the will of the Lord, shall be the mind of the Lord, shall be the word of the Lord, shall be the voice of the Lord, and the power of God unto salvation [the Gospel].[12]

In the closing remarks of his last General Conference, President Harold Lee said:

> Now, you Latter-day Saints, I think you have never attended a conference where in these three days you have heard more inspired declarations on most every subject and problem about which you have been worrying. *If you want to know what the Lord would have the Saints know and to have his guidance and direction for the next six months, get a copy of the proceedings of this conference, and you will have the latest word of the Lord as far as the Saints are concerned.* And also all others who are not of us, but who believe what has been said has been "the mind of the Lord, the will of the Lord, and the voice of the Lord and the power of God unto salvation."[13]

Any of the General Authorities may speak the mind of the Lord and thus proclaim scripture, but only the living Prophet has the keys necessary to declare, clarify, or introduce doctrines and commandments for the entire Church. Christ explained that "there is none other appointed unto you to receive commandments and revelations until he [the Prophet] be taken, if he abide in me." Then the Lord continued by stating that "none else shall be appointed unto this gift except it be through him. . . ."[14] President Joseph Fielding Smith taught:

> *There is only one man at a time who holds the keys of revelation for the Church. The Twelve Apostles may receive revelation to guide them in their labors and to assist them in setting in order the priesthood and organizations of the Church.* When they are sent out into a stake by authority, to have all the power to receive revelation, to make changes, and to conduct the affairs according to the will of the Lord. *But they do not receive revelations for the guidance for the whole church,* only wherein one of them may succeed to the Presidency. In other words the right to receive revelation and guidance for the whole Church is vested in each one of the Twelve which he could exercise should he succeed to the Presidency. But this power is dormant while the President of the Church is living.[15]

THE NEED FOR MODERN SCRIPTURE

One of the great doctrines of this latter day is that the messages of the standard works, though profoundly important to the children of the covenant, are not enough to bring God's people into His presence.[16] A grand distinguishing feature between existing Christianity and the Restored Church is the presence (in the latter) of modern and continuing revelation. Joseph Smith spoke of the importance of this principle: "God said, 'Thou shalt not kill;' at another time He said, 'Thou shalt utterly destroy.' This is the principle on which the government of heaven is conducted—by *revelation adopted to the circumstances in which the children of the kingdom are placed.*[17] President Brigham Young spoke in a similar vein:

> *When God speaks to the people, He does it in a manner to suit their circumstances and capacities.* . . . Should the Lord Almighty send an angel to rewrite the Bible, it would in many places be very different from what it is now. And I will even venture to say that if the Book of Mormon were now to be rewritten, in many instances it would materially differ from the present translation. According as the people are willing to receive the things of God, so the heavens send forth their blessings.[18]

In teaching of the importance of the Living Oracles and the need for modern scripture, John Taylor said:

> The Bible is good. . . . The Book of Mormon is good, and the book of Doctrine and Covenants, as land marks. . . . Those books are good for example, precedent, and investigation, and for developing certain laws and principles; but they do not, they cannot touch every case required to be adjudicated and set in order; *we require a living tree—a living fountain—living intelligence, proceeding from the living priesthood in heaven, through the living priesthood on earth.*[19]

President Wilford Woodruff also spoke of how the Standard Works without the words of the Brethren, are insufficient. After making reference to the *Bible, Book of Mormon,* and *Doctrine and Covenants,* he said: "We may read them through and every other revelation that has been given to us, and *they would scarcely be sufficient to guide us twenty-four hours.* We have only an outline of our duties written; we are to be guided by the living oracles."[20] President George Q. Cannon elaborated on the importance of revelation that is received daily by the Authorities of the Church:

> The Lord has revealed unto us that which he wants us to do, and though we do not receive written revelations (the men who have held the keys have not always felt led to write revelations as the Prophet Joseph did), the servants of the Lord do receive revelations, and they are

as binding upon the people as though they were printed and published throughout all the stakes of Zion.

The oracles of God are here, and he speaks through his servant whom he has chosen to hold the keys. He gives revelations to the Church. We have been blessed as a people with an abundance of revelation. *Some have deceived themselves with the idea that because revelations have not been written and published, therefore there has been a lessening of power in the Church of Christ. This is a very great mistake,* as we will find out sooner or later.[21]

Many pride themselves as Gospel scholars, and continue to search and research the Standard Works of the Church. Yet, Gospel scholarship implies also a knowledge of and an appreciation for the words of the living authorities. Joseph Fielding Smith encouraged the members of the Church to study *all* of the scriptures.

Everyone of us should be a student of the scriptures. Not only should he be a student of the scripture as that scripture is found recorded in Holy Writ, but he should be obedient to the scripture as it shall come from the constituted authority of the Church. *Somehow it seems so easy to believe that the word of the Lord is printed in a book, but to some people it seems a little difficult when the word of the Lord comes from a living man.*[22]

LIVING VS. DEAD PROPHETS

For some strange reason, many of the Saints of God (and many of the Priesthood) feel that the teachings, writings, and discourses of the dead prophets are of greater significance and have more epical value than the remarks and statements of the living oracles. Nothing could be farther from the truth! The words of the President of the Church and those spoken by the other General Authorities under the influence of the Holy Ghost, are to be received as equally binding as any of the works or discourses by the dead prophets; those called and anointed to preside in this day have been authorized and commissioned to speak to this generation. It is not to be implied here that the teachings of the *Bible, Book of Mormon, Doctrine and Covenants,* or *Pearl of Great Price* are not to be accepted as binding on this people, for they are. However, of equal force with the written word of yesterday is the word of the Lord's Commanding General today.

It is because some have attempted to follow dead prophets and their teachings in preference to the living fountain and intelligence that they have fallen into sin and apostasy. President Harold B. Lee spoke to this subject as follows:

When the Prophet Joseph Smith was martyred, there were many saints who died spiritually with Joseph. So it was with Brigham Young, so it was with John Taylor. And you have people today who are still quoting from what is alleged to have been revelation given to John Taylor. Well, suppose he did have revelations? Did they have any more authority than something that comes from President McKay today? Do you see? *. . . We have the same affliction today—willing to believe someone who is dead and gone and accept his as more authority than the words of a living authority today.*[23]

On another occasion President Lee gave an example of the need for a living tree of life:

Recently, President McKay, acting under the inspiration of his calling moved to enlarge the activities of the seventies, by ordaining some of the presidents of seventies to the office of high priests, with the explanation that it would make them more serviceable and more effective in their work. I was in one of the Arizona stakes, and I had one of the brethren ask, "Was it not true that the Prophet Joseph had said that it was contrary to the order of heaven that a high priest should be in that position?" [HC 2:476] I merely said to him, "*Had you ever thought that what might have been contrary to the order of heaven in the early 1830's might not be contrary to the order of heaven in 1960?*"

Sometimes we forget that today, here and now, we have a prophet to whom the Lord is giving instruction for our good.[24]

Again, we see that the Lord makes known His will to the Living Prophet according to the circumstances which exist at a particular time. What might have been true in the formative years of Church organization may or may not be true today.

President Lee told of another experience he had which demonstrated that sometimes the members of the Church tend to hold the words of dead prophets in greater esteem than those of the Seers and Revelators today. In speaking to a group of Seminary and Institute of Religion faculty at the Brigham Young University he said:

I had an experience here at the Y, and it was long enough ago so that no one will, I am sure, affix any responsibility. I had said something about a very touchy, explosive subject that was very much discussed. . . . I had dragged in something "by the ears" and had made a quotation from a statement of a president of the Church and [I] was the authority for saying this had been said. When I got back home one of the teachers of the Brigham Young University wrote me and asked if I would give him chapter and verse as to where and when this had been said. . . . *He had to have the chapter and verse of somebody who had been dead long enough in order for his statements to take on epical authority. He was following a prophet who was dead. He was not listening to one who was talking to him today. . . . To most people you would have supposed it was enough to say that it was said—that was the authority. And I was almost inclined to say, "I refer you to my talk of such-and-such day at the Brigham Young University." But he would have thought, of course, that that was a display of egotism which I was not quite willing to have tagged upon me.*[25]

One with the witness of the Holy Ghost in his soul is devoted to The Church of Jesus Christ of Latter-day Saints, and to the man God chooses to stand in the position of Head of the Church on earth. He is not devoted to particular personalities, for personalities may fall from prominent positions in the Church. He is willing to sustain the man the Almighty chooses, and to value his words above all that may have been spoken in the past. Though each of us dies to some degree at the passing of each President of the Church, yet the responsibility of the Priesthood holder is to look forward and obtain the witness that (1) God's will has been done, and (2) the new President of the High Priesthood is the only man that God wants to lead the people in this day. To do otherwise is to risk a spiritual death with the dead prophet, against which President Lee warned.

This author recalls vividly the sense of shock, unbelief, and personal loss at the death of President David O. McKay, probably because this great leader had served in the Presidency all of my young life. As I came to appreciate the fact that my beloved prophet-leader was truly gone, and that the Church would go on with another in his place, I remember praying for the witness as to the divine calling of Joseph Fielding Smith. That witness burned in my heart for the first time as this pure and holy man stood before the Church to speak at the April Conference in 1970. As President Smith began to speak, my soul was suddenly filled with a profound love for him, and I wept with tears of joy and appreciation as he spoke in those few moments. The witness had been planted in my soul, and it burned like fire. Less than four years later, the same was true in regard to the sudden passing of President Harold B. Lee; slowly but surely there came an appreciation for the fact that the will of the Lord had been done and that Spencer W. Kimball, one tried and tested and readied over a period of 79 years, was the man God would have to lead his people for a time and season. Such a witness must come to each Priesthood bearer, in order that we might be completely attuned to the words of eternal life that come from the living oracles.

SUSTAINING THE BRETHREN

When the Lord gave the first revelation on Church organization and government in April of 1830, He explained that "no person is to be ordained to any office in this church, where there is a regularly organized branch of the same, *without the vote of that church.*"[26] Three months later a revelation declared that "all things shall be done by *common consent* in the church by much prayer and faith, for all things you shall receive by faith."[27] The Law of Common Consent in the Restored Church demonstrates its theocratic nature—man sustaining what God has proposed. More than anything else, the vote or voice of the people is "*a sanction, a strength and support to that which God chooses. But they* [the people] *do not confer the authority in the first place, nor can they take it away.*"[28] President Joseph Fielding Smith explained:

> No man can preside in this Church in any capacity without the consent of the people. The Lord has placed upon us the responsibility of sustaining by vote those who are called to various positions of responsibility. No man, should the people decide to the contrary, could preside over any body of Latter-day Saints in this Church, and *yet it is not the right of the people to nominate, to choose, for that is the right of the priesthood.*[29]

The Lord (through the living Priesthood) chooses whom He will. The burden of responsibility then rests upon the membership to sustain or reject. The taking of a sustaining vote is a solemn occasion, and one that should be given serious consideration. President Smith continued:

> ... no man has the right to raise his hand in opposition, or with contrary vote, unless he has a reason for doing so that would be valid if presented before those who stand at the head. In other words, *I have no right to raise my hand in opposition to a man who is appointed to any position in this Church, simply because I may not like him, or because of some personal disagreement or feeling I may have, but only on the grounds that he is guilty of wrong doing, of transgression of the laws of the Church which would disqualify him for the position which he is called to hold.*[30]

Interestingly enough, few votes are cast in opposition to persons being sustained. Why is this? Charles W. Penrose taught that it was "because they [the body of membership] are satisfied that the men who are called to occupy these various positions are men of God, that they are fit for the positions."[31]

Those men who magnify their callings in the Priesthood are filled with a quiet reverence for the Presiding Authorities of the Church. Joseph F. Smith taught: "*If you will honor the holy Priesthood in yourself first, you will honor it in those who preside over you,* and those who administer in the various callings, throughout the Church."[32] To "sustain" is to support, to stand behind, or to hold up. In speaking of the First Presidency, the Lord declared that they are to be "upheld by the confidence, faith, and prayer of the church. . . ."[33]

The act of sustaining brethren and sisters in various positions represents a great deal more than "That sounds good to me," or "I guess I can go along with that proposition." As the arm is raised to the square, the participant in the sustaining process enters into covenant to stand behind and support that particular person, in word and deed. At a Solemn Assembly held in October of 1972, President N. Eldon Tanner explained: "When you vote affirmatively *you make a solemn covenant with the Lord that you will sustain, that is, give your full loyalty and support, without equivocation or reservation, to the officer for whom you vote.*"[34] Elder Orson F. Whitney also explained to a large congregation of people that "you who raised your hands to sustain these men in their positions, *made a solemn covenant with God that you would uphold and defend them, that you would exercise your faith for them, and would listen to their counsels.*"[35]

What are some ways that the Elders, Seventies, and High Priests of the Church may sustain leaders of the Kingdom? First, it means to stand behind and uphold them:

> The obligation that we make when we raise our hands under such circumstances is a most sacred one. It does not mean that we will go quietly on our way and be willing that the prophet of the Lord shall direct this work, but it means—if I understand the obligation I assumed when I raised my hand—that *we will stand behind him;* we will pray for him, we will defend his good name. . . .[36]

Second, the Priesthood will pray for the Authorities, that they may be guided by the spirit of prophecy and revelation. President Wilford Woodruff taught on one occasion that "inasmuch as we have voted today to sustain the presidency of this church and kingdom, *let our prayers ascend night and morning unto the ears of the Lord of Sabaoth,* in behalf of the men who now stand at our head. . . ."[37]

Third, sustaining the Brethren entails reading, studying, and abiding by their words of counsel. To sustain the Prophet is to "strive to carry out his instructions as the Lord shall direct him to offer them to us while he remains in that position."[38] George Q. Cannon also spoke of the member's responsibility in this regard: "We ought to listen to their words. When we cannot hear their words, we should read them; for they are the words of the authorized servants of God. I feel that there is a great neglect among us in this respect."[39]

A final way to sustain the Brethren is to carry our share of the load entailed in "bearing off the kingdom." This is done only by perfecting individual homes, wards, and stakes. President Wilford Woodruff pleaded with the Saints:

... I hope my brethren and sisters will feel in their hearts to sustain the Presidency of the Church, by their faith, works, and prayers, *and not suffer them to carry all the load,* while we hide ourselves in the rear. If we should do this we are not worthy, we are not worthy of our position as elders in Israel, and fathers and mothers in Israel. *Let each one bear their share;* and if we will correct our own follies, and set in order our own houses, and do that which is right, we shall then do some good, and help to lift the load that rests upon those who lead.[40]

Members of the Church are under obligation to recognize and obey the directions of local Priesthood authorities, as well as those of the general Church leadership. As was discussed earlier in this chapter, the Lord's words are: "For he that receiveth my servants receiveth me." No man or woman can ever receive the presence and glory of the Master who does not receive the Lord's servants—general and local. Elder B. H. Roberts of the First Council of the Seventy explained:

There should be respect for the Priesthood of God, and *when I speak of respecting the Priesthood, I do not mean merely the President of the Church nor the Apostles of the Church, nor the General Authorities of the Church. I mean them of course; but I also mean all those who hold the Priesthood.* I bespeak respect for the Presidents of stakes, for Bishops of wards; and also for priests, who teach the Gospel at the fireside of the people. I bespeak for the humblest of God's servants, as well as for the highest; for *it is all one authority; it all comes from God.*[41]

President David O. McKay also emphasized the value of recognizing local Priesthood authority:

Recognize those who preside over you, and when necessary, seek their advice. . . . Let us recognize the local authority. The bishop may be a humble man. Some of you may think you are superior to him, and you may be, but he is given authority direct from our Father in Heaven. You recognize it. . . . Recognition of authority is an important principle.[42]

Members of a particular ward or stake occasionally cling too closely to the memories of when their "favorite" Priesthood leader was in office, and often fail to show the proper respect for the present presiding officer. Like those who died spiritually with Joseph and Brigham, many were "released" with Bishop Brown when he left the office of bishop. The author has seen on several occasions how some ward members have criticized the existing leaders with an attitude of "If only Bishop Brown were still in office—he'd do the job the way it ought to be done." Such an attitude is dangerous, and by maintaining it one is liable to the loss of the Holy Spirit. If necessary, one should spend many hours on his knees in obtaining the witness that the new quorum leader, bishop, or stake president has been called by the word of prophecy. With that witness, the individual member is able to sustain wholeheartedly the leaders called to preside.

EVIL SPEAKING OF THE ANOINTED

There is something unholy about speaking unkindly of others. This is especially true if those spoken of in a derogatory manner are leaders of the Church. Some will attempt to justify such an evil practice with a comment such as "I respect his position as Elder's Quorum President, but I just don't care for the man himself." Such an attitude is not possible, for in speaking against the man, the offender also downgrades the office or position. Thus Heber C. Kimball explained that "it is impossible to honor the Priesthood in that man and not honor the vessel that holds it."[43] President George Q. Cannon also taught this principle: "*You cannot show reverence to the priesthood without showing it to the men who bear it.*"[44] President Cannon said on another occasion:

Men have said concerning servants of God: "Oh! These men are but mortal; they are very fallible, and they are as liable to do wrong as anybody else." This may be true. At the same time God does not sustain those who imagine they have a right to criticize, find fault with or in this manner condemn His servants. They are weak and fallible; but they bear the Priesthood. *The Priesthood cannot be separated from the men; and in attacking the men it is evident from the results which have followed such a course that the Lord views such attacks as being made upon His authority.*[45]

Elder Parley P. Pratt spoke of the consequences of "trifling" with the holders of Priesthood:

When I trifle with the Priesthood I trifle with the Almighty; and when I trifle with President Young I trifle with the Priesthood, and *that Priesthood will leave me, and I will fall*, and I will become disgraced in the eyes of heaven, and of all Saints; and I forfeit everything that I had attained while I held that Priesthood, when I forfeit it; *I forfeit my salvation and every blessing I possess.*[46]

Those Priesthood holders who have been endowed in the House of the Lord are under an additional covenant to receive the Lord's servants and avoid speaking evil of them. President George Q. Cannon said: "You who have been in sacred places know one thing, that you cannot speak evil of the Lord's anointed and be justified [free from sin—see Chapter 9], and *if you break your covenants in that respect, you are of course incurring severe condemnation.*"[47] As in the case of those who attempt to exercise unrighteous dominion, those who persist in opposing the servants of God (general or local) will grieve the Spirit of God. President Cannon taught that "whoever arrays himself in any manner against the authority which God has placed in His Church for its government, no matter who it is—one of the Twelve Apostles even or any number of them—unless he repents, *God will withdraw His Spirit and Power from him.*"[48]

It is a dreadful sin to fight against or in any manner oppose the Priesthood of the Son of God, and every one of us should repent of such opposition with all our hearts. . . . *He will have a pure people, who will be led by His servants. When a man ceases to be a true servant of the Lord, the Lord withdraws His Spirit from him, and leaves him to himself* [compare D&C 121:38]. Happy would that man be if he should die before he did this.[49]

Men of the Priesthood must stay on guard against the powers of the Adversary, for Satan would cause unrest and contention. It is therefore essential to obtain the witness of the divine callings of the Lord's servants in order to maintain a safe course, for "those who lift their voices and their heels against the authority of the Holy Priesthood, . . . will go down to hell, unless they repent."[50]

INTELLIGENT OBEDIENCE

As the first law of heaven, obedience is a principle of salvation. No Saint in all the creations of God will grow to the stature of Christ without becoming perfectly obedient to the laws and ordinances of the revealed Gospel, including the words of eternal life as they flow from the lips of the living oracles. Joseph Smith explained that "when we obtain any blessing from God, *it is by obedience to that law upon which it is predicated.*"[51] Though the Priesthood of God are under covenant to be obedient to every word of God, they are also responsible to ensure that all they do (in the name of obedience) is, without question, the will of the Almighty. President Brigham Young was reported to have said: "*The greatest fear I have is that the people of this Church will accept what we say as the will of the Lord without first praying about it and getting the witness within their own hearts that what we say is the word of the Lord.*"[52] President Young asked on another occasion: "How can you know whether we lead you correctly or not? *Can you know by any other power than that of the Holy Ghost? I have uniformly exhorted the people to obtain this living witness,* each for themselves; then no man on earth can lead them astray."[53] Those who pay the price to gain the proper witness will never be guilty of blind obedience, but will have the comforting assurance that the leaders of the Church are in strict harmony with the living tree of life in the heavens. Said President Young:

> I am fearful they [the Saints] *settle down in a state of blind self-security, trusting their eternal destiny in the hands of their leaders with a wreckless confidence that in itself would thwart the purposes of God in their salvation. . . . Let every man and woman know, by the whispering of*

the Spirit of God to themselves, whether their leaders are walking in the path the Lord dictates, or not.[54]

It is not difficult to follow the leaders when what they proclaim or command is consistent with what we already feel or know. There is generally no question involved when what the Brethren advise is logical to the reasoning faculties. But what happens if the Living Prophet should contradict something that has been declared as factual on a previous occasion? What do we do if the Lord's mouthpiece should speak something that is seemingly inconsistent? George Q. Cannon stated beautifully the attitude that the Saints of God should possess whenever such situations arise:

"I do not understand the reasons for this action; I do not see clearly what the presiding authorities have in view in doing this; but I will wait and learn more. This I do know, that this is the work of God and that these men are His servants and that they will not be permitted by Him to lead the Church astray or to commit a wrong of so serious a character as to endanger its progress or perpetuity." This would undoubtedly be the feeling of a man living close to the Lord, because the testimony of God's Spirit would bring this to his mind and make him feel sure that God had not forgotten nor forsaken His Church.[55]

President Harold B. Lee told of an experience in the life of Marion G. Romney, in which President Romney's political views were verbally attacked and called into question by the Church leaders. President Lee reported:

On one such occasion when Church leaders in a tersely-worded editorial had denounced the trends of the political administration then in power, he confided in me something which it might be well if all Church members in public life could emulate: "When I read that editorial," he told me, *"I knew what I should do—but that wasn't enough. I knew that I must feel right about following the counsel of the Church leaders and know that they were right. That took a whole night on my knees to accomplish."* I submit in that statement the difference between "intelligent" and "blind" obedience.[56]

We see, then, that intelligent obedience consists of not only following the dictates of the Lord's Anointed, but doing so with a firm knowledge (gained by the Holy Ghost) that what has been said is the will of the Lord, the mind of the Lord, the word of the Lord, and the voice of the Lord.[57]

One needs never fear in following the constituted authorities of the Church, as long as he learns to "keep his eye on the Captain."

Though the General Authorities may all speak scripture as they are so moved upon, these men do not have the last word in the Kingdom of God on earth—that right rests with the President of the Church. It is a solemn fact that each of the leaders of the Church *may* fall into apostasy and deceive the members, but the Father in Heaven will not permit the President to fall away in such a manner. President Wilford Woodruff said: "It is my faith that the Lord will never permit any man upon whose shoulders he places the authority and power to lead Israel, to go astray, or to lead the children of God from the path of duty. The Lord would remove such a man from his place."[58]

Marion G. Romney told of a conversation he once had with President Heber J. Grant. President Grant said: "My boy, you always keep your eye on the president of the Church, and if he ever tells you to do anything, and it is wrong, and you do it, the Lord will bless you for it. But you don't need to worry. The Lord will never let his mouthpiece lead the people astray." President Romney then continued:

> I have thought much about this statement. I remember that *counselors in the presidency have been deceived. I remember that members of the Twelve have been deceived and left the Church. And men in every other council in the Church have been deceived, and, according to President Grant (and I believe him), there never will be a president of this Church who will lead the people astray.*[59]

The blessings that come to those who learn to obey intelligently the words of the leaders of the Church are numerous. Wilford Woodruff explained that "inasmuch as we do this [intelligently sustain the Brethren] we will grow, we will advance, *the Spirit of God will be poured out upon us,* which will reveal unto us the mind and the will of God concerning us."[60] In a most interesting way, Harold B. Lee closed an address in 1968 by saying: "Listen to the leaders of the Church and follow their footsteps in righteousness, *if you would learn not only by study but also by faith.*"[61] Priesthood bearers who keep their covenant with the Father will therefore receive the endowments of the Holy Spirit from those chosen and anointed to declare the words of eternal life unto this generation. By so doing, they prepare themselves for the full blessings of the glorified state in the world to come.

SUMMARY

1. Those who receive the Melchizedek Priesthood are under covenant to receive the Lord's servants (general and local) and to abide by their words, as if they came directly from the Lord.

2. Though all of the General Authorities have the right to declare scripture as they may be moved upon, only the President of the

Church may declare or clarify new doctrines or commandments for the entire Church.

3. Priesthood bearers are to honor and revere the living prophets, and regard their words as the word of God revealed to those in this generation.

4. To sustain the Brethren is to:
    A. Support them.
    B. Pray for them.
    C. Read, study and abide by their counsel.
    D. Carry our share of the load by building up our families, wards, and stakes.

5. The Priesthood cannot be separated from the man. In speaking evil of a Priesthood holder (especially a leader), we are showing an overt disrespect for the Priesthood.

6. Those who continue to speak evil of the Lord's Anointed will lose the Spirit of God and fall away into apostasy.

7. Intelligent obedience consists of not only following the dictates of the authorities of the Church, but doing so with a firm knowledge (gained via the Holy Ghost) that what has been said is the will of the Lord.

VIII
THE DOCTRINE OF ADOPTION

WE NOW TURN OUR ATTENTION to God's covenant with man in the reception of the Melchizedek Priesthood. This covenant consists of the promised blessings to those who obtain the Priesthood and magnify callings in it, continually seeking to live by every word of God. In the final three chapters we will consider the transcendent privileges that come to the faithful of the Priesthood.

MAN'S STAGES OF EXISTENCE

Among the greatest of all blessings that come to the pondering Latter-day Saint is a knowledge of his divine origin and glorious destiny. In seeking after man's origin and destiny, we learn that the plan of salvation and redemption consists of progression through three major stages of existence: spirit life, physical life, and eternal life.[1] *Spirit life* is made up of the countless ages that antedated mortality, or the existence of man before tabernacling the flesh. The ego or mind or intelligence of man never had a beginning, nor will it ever end. In one of the greatest revelations ever given to man, the Lord explained: "Intelligence, or the light of truth, was not created or made, neither indeed can be."[2] The Prophet Joseph also explained in a powerful funeral sermon that "the intelligence of spirits had no beginning, neither will it have an end."[3] Continuing in the same discourse, the Prophet gave a beautiful analogy:

> I take my ring from my finger and liken it to the mind of man—the immortal part, because it has no beginning. Suppose you cut it in two; then it has a beginning and an end; but join it again, and it continues one eternal round. *So with the spirit [intelligence] of man. As the Lord liveth, if it had a beginning, it will have an end.*[4]

The organization of intelligence[5] was accomplished through a literal birth process, by which the intelligence of man was added upon, so as to evolve to a higher level of progression.[6] At this point in the pre-earth life man possessed what is often termed a "spirit body," composed of that pure, fine, and elastic matter called *spirit,* only to be discerned by spiritual eyes.[7] It was in this spirit state that man continued until mortal birth occurred. And it was as a spirit that man made preparations and covenants in the organizational councils before mortality.

Physical life is that stage of existence realized in the mortal state, and consisting of added attributes, powers, and abilities not available in spirit life. Those who kept the First Estate were added upon. The acquisition of the physical body made it possible for man to learn through experience. Elder Orson Pratt taught:

> There are two different kinds of knowledge; one kind is obtained through reason and reflection, of which self-evident truths are the foundation; the other kind is gained by sensation or experience. The ideas relating to the first kind are obtained by comparing truth with truth; hence they are acquired by spirits in this manner, and can be communicated to them independent of experience. *The ideas of the latter kind cannot be obtained by reasoning or reflection; they can only be learned by experience. Spirits, therefore, can advance to the highest degree of knowledge in some things, while in others they must remain in ignorance until they are placed in circumstances to learn them by experience.*[8]

The physical body serves as a tabernacle for the spirit of man, and is in the image of the spirit body.[9]

Eternal life, the third stage of man's existence, is a state enjoyed by the faithful in the eternities to come. Eternal life is God's life, and represents the *qualitative* aspects of such a life—the glory of the Celestial Kingdom, the glory of the Church of the Firstborn, etc.[10] The expression "eternal life" is therefore not intended to convey the concept of an everlasting duration only (the *quantitative* aspect of God's life), for that concept is embodied in the word "immortality," a state also descriptive of the life of Deity. Eternal life is gained in the resurrection, when man rises to receive a fulness of the glory of the Father.

In each of these three stages of existence there are significant and vital familial relationships. The Father of Christ in spirit life is Elohim, the exalted Man of Holiness. Jesus was the firstborn of all spirit offspring,[11] and thus received the birthright blessings of the Father. Elohim is also the Father of Christ in physical life, inasmuch as He sired the body of Christ through the virgin, Mary.[12] Finally, Elohim is the Father in eternal life for Christ, since the powers of the Spirit were given by the Eternal Father to His Son. By this means, Christ attained unto a fulness of glory in the resurrection.

In the case of man, the paternal relationships in these stages differ in most interesting ways from those of the Savior. The Father of man's spirit is also Elohim, but, unlike Christ, man is given life on earth by two mortal parents. Man's spirit is the hereditary recipient of spiritual attributes and qualities, gained through the genetic processes accompanying the union of exalted and holy parentage. The evolution and development of these sacred qualities are realized as man grows into a union with Christ. Man likewise inherits from mortal parents physical characteristics, attitudes, and dispositions. He also inherits the seeds of corruption, such that the inevitable product of mortal life is death.

In the realm of eternal life, man looks to the Beloved Son for redemption, salvation, and exaltation. Inasmuch as Jesus is the only way by which man may receive the powers of the Spirit of God, and thus come unto the Father,[13] He becomes the Father of man in the eternal stage of existence.

THE ROLE OF CHRIST IN THE GOSPEL PLAN

Jesus the Christ stands in a unique position in the plan of salvation. In a very real sense, He is both Father and Son. In a prophetic declaration to his persecutors, the *Book of Mormon* Prophet Abinadi said:

I would that ye should understand that God himself shall come down among the children of men, and shall redeem his people.

And because he dwelleth in flesh he shall be called the Son of God, and having subjected the flesh to the will of the Father, being the Father and the Son—

The Father, because he was conceived by the power of God; and the Son, because of the flesh; thus becoming the Father and Son—

And they are one God, yea, the very Eternal Father of heaven and earth.[14]

In a modern revelation the Lord explained in a similar vein: "... I am in the Father, and the Father in me, and the Father and I are one—[I am] *The Father because he gave me of his fulness, and the Son because I was made in the world and made flesh my tabernacle, and dwelt among the sons of men.*"[15] From these two scriptural passages we come to understand that Christ is considered the Son because He came into the world and took upon Himself flesh and bones, and dwelt among the children of God. He is the Father because He was conceived by the Eternal Father and thus (having the seeds of eternal life planted within Him) grew to the level of grace so as to receive the fulness of Elohim's glory.

In a doctrinal exposition to the Church in 1916, the First Presidency and the Twelve clearly defined the role of Christ as the Father. *First,* Christ is Father by creation. Since Jehovah was the chief executive in the creation of worlds,[16] He is known as the "Father of the heavens and of the earth and all things that in them are."[17] *Second,* Christ is Father by divine investiture of authority. He has the sacred right to act and speak in the name of the Eternal Father. Jesus thus explained simply: "I am come in my Father's name."[18] Note, for example, that a revelation given in September of 1830 opens with these words: "Listen to *the voice of Jesus Christ,* your Redeemer, the great I Am, whose arm of mercy hath atoned for your sins."[19] Yet, we read in the same revelation forty-one verses later:

"But behold, I say unto you that I, the Lord God, gave unto Adam and unto his seed, that they should not die as to the temporal death, until I, the Lord God, should send forth angels to declare unto them repentance and redemption, through faith on the name of *mine Only Begotten Son*."[20] A similar demonstration of the Son speaking for the Father is contained in a revelation given in March of 1831:

> Thus saith the Lord; for I am God, and have sent *mine Only Begotten Son* into the world for the redemption of the world, and have decreed that he that receiveth him shall be saved, and he that receiveth him not shall be damned—
>
> Behold, *I am Jesus Christ*, and I come quickly. Even so. Amen.[21]

Without an understanding of the role of Christ as Father and God, a reading of the preceding sections of scripture could prove most confusing. However, an appreciation for the fact that all revelation since the Fall of man has been given by Christ, as supreme representative of the Eternal Father,[22] gives added comfort and assurance to one pondering on these scriptures. *Finally,* Christ is Father to all those who abide by the saving principles of His Gospel. In His high priestly prayer just preceding the crucifixion, Jesus spoke:"I have manifested thy name unto *the men which thou gavest me* out of the world: thine they were, and thou gavest them me; and they have kept thy word."[23] The Lord continued His prayer:"I pray for them: I pray not for the world, but *for them which thou hast given me*; for they are thine."[24] The Master reaffirmed this paternal relationship in the latter dispensation in the following words:"Fear not, little children, for *you are mine*, and I have overcome the world, and *you are of them that my Father hath given me*."[25] Abinadi the Prophet spoke of the life and mission of the Messiah, and of those who should take an active part in the Atonement:

> And now I say unto you, who shall declare his [Christ's] generation? Behold, I say unto you, that when his soul has been made an offering for sin he shall see his seed. And now what say ye? And who shall be his seed?
>
> Behold I say unto you, that whosoever has heard the words of the prophets, yea, all the holy prophets who have prophesied concerning the coming of the Lord—I say unto you, that all those who have hearkened unto their words, and believed that the Lord would redeem his people, and have looked forward to that day for a remission of their sins, I say unto you, that *these are his seed, or they are the heirs of the kingdom of God.*
>
> For these are they whose sins he has borne; these are they for whom he has died, to redeem them from their transgressions. And now, are they not his seed?[26]

BIRTH INTO THE KINGDOM OF GOD

Entering into the Kingdom of God through repentance and baptism is often referred to as a "rebirth." This expression finds its true meaning when we consider the great symbolism associated with birth into the Lord's Kingdom. *First*, the Godly anguish and suffering of the repentant soul is very typical of the excruciating pain experienced by the laboring mother as birth of the infant is eminent. *Second*, the water used in the baptismal proceedings is symbolic of a body of water in which dirtiness and uncleaness is washed away. *Third*, the scriptures teach that the process of being taken down into the water is representative of Christ's burial in the tomb for three days. The rise out of the "watery grave" is in the likeness of the Master's rise to a newness of life in the resurrected state.[27] *Fourth*, the innocent and pure state of the new candidate for the Kingdom is like unto the wholly-innocent newborn at delivery.[28]

There are three elements common to the two birth processes of which we have spoken: water, blood, and spirit.[29] The amniotic fluid which surrounds the fetus prior to birth is a watery substance which aids in the development of the infant. The water of the baptismal font serves as a medium through which the spiritual development of man begins. Another factor involved in the development of the infant is blood, the medium through which saving nutrients and life-giving substances are passed to the child. It is through the blood of Christ that the benefits of the Atonement are extended to man, and the saving principles of the Gospel are made a part of his life. At the time the individual spirit enters the new organism life begins in the mortal existence. Similarly, at the time that the Holy Spirit descends upon a man (following baptism), a quickening of his mind and faculties takes place, thus preparing that man for the words of eternal life.

Man must be *born again* to become a part of the Family of Christ. The need for being born again was taught in a most direct manner to the man Nicodemus:

> There was a man of the Pharisees, named Nicodemus, a ruler of the Jews:
> The same came to Jesus by night, and said unto him, Rabbi, we know that thou art a teacher come from God: for no man can do these miracles that thou doest, except God be with him.
> Jesus answered and said unto him, Verily, verily, I say unto thee, *Except a man be born again, he cannot see the kingdom of God.*
> Nicodemus saith unto him, How can a man be born when he is old? can he enter the second time into his mother's womb, and be born?
> Jesus answered, Verily, verily, I say unto thee, *Except a man be born of water and of the Spirit, he cannot enter into the kingdom of God.*[30]

Note the distinction Jesus made between *seeing* and *entering* the Kingdom of God. Joseph Smith taught that "it is one thing to see the kingdom of God, and another thing to enter into it. We must have a change of heart to see the kingdom of God, and subscribe the articles of adoption [first principles and ordinances] to enter therein."[31] The Spirit of God must change a man's heart so as to allow that man to part the veil momentarily and see the Kingdom of God—this is one aspect of being born again. Then that man must continue in the ordained path of baptism and confirmation, for "being born again, comes by the Spirit of God through ordinances."[32] In commenting on the Master's words to Nicodemus, the Prophet Joseph was reported to have made the following clarifications:

> The birth here spoken of was not the gift of the Holy Ghost, which was promised after baptism, but was a portion of the Spirit, which attended the preaching of the gospel by the elders of the Church. The people wondered why they had not previously understood the plain declarations of scripture, as explained by the elder, as they had read them hundreds of times. When they read the Bible it was a new book to them. *This was being born again to see the Kingdom of God. They were not in it, but could see it from the outside, which they could not do until the Spirit of the Lord took the veil from their eyes. It was a change of heart, but not of state;* they were converted, but were yet in their sins. Although Cornelius [see Acts 10] had seen an holy angel, and on the preaching of Peter the Holy Ghost was poured out upon him and his household, they were only born again to see the Kingdom of God. Had they not been baptized afterwards they would not have been saved.[33]

Needless to say, to be born again implies much more than to be baptized into the Church of Jesus Christ. One is not born again until he begins to obtain and utilize the powers and gifts of the Holy Ghost. Elder Bruce R. McConkie explained:

> *Mere compliance to the formality of the ordinance of baptism does not mean that a person has been born again.* No one can be born again without baptism, but the immersion in water and the laying on of hands to confer the Holy Ghost do not of themselves guarantee that a person has been or will be born again. *The new birth takes place only for those who actually enjoy the gift or companionship of the Holy Ghost, only for those who are fully converted, who have given themselves without restraint to the Lord. . . .*
>
> Those members of the Church who have actually been born again are in a blessed and favored state. They have attained their position, not merely by joining the Church, but through faith (1 John 5:1), righteousness (1 John 2:29), love (1 John 4:7), and overcoming the world (1 John 5:4). . . .[34]

To be born of God is to be made pure and clean, even as the new infant. It is to be changed from a state of nature[35] to a spiritual state. It was to the members of the Church that Alma asked the following searching questions: "And now behold, I ask of you, my brethren of the Church, have ye spiritually been born of God? Have ye received his image in your countenances? Have ye experienced this mighty change in your hearts?"[36] Following his miraculous conversion, Alma made the following remarks:

> . . . I have repented of my sins, and have been redeemed of the Lord; behold I am born of the Spirit.
>
> And the Lord said unto me: *Marvel not that all mankind, yea, men and women, all nations, kindreds, tongues and people, must be born again; yea, born of God, changed from their carnal and fallen state, to a state of righteousness, being redeemed of God, becoming his sons and daughters;*
>
> And thus they become new creatures; and unless they do this, they can in nowise inherit the kingdom of God.[37]

President David O. McKay had a beautiful dream while aboard a ship en route to Apia, Samoa. In his world tour diary, under date of May 10, 1921, President McKay wrote:

> I . . . fell asleep, and beheld in vision something infinitely sublime. In the distance I beheld a beautiful white city. Though far away, yet I seemed to realize that trees with luscious fruit, shrubbery with gorgeously-tinted leaves, and flowers in perfect bloom abounded everywhere. The clear sky above seemed to reflect these beautiful shades of color. I then saw a great concourse of people approaching the city. Each one wore a white flowing robe, and a white headdress. Instantly my attention seemed centered upon their Leader, and though I could see only the profile of his features and his body, I recognized him at once as my Savior! The tint and radiance of his countenance were glorious to behold! There was a peace about him which seemed sublime—it was divine!
>
> The city, I understood was his. It was the City Eternal; and the people following him were to abide there in peace and eternal happiness.
>
> But who were they?
>
> As if the Savior read my thoughts, he answered by pointing to a semicircle that then appeared above them, and on which were written in gold words: "THESE ARE THEY WHO HAVE OVERCOME THE WORLD—WHO HAVE TRULY BEEN BORN AGAIN!"[38]

ADOPTION INTO THE ROYAL FAMILY

Those persons who are born into the Kingdom of God through the proper channels become adopted into the Family of Jesus Christ. Inasmuch as men are not born into the divine family initially, adoptive proceedings are obviously necessary. Adoption is simply the act of being accepted by choice into a familial relationship, and then receiving equal status with the rest of the children, eventually possessing and receiving as an heir all things that the father of the family may pass on.[39] Having received of the fulness of the Father's glory,[40] Christ becomes the means by which we gain the endowments and powers of the Spirit. That those who walk the strait path become the adopted children of Christ is very evident from the Scriptures.[41] After the people of Zarahemla had received the great sermon and discourse of King Benjamin, they all experienced a mighty change, in that they had no more desire for evil but a desire to do good continually. They then entered into covenant with the Lord to stay faithful for the remainder of their days.[42] After witnessing this great conversion, King Benjamin declared:

> And now, because of the covenant which ye have made ye shall be called the children of Christ, his sons, and his daughters; for behold, this day he hath spiritually begotten you; for ye say that your hearts are changed through faith on his name; therefore, ye are born of him and have become his sons and his daughters.[43]

In a revelation given in this dispensation to Emma Smith, the Master said: "Hearken unto the voice of the Lord your God, while I speak unto you, Emma Smith, my daughter; for verily I say unto you, all those who receive my gospel are sons and daughters in my kingdom."[44] In a similar way the word of the Lord came to James Covill in January of 1831:

> Hearken and listen to the voice of him who is from all eternity, the great I AM, even Jesus Christ
>
> The light and the life of the world; a light which shineth in darkness and the darkness comprehendeth it not;
>
> The same which came in the meridian of time unto mine own, and mine own received me not;
>
> But *to as many as received me, gave I power to become my sons; and even so will I give unto as many as will receive me, power to become my sons.*[45]

Those who do not live worthy of adoption into the family of Christ remain spiritual orphans and bastards. Those who are true and faithful receive all of the rights, privileges, and blessings that appertain unto the children of Christ; they take upon themselves the name of Christ as their new spiritual surname, and are legal heirs to all things in heaven and on earth.

THE ROLE OF ABRAHAM
IN THE GOSPEL PLAN

Just as Jesus becomes Father to all those who abide in His Gospel, so do great Priesthood figures become the means whereby eternal life is given to the people of God. Abraham stands as a mighty Patriarch to all those born through his lineage, or who enter into the blessings of the House of Israel through adoption. The Lord explained to Abraham that *"as many as receive this Gospel shall be called after thy name, and shall be accounted thy seed, and shall rise up and bless thee, as their father."*[46] Men who receive the Gospel with full purpose of heart are thus called the "seed of Abraham," and as his spiritual progeny (and by virtue of their actual lineal descent) become heirs to all the blessings of Abraham, should they prove true and faithful.

The blessings of Abraham are numerous and glorious. *First,* his posterity was to be an innumerable race, continuing into time and eternity. Joseph Smith was told in 1843 that:

> Abraham received promises concerning his seed, and of the fruit of his loins—from whose loins ye are, namely, my servant Joseph—which were to continue so long as they were in the world; and *as touching Abraham and his seed, out of the world they should continue; both in the world and out of the world should they continue as innumerable as the stars;* or, if ye were to count the sand upon the seashore ye could not number them.[47]

Second, the posterity of Abraham are heirs to the Adoption, Glory, and Covenants.[48] The seed of Abraham may be *adopted* into the Family of Christ through subscribing the Articles of Adoption. This elect group are heirs to the *glory* and powers of Christ, just as Christ received the same from His Father. The seed of Abraham may also be an integral part in the establishment of the eternal *covenants* pertaining to the Divine Patriarchal Order.

Third, through Abraham and his seed, the blessings of the Holy Priesthood were to continue. Christ explained to Abraham that his seed should "bear this ministry and Priesthood unto all nations."[49] The Prophet Joseph taught that "the election of the promised seed still continues, and in the last day, they shall have the Priesthood restored unto them, and they shall be the 'saviors on Mount Zion,' the ministers of our God."[50]

Those who are not of the House of Israel by natural lineage may also become the seed of Abraham, by adoption, through accepting the Gospel and abiding by the principles of salvation. In such persons a radical change is necessary, in order that they may truly be accounted as Israel. Joseph the Seer taught:

> The Holy Ghost ... is more powerful in expanding the mind, enlightening the understanding, and storing the intellect with present

knowledge, of a man who is of the literal seed of Abraham, than one that is a Gentile, though it may not have half as much visible effect upon the body; for as the Holy Ghost falls on one of the literal seed of Abraham, it is calm and serene; and his whole soul and body are only exercised by the pure spirit of intelligence; while *the effect of the Holy Ghost upon a Gentile, is to purge out the old blood, and make him actually the seed of Abraham. That man that has none of the blood of Abraham (naturally) must have a new creation by the Holy Ghost.*[51]

THE SONS OF MOSES AND AARON

Moses and Aaron were great Priesthood figures in their day, just as Abraham was in his. Since the Priesthoods of Moses and Aaron (Melchizedek and Aaronic, respectively) bless the lives of men everywhere, it is a simple fact that "faithful holders of the Melchizedek Priesthood, no matter what their natural lineage, become by adoption the sons of Moses and Aaron."[52]

Now, the *literal* descendants of Moses and Aaron are Levites. But *the Lord was not talking about their lineal descendants;* he was talking about those who are "faithful unto the obtaining these two Priesthoods;" these are they who "become the sons of Moses and of Aaron," Levites, by adoption without regard to lineal descent.

In truth, *all who will have received both the Aaronic and Melchizedek Priesthoods, who will have magnified their callings in these two Priesthoods, will, by adoption, "become the sons of Moses and of Aaron and the seed of Abraham, and the church and kingdom, and the elect of God."*[53]

Those holders of the Melchizedek Priesthood who magnify their callings and remain faithful will have the privilege of officiating in the House of the Lord in the New Jerusalem. In a revelation given in 1832 the Master said:

Therefore, as I said concerning the sons of Moses—for *the sons of Moses and also the sons of Aaron shall offer an acceptable offering and sacrifice in the house of the Lord,* which house shall be built unto the Lord in this generation, upon the consecrated spot as I have appointed—

And the sons of Moses and of Aaron shall be filled with the glory of the Lord, upon Mount Zion in the Lord's house, *whose sons ye are;* and also many whom I have called and set forth to build up my church.[54]

Elder Orson Pratt elaborated upon the role of the sons of Moses and Aaron in a discourse given in March of 1873:

When the Temple is built the sons of the two Priesthoods . . . will enter into that Temple, . . . and all of them who are pure in heart will behold the face of the Lord and that too before he comes in his glory in the clouds of heaven, for he will suddenly come to his Temple, and he will purify the sons of Moses and of Aaron, until they shall be prepared to offer in that Temple an offering that shall be acceptable in the sight of the Lord. In doing this, he will purify not only the minds of the Priesthood in that Temple, but he will purify their bodies until they shall be quickened, renewed and strengthened, and they will be partially changed, not to immortality, but changed in part that they can be filled with the power of God, and they can stand in the presence of Jesus, and behold his face in the midst of that Temple.[55]

THE ROLE OF JOSEPH SMITH IN THE GOSPEL PLAN

As was mentioned in Chapter 1, Joseph Smith and Oliver Cowdery received the keys necessary to establish the Divine Patriarchal Order in the Kirtland Temple. They thus received the same promise as Abraham, that through them and their seed all the nations of the earth would be blessed.[56] In speaking of the importance of Joseph Smith, President Brigham Young explained that:

> ... *no man or woman in this dispensation will ever enter into the celestial kingdom of God without the consent of Joseph Smith.* From the day that the Priesthood was taken from the earth to the winding-up scene of all things, every man and woman must have the certificate of Joseph Smith, Junior, as a passport to their entrance into the mansion where God and Christ are. . . .[57]

Joseph Smith stands as a spiritual father to this dispensation, and, under Christ, is the means of blessing the people of this age. The members of the Church in the formative period understood clearly that *"Joseph is a father to Ephraim and to all Israel in these last days."*[58] In the spring of 1831, Joseph preached to a body of Saints at Kirtland. A most powerful spirit was felt by all, and each person in attendance was awed by the Prophet's manner of speaking and his glorious countenance. Joseph then explained why the Spirit of God was so powerfully evident:

> Yes, brothers and sisters, the Savior has been in your midst this night, and I want you to all remember it. There is a veil over your eyes, for you could not endure to look upon him. You must be fed with milk, not with strong meat. I want you all to remember this as if it were the last thing that escapes my lips. *He has given you all to me*, and commanded me to seal you up to Everlasting life, that where he is there you may be also.[59]

SUMMARY

1. There are three stages to man's existence in the plan of salvation:
    A. Spirit life is that period of spirit existence antedating mortality, in which man made preparations for the world of flesh and bones.
    B. Physical life is that period of existence in which man is added upon, so as to receive the attributes and experiences accompanying the physical body.
    C. Eternal life is the quality of life enjoyed by the faithful, the full endowment of which comes in the resurrection.

2. In each of these stages of existence, man is a part of vital and significant familial relationships:
    A. Elohim is Father of man's spirit life.
    B. Mortal man is father in physical life.
    C. Jesus Christ is Father in eternal life.

3. Christ has a unique role in the Gospel plan as both Father and the Son. He is called the Son because He made flesh His tabernacle and dwelt on earth among men. He is called the Father because:
    A. He was conceived by the power of the Eternal Father, and thus received the powers of eternal life.
    B. He was the chief executive in the creation of worlds.
    C. He may speak and act in the name of Elohim (divine investiture of authority).
    D. He provides the spiritual powers necessary to gain eternal life.

4. Man must be born again to become a part of the Family of Jesus Christ. To be born again is to make the powers of the Holy Ghost an active part in one's life.

5. Those who are born into the Kingdom of God through the proper channels (the Articles of Adoption) become adopted into the Family of Christ, and become heirs to all that Christ has.

6. Abraham stands as a mighty Patriarch to all those born through his lineage, or to those who enter the House of Israel through adoption.

7. The seed of Abraham are those who accept the Gospel with full purpose of heart. Such persons are eventually worthy of the blessings promised to Abraham, which include the following:

A. Their posterity will continue into time and eternity (eternal lives).

B. They are heirs to the Adoption, Glory, and Covenants.

C. The blessings of the Priesthood will continue in their special lineage.

8. Faithful men of the Priesthood, no matter what their natural lineage, may become by adoption sons of Moses and Aaron.

9. Having received the fulness of Priesthood keys and powers, Joseph Smith stands as a father to this dispensation, and, under Christ, provides the means of salvation to all people of this age.

HIGHER BLESSINGS TO THE FAITHFUL

AMONG THE BLESSINGS that come to the faithful Priesthood holder is the right to rise above the world, or to rise from the natural state to the spiritual. Because of the Fall of the first parents, man finds himself in a dreary world, cut off from the source of light and truth. Having inherited through conception the seeds of corruption and death,[1] man spends most of his time in mortality attempting to subdue the physical and yield to the spiritual. The challenge of mortality thus consists of overcoming the world and conquering self, so as to be worthy of the paradisiacal state that Adam and Eve once enjoyed. The Gospel of Jesus Christ is the divine power by which man may climb the ladder of spiritual development to the point of Celestial glory.[2] This ladder is ascended through recognizing, obtaining, and utilizing the powers of God given through the Holy Ghost. The Holy Ghost may lead man to the point where he is truly converted, and is justified, sanctified, and sealed, in preparation for the glories of the resurrection.

TESTIMONY AND CONVERSION:
A CONTRAST

Is a testimony of Jesus and of the Lord's work a necessary and sufficient condition in order to be fully converted to the Master's way of doing things? A testimony is definitely necessary, but may not be sufficient to bring about the type of conversion that the Almighty requires of each Saint. This truth is classically demonstrated in the life of the Apostle Peter.

Simon was a humble man, a fisherman, when he first beheld the Christ. The special nature of Simon Peter's character is demonstrated in the fact that of all Christ's disciples, Simon was among the twelve who were chosen and ordained to serve as especial witnesses or Apostles.[3] Peter was also a member of the First Presidency of the Church in the meridian of time, along with James and John. President Joseph Fielding Smith explained that "the Lord selected Peter, James, and John and set them at the head to act as a First Presidency after his departure. They were separated from the other apostles and given special authority." President Smith continued: "This First Presidency comprising Peter, James, and John was the forerunner of the First Presidency in our day."[4] Peter, as a member of this select Presidency, was often alone with Christ, and took part in many of the great spiritual experiences during the ministry of the Master.[5] No one can doubt the goodness of Peter's character. There is also little doubt that the Big Fisherman had a testimony of Jesus. After preaching the great sermon on the "Bread of Life," Jesus noticed that many persons were offended by the doctrines taught, and "walked no more with him." Disappointed somewhat by the hardness of the people's hearts, Christ turned unto the Twelve and asked: "Will ye also go away?" At this point Peter spoke in a sincere tone, from the depths of his heart: "Lord, to whom shall we go? *thou hast the words of eternal life. And we believe and are sure that thou art that Christ, the Son of the living God.*"[6] As Jesus and the disciples came into the coasts of Caesarea Philippi, Jesus asked:

> Whom do men say that I the Son of man am?
>
> And they said, Some say that thou art John the Baptist: some, Elias; and others, Jeremias, or one of the prophets.
>
> He saith unto them, But whom say ye that I am?
>
> And Simon Peter answered and said, *Thou art the Christ, the Son of the living God.*[7]

Ironically, despite the fact that the New Testament bears record of Peter's faithfulness, the record also indicates that this man of men slipped and stumbled and fell. Not infrequently he was chastened by the Lord for his spiritual near-sightedness and often impulsive ways. Almost immediately following Peter's perfect testimony in Matthew 16 the Lord began to explain the suffering and impending doom which lay ahead.

> Then Peter took him, and began to rebuke him, saying, Be it far from thee, Lord: this shall not be unto thee.
>
> But he turned, and said unto Peter, *Get thee behind me, Satan: thou art an offense unto me; for thou savourest not the things that be of God, but those that be of men.*[8]

Another instance in which Peter failed to "savour the things of God" took place as the Roman soldiers apprehended the Master in Gethsemane. In a fit of rage, Peter drew his sword and smote off the ear of a servant of the high priest.

> Then said Jesus unto him, Put away thy sword into his place: for all they that take the sword shall perish by the sword.
>
> Thinkest thou that I cannot now pray to my Father, and he shall presently give me more than twelve legions of angels?
>
> But how then shall the scriptures be fulfilled, that thus it must be?[9]

Finally, the most classic of Peter's blunders was his open denial of Jesus three times during the night of the betrayal.

Now Peter sat without in the palace; and a damsel came unto him, saying, Thou also wast with Jesus of Galilee.

But *he denied before them all*, saying, I know not what thou sayest.

And when he was gone out into the porch, another maid saw him, and said unto them that were there, This fellow was also with Jesus of Nazareth.

And again *he denied with an oath*, I do not know the man.

And after a while came unto him they that stood by, and said to Peter, Surely thou also art one of them; for thy speech betrayeth thee.

Then began he to curse and to swear, saying, *I know not the man*. And immediately the cock crew.[10]

At this point one cannot help but ask: How could a man who had a testimony of Jesus' divine calling[11] slip as often as Peter did, even to the point of an outright denial? The answer to this puzzling question possibly lies in a conversation between Jesus and Peter at the Last Supper. The Lord said: "Simon, Simon, behold, Satan hath desired to have you, that he may sift you as wheat: But I have prayed for thee, that thy faith fail not: *And when thou art converted, strengthen thy brethren*."[12] Though Peter had a testimony, he was not fully converted. Inasmuch as the Holy Ghost was not given as a gift until the Day of Pentecost,[13] Peter had only flashes of the Spirit's influence, which served to bear witness to him of the sacred mission of Jesus as the Christ. After Pentecost and the accompanying baptism of fire, Peter and the other converted Apostles stood boldly in the conviction of the Savior and His work—the permanent and indelible witness was planted. One notices a marvelous contrast between the man Peter before and after the reception of the Holy Ghost. As Peter and John went through the Gate Beautiful on the way to the temple they passed a lame man who begged alms daily. President Harold B. Lee paraphrased this touching scene:

Here was one who had never walked, impotent from his birth, begging alms of all who approached the gate. And as Peter and John approached, he held out his hand expectantly, asking for alms. Peter, speaking for this pair of missionaries—church authorities—said, "Look on us." And, of course, that heightened his expectation. "Then Peter said, Silver and gold have I none; but such as I have give I thee: *In the name of Jesus Christ of Nazareth rise up and walk*."

Will you see that picture now of that noble soul, that chiefest of the apostles, perhaps with his arms around the shoulders of this man, and saying, "Now, my good man, have courage, I will take a few steps with you. Let's walk together, and *I assure you that you can walk, because you have received a blessing by the power and authority that God has given us as men, his servants*." Then the man leaped with joy.[14]

One other event in the life of Peter following Pentacost dramatically demonstrated the true nature of his conversion. After being brought into custody by the captain of the temple for persisting in their preaching of the resurrected Christ, the record continues:

> And when they brought them, they set them before the council: and the high priest asked them,
>
> Saying, Did not we straitly command you that ye should not teach in this name? and, behold, ye have filled Jerusalem with your doctrine, and intend to bring this man's blood upon us.
>
> Then Peter and the other apostles answered and said, *We ought to obey God rather than men.*
>
> The God of our fathers raised up Jesus, whom ye slew and hanged on a tree.
>
> Him hath God exalted with his right hand to be a Prince and a Saviour, for to give repentance to Israel, and forgiveness of sins.
>
> And *we are his witnesses of these things; and so is also the Holy Ghost, whom God hath given to them that obey him.*[15]

EXCEPT YE BE CONVERTED

In its strictest sense, conversion is *change*—change from a passive belief to an active and powerful faith, and change from the worldly and carnal state to the spiritual. Such a change comes about only through the Holy Ghost. Following King Benjamin's great sermon, many souls were pricked in their hearts and overcome by the Spirit of God.

> And they all cried with one voice, saying: Yea, we believe all the words which thou hast spoken unto us; and also, we know of their surety and truth, because of the Spirit of the Lord Omnipotent, which has wrought *a mighty change in us, or in our hearts, that we have no more disposition to do evil, but to do good continually.*[16]

King Benjamin also taught that true conversion consists in putting off the natural man and yielding to the enticings of the Holy Spirit, so as to be as a little child: "submissive, meek, humble, patient, full of love, willing to submit to all things which the Lord seeth fit to inflict upon him...."[17] The Master's words to His disciples in Jerusalem are related here: "*Except ye be converted, and become as little children, ye shall not enter into the kingdom of heaven.*"[18] These words are most thought provoking. Life seems to be as a grand cycle, in which man begins mortality pure and meek. As life goes on, however, man often grows in pride and haughtiness through the adult years. One aspect of becoming converted through the Holy Ghost thus consists in retracing one's steps, so as to become (again) as a child.

Conversion is also the process of bringing the body and spirit into a pure union, so that the soul will reach out for truth. President Lee taught:

> One is converted when he sees with his eyes what he ought to see; when he hears with his ears what he ought to hear; and when he understands with his heart what he ought to understand. And *what he ought to see, hear, and understand is truth—eternal truth—and then practice it.* That is conversion.[19]

THE JUST SHALL LIVE BY FAITH

It is not possible to be valiant in the testimony of Jesus while burdened with unrepentant sins. Sin has its damning influence, and, unless overcome and removed, will bind one with the chains of hell. The man of the Priesthood who takes the Lord at His word will work to apply the Atonement in his own behalf. This consists of *obtaining* and *retaining* a remission of sins, so as to be right with God.

To *justify* is to exonerate and to make amends for. In the Gospel context, the just man is one who has paid the demands of justice through repentance and thus appropriate restitution. The just man is one who has been forgiven his sins and made clean before God. He is one who does not deceive,[20] and who walks and lives by faith.[21] The Prophet Joseph Smith taught that "to be justified before God we must love one another: we must overcome evil; we must visit the fatherless and the widow in their affliction, and we must keep ourselves unspotted from the world."[22]

A classic example of one who petitioned God until he obtained a remission of sins was the Prophet Enos. Enos tells the following story:

> Behold, it came to pass that I, Enos, *knowing my father that he was a just man*—for he taught me in his language, and also in the nurture and admonition of the Lord—and blessed be the name of my God for it—
>
> And *I will tell you of the wrestle which I had before God, before I received a remission of my sins.*
>
> Behold, I went to hunt beasts in the forests; and *the words which I had often heard my father speak concerning eternal life, and the joy of the Saints, sunk deep into my heart.*
>
> And my soul hungered; and I kneeled down before my Maker, and I cried unto him in mighty prayer and supplication for mine own soul; and all the day long did I cry unto him; yea, and when the night came I did still raise my voice high that it reached the heavens.
>
> And there came a voice unto me, saying: *Enos, thy sins are forgiven thee, and thou shalt be blessed.*[23]

In a revelation given in the modern day to Joseph Smith and six Elders, the Lord said:

> Listen to the voice of Jesus Christ, your Redeemer, the great I AM, whose arm of mercy hath atoned for your sins;
>
> Who will gather his people even as a hen gathereth her chickens under her wings, even as many as will harken to my voice and humble themselves before me, and call upon me in mighty prayer.
>
> Behold, verily, verily, I say unto you, that at this time *your sins are forgiven you*, therefore ye receive these things; but remember to sin no more, lest perils shall come upon you.[24]

As Christ appeared to Joseph and Oliver in the Kirtland Temple, he spoke the following words: "I am the first and the last; I am he who liveth, I am he who was slain; I am your advocate with the Father, Behold, *your sins are forgiven you; you are clean before me*; therefore, lift up your heads and rejoice."[25]

Just as Enos, Joseph Smith, and the other brethren of the Church were made clean, so may every Priesthood holder who is willing to exercise faith in Christ, ponder the words of eternal life, and "wrestle with the Lord" in mighty prayer receive the marvelous assurance that his sins are forgiven, and that he is justified to God. This assurance will not always come in the form of audible speech from the Lord Himself (as above), but may come in more subtle and less dynamic ways. After the people of King Benjamin had viewed themselves in their own carnal state and pleaded with the Master to apply His atoning blood in their behalf, the record continues:

> And it came to pass that after they had spoken these words the Spirit of the Lord came upon them, and *they were filled with joy, having received a remission of their sins, and having peace of conscience*, because of the exceeding faith which they had in Jesus Christ who should come, according to the words which King Benjamin had spoken unto them.[26]

One may know beyond doubt that his sins are forgiven by the state of his soul at a given time: Am I truly happy? Do I find joy in living? Do I have a peace of conscience, that peace of mind which transcends anything worldly, even the peace which Jesus promised to His disciples?[27] Do I feel at one with myself? Am I spiritually whole? After Enos had received a remission of sins, he continued his account:

> And I, Enos, knew that God could not lie; wherefore, *my guilt was swept away.*
>
> And I said: Lord, how is it done?
>
> And he said unto me: *Because of thy faith in Christ*, whom thou has never before heard nor seen. And many years pass away before he

shall manifest himself in the flesh; wherefore, go to, *thy faith hath made thee whole*.[28]

Justification is accomplished through the cleansing actions of the Holy Ghost. The Lord explained to Adam that *"by the Spirit ye are justified."*[29] The *Book of Mormon* leader, Nephi, explained:

> Wherefore, do the things which I have told you I have seen that your Lord and your Redeemer should do; for, for this cause have they been shown unto me, that ye might know the gate by which ye should enter. For the gate by which ye should enter is repentance and baptism by water; and *then cometh a remission of your sins by fire and by the Holy Ghost*.[30]

Since all men commit sins frequently, how is it that man may remain in a justified state? Joseph Smith taught that "repentance is a thing that cannot be trifled with every day. Daily transgression and daily repentance is not that which is pleasing in the sight of God."[31] If this is so, how is it possible to remain right with God and maintain a peace of conscience? King Benjamin spoke to this question of *retaining* a remission of sins (or a justified state) from day to day. He explained that only by exercising strong faith in Christ, and by living the Law of the Gospel[32] and reaching out to assist others may one hope to remain a just man. Said he: "And behold, I say unto you if ye do this [remember the greatness of God] ye shall always rejoice, and be filled with the love of God, and always retain a remission of your sins."[33] King Benjamin later said:

> And now, for the sake of these things which I have spoken unto you—that is, *for the sake of retaining a remission of your sins from day to day, that ye may walk guiltless before God—I would that ye should impart of your substance to the poor*, every man according to that which he hath, such as feeding the hungry, clothing the naked, visiting the sick and administering to their relief, both spiritually and temporally, according to their wants.[34]

BLESSINGS OF THE SANCTIFIED

In addition to serving as a revelator and justifier, the Holy Ghost acts as a *sanctifier*. To be sanctified is to be made pure and clean by the purging actions of divine powers. Elder Orson Hyde said that sanctification "means a purification of, or a putting away from us, as individuals and as a community, everything that is evil, or that is not in accordance with the mind and will of our Heavenly Father."[35]

Orson Pratt said simply that "sanctification comes by the continued obedience to the law of heaven."[36] President Brigham Young explained that sanctification consists:

... in overcoming every sin and bringing all in subjection to the law of Christ. God *has placed in us a pure spirit; when this reigns predominant, without let or hindrance, and triumphs over the flesh* and rules and governs and controls as the Lord controls the heavens and the earth, *this I call the blessing of sanctification.*[37]

President Young spoke on another occasion of how the Spirit may ultimately gain the victory over the flesh and sanctify the individual. He taught that:

... the power of God is greater than the power of the wicked one; and unless the Saints sin against light and knowledge, and wilfully neglect their plain and well-understood duties, and the Spirit of God is grieved and ceases to strive with them, *the Spirit is sure to prevail over the flesh, and ultimately succeed in sanctifying the tabernacle for a residence in the presence of God.*[38]

How then does sanctification differ from justification? What is the difference between the just man and the sanctified man? One way to understand the difference is to note the distinction between the removal of sins and the removal of the *effects* of sin. Though one may receive a remission of sins, yet he may still have a battle to fight in overcoming habits of the flesh. As President Young remarked above, sanctification is the triumph over the flesh, as far as that feat is possible in mortality.[39] Orson Pratt gave the following beautiful explanation, which clarifies the distinction between the justified and sanctified states:

Water baptism is only a preparatory cleansing of the believing penitent; it is only a condition of a cleansing from sin; whereas, the baptism of fire and the Holy Ghost cleanses more thoroughly, by renewing the inner man, and by purifying the affections, desires, and thoughts which have long been habituated in the impure ways of sin. Without the aid of the Holy Ghost, a person ... would have but very little power to change his mind, at once, from its habituated course, and to walk in newness of life. *Though his sins may have been cleansed away, yet so great is the force of habit, that he would, without being renewed by the Holy Ghost, be easily overcome, and contaminated again with sin.* Hence, it is infinitely important that the affections and desires should be, in a measure, changed and renewed, so as to cause him to hate that which he before loved, and to love that which he before hated. To thus renew the mind of man is the work of the Holy Ghost.[40]

RENEWAL BY THE SPIRIT

Priesthood bearers who magnify their callings are given the promise that they shall be "sanctified by the Spirit unto the renewing of their bodies."[41] Perhaps the greatest examples of the realization of this promise are evident in the lives of many of the General Authorities of the Church. Many have wondered how men like David O. McKay and Joseph Fielding Smith were able to preside over a world-wide organization while in their nineties. Harold B. Lee assumed the office of President of the Church at the age of 73, and in so doing was the youngest man to lead the Church in decades! At an age when most men are retired and confined to quarters, many of the Brethren seem to work longer days and endure greater pressures than men half their age. Such is the blessing that comes to men who magnify their callings. Elder Parley P. Pratt gave a detailed description of how the Holy Spirit renews the mind and body of man:

The gift of the Holy Ghost . . . quickens all the intellectual faculties, increases, enlarges, expands, and purifies all the natural passions and affections; and adapts them, by the gift of wisdom, to their lawful use. It inspires, develops, cultivates and matures all the fine-tone sympathies, joys, tastes, kindred feelings and affections of our nature. It inspires virtue, kindness, goodness, tenderness, gentleness, and charity. It develops beauty of person, form of features. *It tends to health, vigor, animation and social feeling. It develops and invigorates all the faculties of the physical and intellectual man.* It strengthens and gives tone to the nerves. In short, it is, as it were, marrow to the bone, joy to the heart, light to the eyes, music to the ears, and life to the whole being.[42]

That the active agent in this "divine alchemy" is the Holy Ghost is obvious from the scriptures. In speaking of an earlier group of Saints who had received the Melchizedek Priesthood and proved to be true and faithful, Alma said:

Therefore they were called after this holy order, and were sanctified, and their garments were washed white through the blood of the Lamb.

Now they, *after being sanctified by the Holy Ghost,* having their garments made white, being pure and spotless before God, could not look upon sin save it were with abhorrence; and there were many, exceeding great many, who were made pure and entered into the rest of the Lord their God.[43]

The Lord gave valuable instructions at the close of His American ministry: "Now this is the commandment: Repent, all ye ends of the earth, and come unto me and be baptized in my name, *that ye may be sanctified by the reception of the Holy Ghost,* that ye may stand spotless before me at the last day." In continuing His remarks, Christ said simply: "Verily, verily I say unto you, *this is my gospel.*"[44] To all men of the Priesthood, the words of Moroni should find special meaning:

Yea, come unto Christ, and be perfected in him, and deny yourselves of all ungodliness; and if ye shall deny yourselves of all ungodliness and love God with all your might, mind, and strength, then is his grace sufficient for you, that by his grace ye may be perfect in Christ; and if by the grace of God ye are perfect in Christ, ye can in nowise deny the power of God.

And again, if ye by the grace of God are perfect in Christ, and deny not his power, *then are ye sanctified in Christ by the grace of God*, through the shedding of the blood of Christ, which is in the covenant of the Father unto the remission of your sins, that ye become holy, without spot.[45]

SUMMARY

1. The Apostle Peter, during the era when Jesus was still with His disciples in the flesh, stood as a classic example of one who had a testimony of Jesus and yet was not fully converted.

2. Conversion is change—change from the natural state to the spiritual. Such a change comes only through obtaining and utilizing the powers of the Holy Ghost. Conversion also means to:
   A. Become as a little child.
   B. See, hear, and understand eternal truth.

3. To be justified is to be right with God. It is to have a remission of sins, and be free from the demands of justice.

4. One may know that he is justified by the peace of conscience which he experiences.

5. The process whereby a man may retain a remission of sins from day to day centers in the Law of the Gospel. Only through active service to others may one remain in a justified state.

6. The Priesthood holder who magnifies his callings may be sanctified by the Holy Spirit. To be sanctified is to be made pure and holy by the cleansing actions of divine powers.

7. Whereas justification consists in the removal of sins, sanctification consists in removal of the effects of sin.

8. Though sanctification is made possible through the blood of Christ, the Holy Ghost is the active agent in the purging process.

THE ROAD TO
ETERNAL LIFE

AFTER A MAN HOLDING THE Melchizedek Priesthood has gained the spiritual powers necessary to sanctify his mind and body, he places himself in a marvelous position to receive even greater endowments of light and truth. The Lord instructed the Saints in 1831: "Sanctify yourselves and ye shall be endowed with power. . . ."[1] He explained in a later revelation: "And unto him that repenteth and sanctifieth himself before the Lord shall be given eternal life."[2] Many of these blessings are specified in scripture, and we find some of the clearest explanations in Sections 76, 84 and 107 of the *Doctrine and Covenants*. The comparisons below will prove helpful in the discussions that follow.

D&C 76	D&C 84	D&C 107
They are sealed by the Holy Spirit of Promise (v. 53)	They become sanctified (v. 33)	They receive the Mysteries (v. 19)
They become the Church the Firstborn (v. 54)	They become adopted (v. 34)	They enjoy communion of the Son and the Father (v. 19)
The Father gives all things to them (vs. 55, 59)	They become the elect of God (v. 34) and Kingdom of God (v. 34)	They commune with the Church of the Firstborn (v. 19)
They are Priests and Kings (v. 56)	They Receive Christ (vs. 35–36)	
They have come unto the Church of the Firstborn (v. 67)	They receive the Father (v. 37)	
	They receive all that the Father hath (v. 38)	

THE ELECT OF GOD

Those who continue faithful will eventually receive the blessings promised to them at the time they were called and elected in the pre-earth councils. When one arrives at this state of righteousness, his calling and election is made sure, and he has thus met the challenge of mortality. The Prophet Joseph taught:

> After a person has faith in Christ, repents of his sins, and is baptized for the remission of his sins and receives the Holy Ghost, (by the laying on of hands), which is the first Comforter, then let him continue to humble himself before God, *hungering and thirsting after righteousness, and living by every word of God, and the Lord will soon say unto him, Son, thou shalt be exalted.* When the Lord has thoroughly proved him, and finds that the man is determined to serve Him at all hazards, *then the man will find his calling and his election made sure. . . .*[3]

One's calling and election is made sure unto eternal life as the Lord seals an exaltation upon the man through the Holy Spirit of Promise (Holy Ghost). That man is then "sealed up unto eternal life," and will obtain the resurrection of the pure in heart unless he breaks this seal through willful and grievous transgression. Note how the Prophet Nephi's words parallel Joseph Smith's statement above:

> Wherefore, ye must press forward with a steadfastness in Christ, having perfect brightness of hope, and a love of God and of all men. Wherefore, *if ye shall press forward, feasting upon the word of Christ, and endure to the end, behold, thus saith the Father: Ye shall have eternal life.*
>
> And now, behold, my beloved brethren, this is the way; and there is none other way nor name given under heaven whereby man can be saved in the kingdom of God. And now, behold, *this is the doctrine of Christ, and the only and true doctrine of the Father. . . .*[4]

This knowledge that a man receives that his exaltation is secure is known as the *more sure word of prophecy.* It is the realization of the word of prophecy issued in the pre-mortal organizational councils, and, in this sense, is more sure than the contingent word of prophecy made before the foundations of the world. Joseph Smith explained that "the more sure word of prophecy means a man's knowing that he is sealed up unto eternal life, by revelation and the spirit of prophecy, through the power of the Holy Priesthood. *It is impossible for a man to be saved in ignorance.*"[5] Elder Bruce R. McConkie also explained:

> Those members of the Church who devote themselves wholly to righteousness, living by every word that proceedeth forth from the mouth of God, *make their calling and election sure.* That is, they receive the more sure word of prophecy, which means that *the Lord seals their exaltation upon them while they are yet in this life.*[6]

The relationship between the more sure word of prophecy (the *knowledge* that one is sealed unto eternal life) and making one's calling and election sure (the entire process by which man is so sealed) is clarified by the Prophet in the following statement: "I would exhort you to go on and continue to call upon God until you make your calling and election sure for yourselves, by obtaining this more sure word of prophecy, and wait patiently for the promise until you obtain it."[7] Though it is true that "the fulness of eternal life is not attainable in mortality, . . . *the peace which is its harbinger and which comes as a result of making one's calling and election sure is attainable in this life.*"[8] This peace, which is the assurance of the glories of God, surpasseth all understanding. The Lord said that "he who doeth the works of righteousness shall receive his reward, even *peace in this world, and eternal life in the world to come.*"[9] Since one is *adopted* into the family of Christ through being born of the Spirit, he is thus *sealed* into the divine family through making his calling and election sure. King Benjamin instructed the converted Saints in this manner: "Therefore, I would that ye should be steadfast and immovable, always abounding in good works, *that Christ, the Lord God Omnipotent, may seal you his, that you may be brought to heaven, that ye may have everlasting salvation and eternal life. . . .*"[10]

That this doctrine of sealing was taught and understood in the Hebrew Church following the resurrection of Christ is beyond disputation. After instructing the Saints to incorporate the saving principles of faith, virtue, knowledge, temperance, patience, etc., Peter said:

> For if these things be in you, and abound, they make you that ye shall neither be barren nor unfruitful in the knowledge of our Lord Jesus Christ.
>
> But he that lacketh these things is blind, and cannot see afar off, and hath forgotten that he was purged from his old sins.
>
> Wherefore the rather, brethren, *give diligence to make your calling and election sure:* for if ye do these things ye shall never fall:
>
> For so an entrance shall be ministered unto you abundantly into the everlasting kingdom of our Lord and Saviour Jesus Christ.[11]

In speaking of his experience with Christ on the Mount of Transfiguration, Peter wrote the following:

> For he [Christ] received from God the Father honour and glory, when there came such a voice to him from the excellent glory, This is my beloved Son, in whom I am well pleased.
>
> And this voice which came from heaven we heard, when we were with him in the holy mount.
>
> *We have also a more sure word of prophecy;* where unto ye do well that ye take heed, as unto a light that shineth in a dark place, until the day dawn and the day star arise in your hearts.[12]

Joseph Smith made the following explanation of Peter's words:

> Now, there is some grand secret here, and keys to unlock the subject. Notwithstanding the apostle exhorts them to add to their faith, virtue, knowledge, temperance, etc., yet he exhorts them to make their calling and election sure. And though they had heard an audible voice from heaven bearing testimony that Jesus was the Son of God, yet he says we have a more sure word of prophecy, whereunto ye do well that ye take heed as unto a light shining in a dark place. Now, wherein could they have a more sure word of prophecy than to hear the voice of God saying, This is my beloved Son.
>
> Now for the secret and grand key. *Though they might hear the voice of God and know that Jesus was the Son of God, this would be no evidence that their election and calling was made sure, that they had part with Christ, and were joint heirs with Him. They then would want that more sure word of prophecy, that they were sealed in the heavens and had the promise of eternal life in the kingdom of God.*[13]

The principle that man may receive this ultimate peace that precedes eternal life has also been taught and practiced in the Dispensation of the Fulness of Times. The word of Christ to a group of Elders in 1831 is most emphatic: "And of as many as the Father shall bear record, to you shall be given power to seal them up unto eternal life."[14] In a communication to William Clayton the Prophet said: "Your life is hid with Christ in God, and so are many others. Nothing but the unpardonable sin can prevent you from inheriting eternal life, for you are sealed up by the power of the Priesthood unto eternal life, having taken the steps necessary for that purpose."[15] Finally, Joseph Smith was sealed unto eternal life. The word of God was heard: "For I am the Lord thy God, and will be with thee even unto the end of the world, and through all eternity; for verily *I seal upon you your exaltation, and prepare a throne for you in the kingdom of My Father, with Abraham your father.*"[16]

The "elect of God" are those who press forward in righteousness until they receive the assurance of eternal life—they make their calling and election sure. Elder Bruce R. McConkie referred to the elect of God as "a very select group, an inner circle of faithful members of the Church of Jesus Christ of Latter-day Saints." Continuing, Elder McConkie said: "To gain this elect status they must be endowed in the temple of the Lord (D&C 95:8), enter into that 'order of the priesthood' named 'the new and everlasting covenant of marriage' (D&C 131:1–4), and overcome by faith until, as the sons of God, they merit membership in the Church of the Firstborn (D&C 76:50–70, 94–96)."[17]

RECEIVING THE LORD

The role of the Holy Ghost is to endow man and bring him to a point of spirituality where he may partake of higher powers. Man's goal should thus be to "grow up in the Lord" to the point where he may receive a fulness of the Holy Ghost.[18] Those holding the Melchizedek Priesthood have the right to enjoy the communion and presence of God Himself, should Deity deem it necessary for a man to receive such a manifestation.[19] Joseph Smith taught that those who are diligent in seeking after God shall eventually "obtain faith in God, and power with Him to behold Him face to face."[20] Orson Pratt explained that the privilege of communing with God in mortality was in preparation for the life to come, in which man will live in the Celestial realms forever:

> It [the Higher Priesthood] holds not only the power of the ministration of holy angels to be seen personally, but also the power of beholding the face of God the Father, that through the power and manifestations of the Spirit of God and of his angels *we may be prepared to enter into the presence of God the Father in the world to come, and enjoy continual communion with him. . . .*[21]

The Lord has made it very clear who it is that will enjoy the unspeakable blessings related to seeing Him face to face. He said that "every soul who forsaketh his sins and cometh unto me, and calleth on my name, and obeyeth my voice, and keepeth my commandments, shall see my face and know that I am."[22] He explained to the Elders in 1832: "Therefore sanctify yourselves that your minds become single to God, and the days will come that you shall see him; for he will unveil his face unto you, and it shall be in his own time, and in his own way, and according to his own will."[23]

Those who prove valiant by cleansing their souls, so as to be pure in heart,[24] may thus receive Another Comforter:

> Now what is this other Comforter? *It is no more nor less than the Lord Jesus Christ Himself;* and this is the sum and substance of the whole matter; that *when any man obtains this last Comforter, he will have the personage of Jesus Christ to attend him, or appear unto him from time to time, and even He will manifest the Father unto him, and they will take up their abode with him,* and the visions of the heavens will be opened unto him, and the Lord will teach him face to face, and he may have a perfect knowledge of the mysteries of the Kingdom of God.[25]

Jesus taught His Apostles of the Second Comforter while yet in Jerusalem. Note His words to them, as recorded in the 14th Chapter of John:

> And I will pray the Father, and *he shall give you another Comforter,* that he may abide with you forever;

Even the Spirit of truth; whom the world cannot receive, because it seeth him not, neither knoweth him: but *ye know him; for he dwelleth with you* and shall be in you.

I will not leave you comfortless: I will come to you.

He that hath my commandments, and keepeth them, he it is that loveth me: and he that loveth me shall be loved of my Father, *and I will love him, and will manifest myself to him.*

If a man love me, he will keep my words: and my Father will love him, and *we will come unto him, and make our abode with him.*[26]

The blessings of the Second Comforter were enjoyed in the Americas among the people of Nephi. Nephi and Jacob were among the men who came into the presence of the Lord.

And now I, Nephi, write more of the words of Isaiah, for my soul delighteth in his words. For I will liken his words unto my people, and I will send them forth unto all my children, for he verily saw my Redeemer, *even as I have seen him.*

And my brother, Jacob, also has seen him as I have seen him.[27]

The Brother of Jared was an example of one who could not be withheld from penetrating the veil, because of faith ripening into knowledge. The record explains: "Behold, the Lord showed himself unto him, and said: Because thou knowest these things *ye are redeemed from the fall; therefore ye are brought back into my presence; therefore I show myself unto you.*"[28]

In this dispensation many of the Saints of God have lived so as to merit the blessings of the Second Comforter. The Prophet reported one such occasion in 1836:

The heavens were opened upon us, and I beheld the celestial kingdom of God, and the glory thereof, whether in the body or out I cannot tell. I saw the transcendant beauty of the gate through which the heirs of that kingdom will enter, which was like unto circling flames of fire; also *the blazing throne of God, whereon was seated the Father and the Son.*[29]

The Modern Seer reported another incident in which the veil was lifted and many saw a vision of the Savior:

I exhorted the brethren to faithfulness and diligence in keeping the commandments of God, and gave much instruction for the benefit of the Saints, with a promise that the pure in heart should see a heavenly vision; and after remaining a short time in secret prayer, the promise was verified; for *many present had the eyes of their understanding opened by the Spirit of God, so as to behold . . . a heavenly vision of the Savior,* and concourses of angels, and many other things, of which each one has a record of what he saw.[30]

THE CHURCH OF THE FIRSTBORN

Those of the Priesthood who choose the strait path which leads to eternal life prepare themselves for interactions and associations with exalted beings from times past. Those persons who become sanctified by the Spirit may have the privilege of enjoying the communion and presence of this elect body of Saints, and may ultimately become a part of this organization themselves. The *Church of the Firstborn* or inner Church (within the veil) is comprised of a membership of exalted men and women, those who have truly become the sons and daughters of Christ, and are spiritually begotten by Him.[31] Whereas baptism is the gate into The Church of Jesus Christ of Latter-day Saints, eternal marriage and an ultimate sealing is the gateway to membership in the Church of the Firstborn.[32]

No greater blessing could come to one in mortality than to merit the association of holy beings. Inasmuch as the quality of a man's life is largely determined by the types of persons with whom he associates, contemplate the sublime totality that is affixed to the life of one who communes regularly with members of the Church of the Firstborn! And such *is* the right of every holder of the Melchizedek Priesthood who pays the price of devotion to duty and conquest of self.[33] Elder Orson Pratt explained: "The higher Priesthood after the order of the Son of God, we are told, in a modern revelation, holds the power to commune with the Church of the Firstborn that are in heaven, and that too *not in a spiritual sense alone; . . . but in the literal sense, even the same as one man communes with another.*"[34] Elder B. H. Roberts explained how faith may be perfected and evolve into a principle of power:

> . . . by a union of these three elements, that is, a belief in the existence of God, a correct conception of his character, and a knowledge that the course of life pursued is approved of him—will render faith perfect, will constitute it a principle of power, the incentive to all action—as really it is, whether in temporal or spiritual things—leading from one degree of knowledge or excellence to another, from righteousness to righteousness, *until the heavens will be opened to them and they will hold communion with the Church of the Firstborn, with Jesus Christ, and with God the Father, and thus will they make their calling and election sure—through faith ripening into knowledge.*[35]

To become a member of the Church of the Firstborn is to be in a blessed state. President Joseph Fielding Smith explained: "To become a member of the Church of the Firstborn, as I understand it, is to become one of the inner circle."[36] President Smith said on another occasion:

> Some earths that have been built and some that are now being created are for habitations for those who receive immortality; *others are to*

become celestial earths and the eternal abodes of those who become members of the "Church of the Firstborn," in other words, are true and faithful to every commandment, covenant and obligation required for exaltation in the Gospel of Jesus Christ.[37]

One final statement in this area is most revealing:

When he [a man] has proved himself by a worthy life, having been faithful in all things required of him, then it is his privilege to receive other covenants and to take upon himself other obligations which will make of him an heir, and *he will become a member of the "Church of the Firstborn." Into his hands "the Father has given all things." He will be a priest and a king, receiving of the Father's fulness and of his glory . . . and the fulness of these blessings can only be obtained in the temple of the Lord.*[38]

JOINT HEIRS THROUGH CHRIST

Family relationships on earth are in the similitude of the heavenly order. In mortality, children are legal *heirs* to all of the rights and powers of the parent. So it is with the divine family unit. All those who become the sons and daughters of Christ by adoption are entitled to the inheritance of the Father through Christ. In Paul's message to the Romans, he taught:

For as many as are led by the Spirit of God, they are the sons of God.

For ye have not received the spirit of bondage again to fear; but *ye have received the Spirit of adoption,* whereby we cry, Abba Father.

The Spirit itself beareth witness with our spirit, that we are the children of God:

And if children, then heirs; *heirs of God, and joint heirs with Christ;* if so be that we suffer with him, that we may be also glorified together.[39]

God's promise to the Priesthood holder is glorious: "And he that receiveth my Father receiveth my Father's kingdom; therefore *all that my Father hath shall be given unto him.*"[40] In another revelation the Lord explained: "They are they into whose hands the Father has given all things—Wherefore, all things are theirs. . . ."[41] In addition to receiving all that is in heaven or on earth, heirs of God inherit the glory of the Father,[42] as well as receiving all knowledge and power.[43] As with all of the blessings, that pertain to the Patriarchal Order, divine heirship centers in the Temple of God. Only through receiving the endowment and complying with the eternal order of marriage may one qualify as an heir in the family of God. President Heber C. Kimball thus said: "After receiving the Priesthood, when a person receives his endowment, he is an heir to the Priesthood—an heir of God, and a joint-heir with Jesus Christ; that is, *he has commenced his heirship.*"[44]

A FULNESS OF THE PRIESTHOOD

Those men who magnify and honor their callings in the Melchizedek Priesthood shall eventually receive a *fullness of the Priesthood.* That is, they gain all of the Priesthood rights available—they become Kings and Priests unto God. Joseph Smith therefore explained that "those holding the fulness of the Melchizedek Priesthood are kings and priests of the Most High God, holding the keys of power and blessings."[45] Brigham Young likewise stated that "for any person to have a fulness . . . he must be a king and a priest. . . ."[46] President Young also explained: "*A man may be anointed king and priest long before he receives his kingdom.*"[47] In speaking of the fulness of the Priesthood, a friend of the Prophet (Daniel Tyler) said:

> These additional powers included all of the keys that belong to the holy priesthood on the earth, or were ever revealed to man in any dispensation, and *which admit men and women within the veil.* They enable them to pass by the angels and the gods, until they get into the presence of the Father and the Son. *They make of them kings and priests, queens and priestesses to God, to rule and reign as such over their posterity and those who may be given to them by adoption. . . .*[48]

President Brigham Young made it clear that a man might become a King and a Priest in this life,[49] but he would not receive his kingdom until the resurrection. Said he:

> We have not yet received our kingdoms, neither will we, until we have finished our work on earth, passed through the ordeals, are brought up by the power of the resurrection, and are crowned with glory and eternal lives. Then *he that has overcome and is found worthy, will be made a king of kings, and lord of lords over his own posterity, or in other words: A father of fathers.*[50]

The fulness of the Priesthood may only be obtained in the House of the Lord, through the channels of authority that God has ordained.[51] Joseph the Prophet explained that "if a man gets a fulness of the priesthood of God he has to get it in the same way that Jesus Christ obtained it, and that was by keeping all the commandments and obeying all the ordinances of the house of the Lord."[52] Joseph Fielding Smith also taught the role of the temples in gaining these sacred powers:

> I do not care what *office* you hold in this Church—you may be an apostle, you may be a patriarch, a high priest, or anything else—you cannot receive the *fulness of the priesthood* unless you go into the temple of the Lord and receive the ordinances of which the Prophet [Joseph Smith] spoke. *No man can get the fulness of the priesthood outside the temple of the Lord.*[53]

As was pointed out in Chapter 1, The Church of Jesus Christ exists to serve and strengthen individuals and families. The Church is an organization of offices, quorums, and councils, and exists to build the family in spiritual matters. The Patriarchal Order is the order of heaven and will exist into eternity. In this latter order (which has its basis in the marriage ceremony performed in the Temple), the basic unit is the family, with rights and powers centering in the righteous father. The program of the Temple thus introduces man into the "highest order of the Melchizedek Priesthood," where he may gain the "fulness of those blessings . . . prepared for the Church of the Firstborn, and come and abide in the presence of the Eloheim [Gods] in the eternal worlds."[54]

It is by acquiring the fulness of the priesthood that man is able to receive the fulness of Godhood and eternal lives. A beautiful explanation of the ultimate state of the faithful Priesthood holder was given by George Q. Cannon:

> God designs to have us lead in that path which will bring us into his presence. He designs that his whole people called Latter-day Saints shall have the laws of His celestial kingdom revealed unto them line upon line, precept upon precept, here a little and there a little, until . . . *by means of this Priesthood, this higher Priesthood, every man will be prepared to receive the fulness of the celestial glory* . . . [55]

Finally, the challenge for man to seek after the fulness of the Priesthood while yet in mortality was stressed by President Lorenzo Snow:

> We expect in the resurrection to exercise the powers of our priesthood—we can exercise them only in proportion as we secure its righteousness and perfection; these qualifications can be had only as they are sought and obtained, so that *in the morning of the resurrection we will possess those acquisitions which we secured in this world! Godliness cannot be conferred but must be acquired.*[56]

How powerful are President Snow's words: "Godliness cannot be conferred but must be acquired!" Indeed, the fulness of truth which centers in God shall be the natural and consequential blessing to the valiant. Those "who are quickened by a portion of celestial glory shall then receive of the same, even a fulness."[57] The laws are set. The transcendent blessings and privileges automatically come to the pure in heart. All that remains is for the man of the Priesthood to partake of the enlivening powers inherent in the Gospel of Christ. To all who bear the Holy Priesthood comes the beckoning call: "IF FAITHFUL . . . THE CUP IS WITHIN THY REACH; DRINK THEN THE HEAVENLY DRAUGHT AND LIVE."[58]

SUMMARY

1. Priesthood holders who continue faithful will eventually receive the blessings promised to them in the pre-earth councils. To do so is to make one's calling and election sure to eternal life. That man's exaltation is secure, unless he commits the unpardonable sin.

2. The more sure word of prophecy means a man's knowing that he is sealed up into eternal life through (a) the spirit of prophecy and revelation, and (b) the powers of the Holy Priesthood.

3. The doctrine of making one's calling and election sure was taught and understood in the meridian of time, as well as in Joseph Smith's day.

4. Those bearing the Melchizedek Priesthood have the right (should Deity deem it proper) to enjoy the communion and presence of the Lord Jesus Christ and also the Eternal Father. This is known as the Second Comforter, and comes only to the pure in heart.

5. The Higher Priesthood also entitles one to commune with, and eventually become a member of, the Church of the Firstborn, the inner Church composed of those who have been exalted in the Kingdom of God.

6. Those who truly become the sons and daughters of Christ through adoption also become heirs of God the Father and joint-heirs with Christ. All that the Father hath shall be given to them.

7. To receive a fulness of the Priesthood is to become a King and a Priest (Queen and Priestess) in the Divine Patriarchal Order. The fulness of the Priesthood is only obtained in the blessings received in the Temples of God.

BIBLIOGRAPHY

LATTER-DAY SAINT SCRIPTURES

The Book of Mormon. (trans.) Joseph Smith, Salt Lake City: The Church of Jesus Christ of Latter-day Saints, 1969.

The Doctrine and Covenants of The Church of Jesus Christ of Latter-day Saints. Salt Lake City: The Church of Jesus Christ of Latter-day Saints, 1969.

The Holy Bible, King James Version; Salt Lake City: The Church of Jesus Christ of Latter-day Saints, 1950.

The Pearl of Great Price. Salt Lake City: The Church of Jesus Christ of Latter-day Saints, 1969.

LATTER-DAY SAINT HISTORICAL AND DOCTRINAL SOURCES

Andrus, Hyrum L., *Doctrinal Commentary on the Pearl of Great Price.* Salt Lake City: Deseret Book Company, 1967.

Andrus, Hyrum L., *Doctrines of the Kingdom.* Salt Lake City: Bookcraft, 1973.

Andrus, Hyrum L., *Principles of Perfection.* Salt Lake City: Bookcraft, 1970.

Conference Reports of the Church of Jesus Christ of Latter-day Saints. Salt Lake City: The Church of Jesus Christ of Latter-day Saints, 1897–1973.

Crowther, Duane S., *Gifts of the Spirit.* Salt Lake City: Bookcraft, 1965. (Now Bountiful, Utah: Horizon Publishers & Distributors, Inc.)

Durham, G. Homer, (comp.) *The Gospel Kingdom—Selections From the Writings and Discourses of John Taylor.* Salt Lake City: Bookcraft, 1964.

Durham, G. Homer, (comp.) *The Discourses of Wilford Woodruff.* Salt Lake City: Bookcraft, 1946.

Hymns of the Church of Jesus Christ of Latter-day Saints. Salt Lake City, 1962.

Journal of Discourses. 26 Vols.; Los Angeles, California: General Printing and Lithograph Company, 1961.

Ludlow, Daniel H., *Latter-day Prophets Speak.* Salt Lake City: Bookcraft, 1948.

Lundwall, N.B. (comp.) *Lectures on Faith,* as delivered by Joseph Smith to the School of the Prophets. Salt Lake City, n.d.

Lundwall, N.B. (comp.) *Temples of the Most High.* Salt Lake City: Bookcraft, 1968.

Lundwall, N.B. (comp.) *The Vision.* Salt Lake City: Bookcraft, n.d.

Madsen, Truman G., *Eternal Man.* Salt Lake City: Deseret Book Company, 1966.

McConkie, Bruce R. (comp.) *Doctrines of Salvation—Sermons and Writings of Joseph Fielding Smith.* 3 Vols.; Salt Lake City: Bookcraft, 1954–56.

McConkie, Bruce R., *Mormon Doctrine.* Salt Lake City: Bookcraft, 1966.

McKay, David O., *Gospel Ideals.* Salt Lake City: An Improvement Era Publication, 1953.

McKay, David O., *True to the Faith*. Salt Lake City: Bookcraft, 1966.

Middlemiss, Clare (comp.) *Cherished Experiences From the Writings of David O. McKay*. Salt Lake City: Deseret Book Company, 1955.

Millet, Robert L., *The Perfected Millennial Kingdom*. Salt Lake City: Hawkes Publications, 1974.

Palmer, Lee A., *Aaronic Priesthood Through the Centuries*. Salt Lake City: Deseret Book Company, 1964.

Pratt, Parley P., *Autobiography of Parley P. Pratt*. Salt Lake City: Deseret Book Company, 1966.

Pratt, Parley P., *Key to the Science of Theology*. 9th ed. Salt Lake City: Deseret Book Company, 1965.

Roberts, B. H., *The Gospel and Man's Relationship to Deity*. Salt Lake City: Deseret Book Company, 1966.

Romney, George J. (comp.) *Look to God and Live—Discourses of Marion G. Romney*. Salt Lake City: Deseret Book Company, 1971.

Smith, Joseph, *History of the Church of Jesus Christ of Latter-day Saints*. 7 Vols.; 2nd ed. rev.; Salt Lake City: The Deseret Book Company, 1959.

Smith. Joseph F., *Gospel Doctrine*. Salt Lake City: Deseret Book Company, 1939.

Smith, Joseph Fielding. *Answers to Gospel Questions*. 5 Vols.; Salt Lake City: Deseret Book Company, 1957–66.

Smith, Joseph Fielding, *Man: His Origin and Destiny*. Salt Lake City: Deseret Book Company, 1954.

Smith, Joseph Fielding, *The Way to Perfection*. Salt Lake City: Deseret Book Company, 1970.

Smith, Joseph Fielding, (comp.) *Teachings of the Prophet Joseph Smith*. Salt Lake City: The Deseret News Press, 1938.

Sperry, Sidney B., *Doctrine and Covenants Compendium*. Salt Lake City: Bookcraft, 1960.

Talmage, James E., *A Study of the Articles of Faith*. Salt Lake City: The Church of Jesus Christ of Latter-day Saints, 1961.

Taylor, John, *The Mediation and Atonement of Our Lord and Savior Jesus Christ*. Salt Lake City: Deseret News, 1882.

Widtsoe, John A., *Evidences and Reconciliations*. Salt Lake City: Bookcraft, 1960.

Widtsoe, John A., *Priesthood and Church Government*. Salt Lake City: Deseret Book Company, 1939.

Widtsoe, John A., *Program of the Church*. Salt Lake City: Deseret News Press, 1938.

Widtsoe, John A., *A Rational Theology*. Salt Lake City: Deseret Book Company, 1937.

PERIODICALS

Deseret News, June 7, 1873; June 8, 1873; March 30, 1935; April 20, 1935.

Deseret Weekly, Vols. LV, LII, LIV.

Doxey, Roy W., "Great Truths; The School of the Prophets." *The Relief Society Magazine*, November 1965.

Pratt, Orson, (Ed.) *The Seer*. Washington, D.C.: 1853–54.

Richards, Joel, "Education Among the Latter-day Saints." *Liahona—The Elder's Journal*, Vol. 8, No. 9 (August 16, 1910).

The Ensign. Salt Lake City: The Church of Jesus Christ of Latter-day Saints., January 1974, February 1974.

The Improvement Era. Salt Lake City: The Church of Jesus Christ of Latter-day Saints, June 1905, August 1906, October 1919, January 1953, November, 1966.

The Instructor. Salt Lake City: The Church of Jesus Christ of Latter-day Saints, September, 1963.

The Juvenile Instructor. Salt Lake City: The Church of Jesus Christ of Latter-day Saints. Vols. XV, XXVII, XXXI, XXXVII, XLVII.

The Latter-Day Saints' Millennial Star, Vols. I, IX, XIII, XIV, XXIV, XXVII, XLIX, LII, LVI.

Times and Seasons, Vol. VI (June 1, 1845).

Young, Lorenzo Dow., "Biography of Lorenzo Dow Young." *Utah Historical Quarterly*, Vol. XIV (1946).

Young Woman's Journal, Vols. II, XVI.

MISCELLANEOUS

Lee, Harold B., Brigham Young University Devotional Address, September 11, 1973.

Lee, Harold B., "The Place of the Living Prophet, Seer, and Revelator." Address given to Seminary and Institute of Religion Faculty, Brigham Young University, July 1964.

Pratt, Orson, *The Holy Spirit*. Liverpool, 1856.

Rigdon, Sidney, "Oration Delivered by Mr. S. Rigdon on the 4th of July, 1838." Far West, Missouri, 1838.

Taylor, John, "The Mormon," New York City, August 29, 1857.

The First Presidency and Council of the Twelve, "The Father and the Son," June 30, 1916.

ENDNOTES

CHAPTER I

1. 1 Cor. 2:11.

2. Joseph Smith, *History of The Church of Jesus Christ of Latter-day Saints*, (second edition; Salt Lake City, Utah: Deseret Book Company: 1959), Vol. III, p. 295. This work is the official published history of the Church in its early period, and is composed of six volumes covering the life of Joseph Smith and a seventh volume covering the years between 1844–1847. Further references to this source will be shown as HC 3:295.

3. D&C 121:45. (Italics by the writer.) Hereafter all italics will be added by the writer unless otherwise indicated.

4. Bruce R. McConkie, comp., *Doctrines of Salvation—Sermons and Writings of Joseph Fielding Smith* (3 Vols.: Salt Lake City: Bookcraft, 1954–56), Vol. III, p. 80.

5. *Conference Reports of The Church of Jesus Christ of Latter-day Saints*, October 1965. pp. 103–106; cited hereafter as CR.

6. D&C 107:3.

7. HC 6:305.

8. *Journal of Discourses* (Los Angeles, California: General Printing and Lithograph Co., 1961; Photo Lithographic Reprint of exact original edition published in 1882), Vol. XV, p. 127. This work is a collection of discourses by most of the authorities of the Church between the years of 1851 and 1886. Further references to this source will be shown as *JD* 15:127.

9. *The Latter-day Saints' Millennial Star* (Liverpool, England. February 1841). Vol I. p. 257. Hereafter this source will be abbreviated as *MS*, followed by the appropriate volume and page number.

10. *JD* 6:25.

11. CR, October 1904, p. 5.

12. CR, October 1901, p. 2.

13. Joseph Fielding Smith, *The Way to Perfection* (Salt Lake City: Deseret Book Company, 1970). p. 70.

14. *Ibid.*, p. 219.

15. HC 3:295.

16. D&C 107:18.

17. See, for example, D&C 84:17; Heb. 7:3.

18. HC 3:386.

19. *JD* 26:245.

20. *Hymns of The Church of Jesus Christ of Latter-day Saints* (Salt Lake City, 1985), No. 284.

21. *JD* 10:5; compare also a statement by Lorenzo Snow in *Deseret Weekly News*, Vol. XXXVIII, p. 450.

22. HC 4:598.

23. *JD* 19:52; see also a statement by John Taylor in *JD* 19:137.

24. *Ibid.*, 19:176.

25. CR, October 1972, pp. 129–130.

26. *JD* 22:308–309.

27. *Ibid.*

28. *Ibid.*, 3:188–189.

29. These subjects will be discussed in greater detail in Chapter 10.

30. *JD* 2:371.

31. John Taylor, *MS* 9:321–322.

32. John Taylor, *Ibid.*, 9:323.

33. *JD* 7:84.

34. *MS* 9:322.

35. *JD* 16:240.

36. John Taylor, *Ibid.*, 19:56; See also a similar statement in *Ibid.*, 19:137–138.

37. *Ibid.*, 22:333–334.

38. *HC* 3:386.

39. *JD* 22:308; compare also *JD* 18:2.

40. *HC* 4:207.

41. Joseph Fielding Smith, comp., *Teachings of the Prophet Joseph Smith* (Salt Lake City: The Deseret News Press, 1938), p. 180; cited hereafter as *TPJS.*

42. *HC* 5:555.

43. Eph. 4:11–13.

44. D&C 107:99.

45. *Ibid.*, 84:109.

46. *MS* 14:290.

47. John A. Widtsoe, *Priesthood and Church Government* (Salt Lake City: Deseret Book Company, 1939), p. 3.

48. *The Juvenile Instructor*, Vol. XXXVII., pp. 50–51 (January 15, 1902); hereafter cited as *JI.*

49. *HC* 3:381.

50. D&C 107:8.

51. Bruce R. McConkie, *Doctrines of Salvation, op cit.*, III, p. 104

52. Whether this angelic minister was Noah or Melchizedek or Abraham himself is not certain.

53. D&C 110:12.

54. *Ibid.*, 84:25.

55. *Ibid.*, 13:107:20.

56. *Ibid.*, 107:14, 20.

57. Joseph F. Smith, *Improvement Era*, Vol. VIII, p. 620 (June 1905); hereafter cited as *IE.*

58. D&C 84:18; compare also Ex. 30:30–31; Ex. 40:13–15; *HC* 5:257.

59. *JD* 18:363.

60. Joseph Fielding Smith, *Answers to Gospel Questions* (5 Vols.; Salt Lake City: Deseret Book Company, 1957–1966), Vol. I, pp. 119–120.

61. D&C 84:19–21.

62. *HC* 4:207.

63. John A. Widtsoe, *Program of the Church* (Salt Lake City, Deseret News Press, 1938). p. 130.

64. *HC* 2:477.

65. *Ibid.*, 6:363.

66. *JD* 3:192–193.

67. *Ibid.*, 3:192.

68. See D&C 93:19–20.

69. *MS* 52:578.

70. *JD* 21:298.

71. John A. Widtsoe, *Program of the Church, op cit.*, p. 130.

72. D&C 50:27.

73. *JD* 19:17.

74. D&C 107:19.

75. CR, October 1964, pp. 91–93.

76. *JD* 18:363; see also John Taylor, *JD* 19:78.

77. *Ibid.*, 18:363.

CHAPTER II

1. Joseph Fielding Smith, CR, October 1970, p. 92.

2. Bruce R. McConkie, *Mormon Doctrine* (Salt Lake City: Bookcraft, 1966), pp. 486–488.

3. Genesis 26:3–4; compare Genesis 22:16, Abraham 2:9–11.

4. Psalms 110:4; Compare Heb. 5:6; 7:17, 21.

5. 1 Nephi 4:33–37.

6. *Ibid.*, 4:37.

7. Moses 5:29–31.

8. See, for example, Alma 37:27, 29; Helaman 6:21, 25, 30; 4 Nephi 42; Ether 8:15, 20; 10:33.

9. Moses 5:29.

10. Matt. 5:33–37.

11. *HC* 1:269.

12. CR, April 1955, p. 29.

13. *JD* 17:255.

14. *Ibid.*, 4:141–142.

15. *Ibid.*, 17:247.

16. D&C 132:4.

17. Bruce R. McConkie, *Doctrines of Salvation, op cit.*, I, p. 157.

18. *MS* 56:452.

19. CR, April 1928, p. 69.

20. *JD* 7:314–315.

21. See Romans 1:16.

22. Bruce R. McConkie, *Doctrines of Salvation, op cit.*, I, p. 156.

23. D&C 66:2; Compare D&C 1:22; 39:11; 45:9; 49:9; 76:101; 88:131; 98:14; 101:39; 133:57.

24. Heb. 12:24; D&C 76:69; *HC* 6:51.

25. *HC* 6:78; Compare D&C 1:22.

26. Mosiah 18:8–10.

27. *IE*, October 1919.

28. *IE*, Editor's Page, January 1953.

29. *IE*, October 1919.

30. D&C 20:77–79; Moroni 4, 5.

31. Brigham Young, *JD* 2:31; Compare a statement by Brigham Young in *JD* 12:163–164.

32. *HC* 2:309; Compare D&C 76:60.

33. *IE* 9:813 (August 1906); See also a statement by John Taylor in *JD* 25:165.

34. See *JD* 9:195; *JD* 1:77.

35. See Chapter 4, the section entitled "Blessing the Family."

36. D&C 132.

37. *JD* 2:90.

38. Joseph Fielding Smith, *The Way to Perfection, op cit.*, pp. 249–250.

39. *IE*, Editor's Page, January 1953.

40. *IE*, October 1919.

41. D&C 84:33–44.

42. See a statement to this effect by Joseph Fielding Smith in CR, October 1970, p. 92.

43. CR, October 1948, p. 101.

44. *HC* 5:555.

45. Heb. 7:20–21.

46. CR. April 1965, p. 95.

47. *JD* 23:331.

48. CR. October 1945, pp. 88–89.

49. Note. for example. D&C 76:34; Matt. 12:32; Heb. 6:6.

50. *Church News*, March 30. 1935, p. 6 (italics in the original).

51. CR October 1960.

52. *Inspired Version*, Genesis 14:27–28. 30–31.

53. *JD* 22:209.

54. *Ibid.*, 23:329–330.

55. George Q. Cannon, *JD* 25:290–291.

56. CR April 1962, p. 17.

57. CR October 1945, pp. 98–99 (italics in the original).

CHAPTER III

1. Moses 1:39.

2. John Taylor, "The Mormon," (New York City, August 29, 1857), as cited in N. B. Lundwall, *The Vision* (Salt Lake City. Utah: Bookcraft Publishing Co., n.d.), pp. 146–147.

3. *Deseret Weekly*, Vol. LV, p. 354 (August 22, 1897).

4. See a statement by the First Presidency and Council of the Twelve

entitled "The Father and the Son." June 30. 1916; as cited in James E. Talmage, *Articles of Faith* (Salt Lake City. 1961). pp. 465–473.

5. Moses 1:33.

6. John 1:1–3, 10.

7. Heb. 1:2.

8. D&C 76:24.

9. Orson Pratt, The Seer, Vol. I, No. 10, October 1853, p. 147.

10. *HC* 6:308.

11. Orson F. Whitney, "Elias: An Epic of the Ages," as cited by Marion G. Romney in CR, October 1973, p. 51.

12. *HC* 6:307.

13. Abraham 4:1.

14. See Moses 4:2 as evidence that the plan presented by Jehovah was the plan of the Eternal Father.

15. Orson F. Whitney."Elias: An Epic of the Ages," *op cit.*

16. *TPJS*, p. 181.

17. *MS* 56:452.

18. John Taylor, "The Mormon," *op cit.*

19. Acts 17:24–26.

20. *JD* 21:193.

21. *HC* 4:258.

22. *JD* 1:257–258.

23. CR, October 1973, p. 7.

24. *Ibid.*

25. *HC* 4:260. 261.

26. Abraham 2:11.

27. *JD* 1:260–261.

28. D&C 86:8–10.

29. *JD* 7:289–290.

30. *Ibid.*, 15:250.

31. *HC* 4:360.

32. *Ibid.*, 6:364.

33. 1 Peter 1:20.

34. *Deseret Weekly*, Vol. XXXVIII, p. 389 (March 3. 1889).

35. Abraham 3:23.

36. Jeremiah 1:5.

37. *JD* 22:267; Compare also statements in *JD* 22:28; 7:290; *HC* 6:364.

38. Bruce R. McConkie, *Doctrines of Salvation, op cit.*, III, p. 81.

39. *JD* 21:318.

40. Wilford Woodruff. *Ibid.*, 21:317; Compare also a statement by George Q. Cannon in *Ibid.*, 26:243.

41. Alma 13:1–9.

42. D&C 84:24.

43. Article of Faith #5.

44. *JD* 23:177; Compare also a statement by Brigham Young in *JD* 7:289.

45. *Ibid.*, 22:267.

46. John A. Widtsoe, *Program of the Church, op cit.*, p. 131.

47. See John A. Widtsoe, *Priesthood and Church Government, op cit.*, p. 50; Bruce R. McConkie, *Doctrines of Salvation, op cit.*, 111, p. 106.

CHAPTER IV

1. *JD* 21:49.

2. D&C 84:33.

3. D&C 88:67; A more comprehensive study of "An Eye Single to the Glory of God" will be undertaken in Chapter 5.

4. Moroni 10:5.

5. *JD* 19:241–242.

6. *JI* 31:101–102 (February 15, 1896).

7. *JD* 2:157.

8. *Ibid.*, 19:245.

9. D&C 82:3.

10. *Ibid.*, 107:99–100.

11. *Ibid.*, 84:109.

12. Joseph Fielding Smith, *The Way to Perfection, op cit.*, p. 219; See also CR, April 1966, p. 102.

13. *JD* 19:51.

14. D&C 64:33.

15. *JD* 21:48–49.

16. *Ibid.*, 26:62.

17. George Q. Cannon, *MS* 24:536–538 (August 23, 1862).

18. John A. Widtsoe, *A Rational Theology* (Salt Lake City: Deseret Book Company, 1937), pp. 102–103.

19. John Taylor, *Mediation and Atonement of Our Lord and Savior Jesus Christ* (Salt Lake City, Utah: Deseret News, 1882) pp. 87–88.

20. *JD* 7:84.

21. CR, October 1965, pp. 103–106.

22. *JD* 1:312.

23. For an excellent treatment of the various gifts of the Spirit, see Duane S. Crowther, *Gifts of the Spirit* (Salt Lake City: Bookcraft, 1965).

24. Rev. 19:10.

25. *HC* 6:58.

26. *MS* 28:516–518.

27. Moroni 10:24.

28. *JD* 21:191.

29. *Autobiography of Parley P. Pratt* (Salt Lake City: Deseret Book Company, 1966), p. 294.

30. *JD* 12:125.

31. *JI* 27:492 (August 1892).

32. Lorenzo Dow Young, "Biography of Lorenzo Dow Young," *Utah Historical Quarterly*, Vol. XIV (1946), pp. 45–46.

33. Joseph Smith, *MS* 4:116; also cited in *Autobiography of Parley P. Pratt, op cit.*, pp. 69–71.

34. *Autobiography of Parley P. Pratt, op cit.*, pp. 210–211.

35. CR, April 1973, p. 130.

36. CR, April 1964, p. 5.

37. CR, April 1964.

38. *Ibid.*

39. See D&C 2:3.

40. CR, October 1964, pp. 91–93.

41. CR, April 1965, pp. 60–65.

42. *HC* 3:301.

43. D&C 107:53–56.

44. *JD* 17:372.

45. Eliza R. Snow, in Edward Tullidge, *Women of Mormondom*, p. 96; as cited in Hyrum L. Andrus, *Doctrines of the Kingdom* (Salt Lake City: Bookcraft, 1973), p. 434.

46. See a statement by John Taylor in *Times and Seasons*, Vol. VI, p. 921 (June I. 1845).

47. Bruce R. McConkie, *Doctrines of Salvation, op cit.*, III, p. 172.

48. *JD* 8:62.

49. *Ibid.*, 11:209; Compare also a statement by Orson Pratt in *The Seer, op cit.*, pp. 155–156.

50. CR, October 1904, p. 5.

51. *JD* 26:100.

52. *Ibid.*, 8:23.

53. CR, October 1901, p. 83.

54. See statements by Lorenzo Snow (*JD* 23:341–342) and John Taylor (*JD* 20:22).

CHAPTER V

1. *HC* 4:209.

2. D&C 50:9.

3. *JD* 11:80.

4. D&C 133:5; Compare also D&C 38:42.

5. *Ibid.*, 50:27–28.

6. The process of obtaining and retaining a remission of sins will be discussed in Chapter 9.

7. JD 6:161.

8. Ibid., 9:166.

9. CR, April 1949, p. 17.

10. As cited by David O. McKay in IE 52:558:560, 600–602 (1949).

11. See Alma 39:5.

12. D&C 42:24.

13. CR, October 1972, pp. 127–128.

14. CR, April 1969, p. 94.

15. Matt. 5:27–28.

16. Prov. 3:1.

17. D&C 42:23.

18. David O. McKay, CR, April 1950, pp. 33–34; citing William James, Psychology, Henry Holt and Co., N.Y. 1892, p. 150.

19. David O. McKay, CR, October 1951, p. 8.

20. Prov. 23:7.

21. David O. McKay, True to the Faith (Salt Lake City; Bookcraft, 1966), p. 270.

22. D&C 50:27.

23. Ibid., 121:34; compare also Ibid., 121:40; Matt. 20:16, 22:14.

24. CR, October 1973.

25. Alma 13:4.

26. D&C 95:5–6.

27. Ibid., 121:34–35.

28. Luke 12:16–21.

29. Undoubtedly, this system of economics was what we have termed the Law of Consecration and Stewardship; see Acts 4, 5.

30. Matt. 6:24; Luke 16:13.

31. N. B. Lundwall, comp., Lectures on Faith—a series of lectures delivered by the Prophet Joseph Smith before the School of Prophets, n.d.; Lecture #6.

32. JD 21:284.

33. Joseph Fielding Smith, The Way to Perfection, op cit., p. 255.

34. Matt. 6:19–21.

35. D&C 121:35.

36. Matt. 6:2, 5, 16.

37. JI 27:129.

38. Ibid.

39. 2 Nephi 9:28–29.

40. D&C 121:36–37.

41. JD 19:138.

42. Mor. 7:47.

43. 1 Cor. 13:4; compare also Mor. 7:45.

44. MS 24:548 (August 10, 1862).

45. Ibid., 24:536–538.

46. Ibid.

47. D&C 121:39–40.

48. HC 5:285.

49. JD 13:55.

50. Charles W. Penrose, JD 24:306; compare also a statement by John Taylor in JD 20:261–262.

51. D&C 121:37–38.

52. MS 49:546.

53. See, for example, D&C 20:60; HC 5:555.

54. As cited by Wilford Woodruff in JD 21:284.

55. Ibid., 21:190–191.

56. Joseph Smith, HC 6:314–315.

57. D&C 121:41–45.

58. Hymns of The Church of Jesus Christ of Latter-day Saints, op cit., No. 240.

59. 3 Nephi 12:5; Matt. 5:5; Inspired Version, Matt. 5:7.

60. HC 3:380–381.

61. Mor. 7:47.

62. As cited in JD 10:57–58; Ibid., 24:159.

63. *Ibid.*, 10:190.

64. *Ibid.*, 15:216.

65. D&C 58:27–28.

66. *Ibid.*, 50:26.

67. As cited in *Young Woman's Journal*, II (May, 1891), p. 366.

68. D&C 38:27.

69. John Taylor, *JD* 18:137.

70. *HC* 4:345.

71. *JD* 12:363.

72. *Ibid.*, 1:45.

73. *Ibid.*, 12:257.

74. Moses 1:39.

75. *Deseret News Church Section*, April 20, 1935, p. 3.

76. D&C 25:10.

77. CR, April 1909, p. 2.

78. *JD* 11:115.

79. *Ibid.*, 10:150; compare also *Ibid.*, 20:20.

80. Prov. 3:5–6.

81. Alma 37:36–37.

82. Matt. 6:22.

83. D&C 88:67.

84. Notice how the Lord uses the terms "eye" and "mind" interchangeably in *Ibid.*, 88:67–68.

85. See *Ibid.*, 84:45.

86. *Ibid.*, 50:24.

87. *Ibid.*, 93:28.

88. *JD* 19:142.

89. Matt. 6:33.

90. *JD* 2:125.

91. Jacob 2:17–19.

CHAPTER VI

1. D&C 84:43.

2. *Ibid.*, 88:4.

3. *Ibid.*, 84:45.

4. Moses 6:59.

5. A more detailed discussion of the Living Oracles will be undertaken in Chapter 7.

6. Matt. 4:4; compare Deut. 8:3.

7. D&C 84:44.

8. *Gospel Doctrine, op cit.*, pp. 116–17.

9. Bruce R. McConkie, "To Honest Truth Seekers," letter prepared by Elder McConkie on answering gospel questions, July 1, 1980.

10. *JD* 22:335.

11. *Relief Society Magazine*, July 1969.

12. See a statement to this effect by Harold B. Lee in "The Place of the Living Prophet, Seer and Revelator." Address given to Seminary and Institute of Religion Faculty, Brigham Young University, July 1964.

13. 2 Tim. 3:16–17.

14. *HC* 4:461.

15. D&C 20:9; compare also Smith 2:34.

16. *IE* 30:736–738.

17. D&C 42:12.

18. *JD* 22:146.

19. *Ibid.*, 8:129.

20. *Relief Society Magazine*, July 1969.

21. See a statement by Marion G. Romney in CR, April 1973, p. 116.

22. CR, October 1902, p. 88.

23. CR, October 1917, pp. 41, 43–44.

24. JE 47:204.

25. Truman G. Madsen, *Eternal Man* (Salt Lake City: Deseret Book Company, 1966), p. 20.

26. Orson F. Whitney, *Life of Heber C. Kimball* (Salt Lake City: Bookcraft, 1945), p. 322.

27. Ex. 3:14.

28. *HC* 6:303.

29. *JD* 13:312.

30. *Ibid.*, 16:75.

31. *HC* 3:295.

32. *The Instructor,* September 1963; Compare also statements in CR, April 1946.

33. *Ibid.*

34. CR, October 1962, pp. 82–83.

35. CR, April 1973, p. 117.

36. 2 Nephi 4:15–16.

37. D&C 76:15, 19.

38. Joseph F. Smith, *Gospel Doctrine* (Salt Lake City: Deseret Book Company, 1939), p. 472; See also *IE* 22:166–170 (December 1918).

39. See D&C 43:34; 84:85.

40. Psalms 130:5.

41. As cited in N.B. Lundwall, *Temples of the Most High* (Salt Lake City: Bookcraft, 1968), pp. 139–141.

42. Enos 4.

43. As cited in *IE* 69:992 (November 1966).

44. *HC* 2:31.

45. D&C 42:14; Compare *Ibid.*, 63:64.

46. 2 Nephi 32:8.

47. *JD* 13:155.

48. *Ibid.*, 24:55.

49. *HC* 6:308.

50. See Eph. 6:18; Jude 20.

51. D&C 46:30, 32.

52. *JD* 12:103.

53. *Ibid.*, 9:150.

54. John A. Widtsoe, *Program of the Church, op cit.*, p. 130.

55. *HC* 2:477.

56. *JD* 7:203.

57. John A. Widtsoe, *Program of the Church, op cit.*, p. 130.

58. *HC* 3:381.

59. D&C 93:36.

60. *Ibid.*, 8:2–3.

61. *Ibid.*, 9:8–9.

62. *Ibid.*, 85.

63. *Ibid.*, 130:12–13.

64. *Ibid.*. 76, 110.

65. 1 Nephi 2.

66. CR, April 1964.

67. The importance of birth into the Kingdom of God will be treated in Chapter 8.

68. *Deseret News,* June 7, 1873.

69. D&C 84:19.

70. *Ibid.*, 107:18–19.

71. Bruce R. McConkie, *Mormon Doctrine, op cit.*, p. 523.

72. *Deseret News,* June 8, 1873.

73. *HC* 3:380.

74. *Ibid.*, 5:136.

75. D&C 63:23.

76. *Ibid.*, 42:61.

77. *HC* 5:424–425.

78. *JD* 5:83.

79. John Taylor, *JD* 10:148.

80. *HC* 6:184–185.

81. Alma 12:9–11.

82. BYU Devotional Address, September II, 1973.

83. D&C 63:64.

84. John A. Widtsoe, *Evidences and Reconciliations* (Salt Lake City: Bookcraft, 1960), pp. 98–99.

85. D&C 88:118.

86. *JD* 20:177.

87. *HC* 2:8.

88. Joseph Smith, *Lectures on Faith,* Lecture #2.

89. BYU Devotional Address, September 11, 1973; Compare an address by President Lee in CR, April 1968,

also found in *IE* 71:102–104 (June 1968); The reader is also referred to B. H. Roberts, *Discourses of B. H. Roberts*, pp. 25–26; as cited in Roy W. Doxey, "Great Truths; The School of the Prophets," *The Relief Society Magazine*, November 1965, p. 867.

90. Joel Richards, "Education Among the Latter-day Saints." *Liahona— The Elder's Journal*, Vol. 8, No. 9 (August 16, 1910), p. 131.

91. *HC* 2:23.

92. CR, April 1964.

93. Rigdon, "Oration Delivered by Mr. S. Rigdon on the 4th of July, 1838" (Far West, Missouri, 1838), pp. 9–10.

94. *HC* 4:425.

95. *Ibid.*, 6:50.

96. Moses 1:27.

97. A marvelous discourse is given by Orson Pratt in *JD* 16:362–363, which is closely related to this.

98. As cited in N. B. Lundwall, *The Vision, op cit.*, p. 11.

CHAPTER VII

1. D&C 84:36.

2. CR, October 1960.

3. D&C 1:38.

4. Revelation given through John Taylor, June 27, 1882 at Salt Lake City, Utah: cited by Hyrum L. Andrus in *Doctrines of the Kingdom* (Salt Lake City: Bookcraft. 1973), p. 165.

5. D&C 21:4–6.

6. *JD* 9:279; Compare also a statement by Wilford Woodruff in *Ibid.*, 4:94–95.

7. BYU Devotional Address, September 11, 1973.

8. Rev. 19:10; *HC* 3:28.

9. Mosiah 8:15–17.

10. In speaking of his new first counselor, Harold B. Lee, Joseph Fielding Smith said in his first address to the Church as its President: "President Harold B. Lee is a pillar of truth and righteousness, a true seer who has great spiritual strength and insight and wisdom, and whose knowledge and understanding of the Church and its needs is not surpassed." (CR, April 1970, as found in *IE*, June 1970, p. 27.).

11. Statements of Harold B. Lee in the *Ensign*, January 1974, p. 126, and in "The Place of the Living Prophet, Seer, and Revelator," *op cit.*, indicate his view that the Lord was speaking of the General Authorities in this passage.

12. D&C 68:3–4.

13. CR, October 1973, as found in the *Ensign*, January 1974, p. 128; See also CR, April 1973, p. 176.

14. D&C 43:3–4.

15. Bruce R. McConkie, *Doctrines of Salvation, op cit.*, III, pp. 156–157.

16. See a statement by Brigham Young in *JD* 9:279.

17. *HC* 5:135.

18. *JD* 9:311.

19. *MS* 9:323.

20. *JD* 9:324.

21. CR, October 1900, p. 64.

22. CR, April 1943, p. 76.

23. "The Place of the Living Prophet, Seer, and Revelator," *op. cit.*

24. CR, October 1961, pp. 77–82.

25. "The Place of the Living Prophet, Seer, and Revelator," *op. cit.*

26. D&C 20:65.

27. *Ibid.*, 26:3; Compare also *Ibid.*, 28:13.

28. Parley P. Pratt, *MS* 5:150 (1844); Compare also a statement by John Taylor in *JD* 9:11.

29. CR, June 1919, p. 92.

30. *Ibid.*

31. *JD* 24:307.

32. *IE* 21:106 (December 1917).

33. D&C 107:22.

34. CR, October 1972, p. 6.

35. CR, April 1907, p. 113; See also remarks by Brigham Young in *JD* 1:76.

36. Rudger Clawson, CR, June 1919, p. 40.

37. *JD* 21:318.

38. Rudger Clawson, CR, June 1919, p. 40.

39. CR, 1897, p. 38; Compare also Brigham Young's statement in *JD* 1:76.

40. *JD* 2:199–200.

41. CR, 1901, p. 59.

42. CR, October 1965, pp. 103–106.

43. *JD* 11:80.

44. CR, April 2900, p. 14.

45. *JI* 31:101–102 (February 15, 1896).

46. *JD* 2:157.

47. CR, April 1900, p. 14.

48. *Deseret Weekly* 52:385–386 (February 26, 1896).

49. George Q. Cannon, *Deseret Weekly* 54:674 (April 5, 1897).

50. George Q. Cannon, *Deseret Weekly* 52:385–586: Compare D&C 121:16–22.

51. D&C 130:21.

52. As cited by Harold B. Lee in "The Place of the Living Prophet, Seer, and Revelator." *op. cit.*

53. *JD* 6:100: Compare *JD* 9:149.

54. Brigham Young. *Ibid.*, 9:150.

55. *JI* 31:618 (October 15, 1896).

56. As cited in George J. Romney, comp., *Look to God and Live—Discourses of Marion G. Romney* (Salt Lake City: Deseret Book Company, 1971), pp. xi–xii.

57. See again D&C 68:4.

58. *MS* 52:578 (1890).

59. CR, October 1960; Compare a statement by Wilford Woodruff in *JD* 9:166.

60. *JD* 21:319.

61. CR, April 1968; Compare also D&C 50:36.

CHAPTER VIII

1. An excellent treatment of this aspect of the Gospel may be found in Hyrum L. Andrus' *Doctrinal Commentary on the Pearl of Great Price* (Salt Lake City: Deseret Book Company, 1967), Chapters 3 and 4.

2. D&C 93:29. It is interesting to note that in Section 93 of the *Doctrine and Covenants* the Lord describes two kinds of intelligence: (1) the central primal intelligence or ego of man (v. 29), and (2) the light and truth (spirit or glory) that is an added endowment to the faithful (v. 28), and that which emanates from God (v. 36).

3. HC 6:311.

4. *Ibid.*

5. See Abraham 3:22.

6. See the statement by the First Presidency and the Twelve, "The Father and the Son," *op. cit.*

7. D&C 131:7–8; HC 4:575.

8. *The Seer,* Vol. I, No. 4 (April 1853), p. 49.

9. See D&C 77:2.

10. *Ibid.,* 88:4–5.

11. Rom. 8:29; Col. 1:15.

12. See again "The Father and the Son," *op cit.*

13. Mosiah 3:17; Acts 4:12.

14. Mosiah 15:1–4.

15. D&C 93:3–4.

16. Heb. 1:2; D&C 76:24; Moses 1:33.

17. Ether 4:7; Compare Alma 11:38–39.

18. John 5:43; Compare John 10:25.

19. D&C 29:1.

20. *Ibid.*, 29:42.

21. *Ibid.*, 49:5, 28; Compare Moses 1:6.

22. See a statement to this effect by Joseph Fielding Smith in Bruce R. McConkie, *Doctrines of Salvation, op cit.*, 1, pp. 26–27.

23. John 17:6.

24. *Ibid.*, 17:9.

25. D&C 50:41.

26. Mosiah 15:10–12.

27. Rom. 6:3–5; Col. 2:12.

28. See D&C 93:38.

29. 1 John 5:8; Moses 6:60.

30. John 3:1–5.

31. *HC* 6:58.

32. *Ibid.*, 3:392.

33. "Recollections of the Prophet Joseph Smith." by Daniel Tyler, *JI* 27:93–94 (February 1, 1892).

34. Bruce R. McConkie, *Mormon Doctrine, op cit.*, p. 101. President David O. McKay made the following interesting observation:

    ... He [the Lord] told Nicodemus that before he could solve the question that was troubling his mind, his spiritual vision would have to be changed by an entire revolution of his "inner man." His manner of thinking, feeling and acting with reference to spiritual things would have to undergo a fundamental and permanent change with reference to spiritual matters.

    It is easy to see temporal things. It is easy to yield to lascivious things. It requires little or no effort to indulge in anything physical and animallike. But to be born out of that world into a spiritual world is advancement that the Lord requires of each of us. (CR, April 1960, p. 26)

35. Alma 41:11.

36. *Ibid.*, 5:14. Interestingly enough, those who become the children of Christ take on the image of Christ, just as man is born in the image of his mortal father.

37. Mosiah 27:25–26.

38. Clare Middlemiss, comp., *Cherished Experiences From the Writings of David O. McKay* (Salt Lake City: Deseret Book Company, 1955), pp. 101–102.

39. The concept of becoming heirs of God through Christ will be discussed in Chapter 10.

40. D&C 93:16.

41. See Gal. 4:5; Eph. 1:5.

42. Mosiah 5:1–5.

43. *Ibid.*, 5:7.

44. D&C 25:1.

45. *Ibid.*, 39:1–4; Compare also John 1:12; D&C 34:1–3, 35:2.

46. Abraham 2:10.

47. D&C 132:30.

48. Rom. 9:4; *HC* 4:360.

49. Abraham 2:9.

50. *HC* 4:360: Compare also a statement by Parley P. Pratt in *JD* 1:261.

51. *HC* 3:380; Compare also *JD* 12:270.

52. Bruce R. McConkie, *Mormon Doctrine, op cit.*, pp. 745–746.

53. Lee A Palmer, *Aaronic Priesthood Through the Centuries* (Salt Lake City: Deseret Book Company, 1964), pp. 319–320; See also remarks by Joseph Fielding Smith in Bruce R.

McConkie, *Doctrines of Salvation, op cit.,* III, p. 93.

54. D&C 84:31–32.

55. *JD* 15:365–366.

56. D&C 110:12; See also *Ibid.,* 124:58; *Ibid.,* 132:30–32; *JD* 25:367–368.

57. *JD* 7:289.

58. *Journal History,* April 9, 1837.

59. As cited by Mary Elizabeth Rollins Lightner in *Young Woman's Journal,* Vol. 16, pp. 556–557 (December 1905). It is interesting to compare these words of the Prophet with the words of Christ cited earlier in John 17:6, 9 and D&C 50:41.

CHAPTER IX

1. See Moses 6:55.

2. Rom. 1:16.

3. Luke 6:13.

4. Joseph Fielding Smith. "The First Presidency and the Council of the Twelve, *IE* 69:977 (November 1966).

5. See, for example, Matt. 14:28–29; Matt. 17: Matt. 26:37.

6. John 6:66–69.

7. Matt. 16:13–16.

8. *Ibid.,* 16:21–23.

9. *Ibid.,* 26:50–54; John 18:10–11.

10. Matt. 26:69–74.

11. That Peter's testimony was genuine is evident from Christ's statement that "flesh and blood hath not revealed it unto thee, but my Father which is in heaven." (Matt. 16:17)

12. Luke 22:31–32. Note President Harold B. Lee's words: "You cannot lift another soul until you are standing on higher ground than he is. You must be sure, if you would rescue the man, that you yourself are setting the example of what you would have him be. You cannot light a fire in another soul unless it is burning in your own soul." (CR, April 1973, p. 178.)

13. For some reason, Christ needed to leave the earth before the Holy Ghost could be given. See John 7:39, 16:7.

14. CR, April 1973, p. 178; citing Acts 3:1–8.

15. Acts 5:27–32.

16. Mosiah 5:2; Compare Alma 5:14.

17. Mosiah 3:19.

18. Matt. 18:3.

19. As cited in the *Ensign,* February 1974, p. 78.

20. D&C 129:7.

21. Gal. 3:11; Rom. 1:17; *HC* 4:11.

22. *HC* 2:229.

23. Enos 1–5.

24. D&C 29:1–3.

25. *Ibid.,* 110:4–5.

26. Mosiah 4:3.

27. John 14:27.

28. Enos 6–8.

29. Moses 6:60.

30. 2 Nephi 31:17.

31. *HC* 3:379.

32. See D&C 104:18.

33. Mosiah 4:12.

34. *Ibid.,* 4:26.

35. *JD* 1:71.

36. *Ibid.,* 17:112.

37. *Ibid.,* 5:173.

38. *Ibid.,* 11:237; Compare also a statement by Brigham Young in *Ibid.,* 10:173.

39. The fact that man may still commit inadvertent sin after he is sanctified is evident from D&C 20:31–34. See also remarks of Brigham Young in *JD* 10:173.

40. Orson Pratt, *The Holy Spirit* (Liverpool, 1856), pp. 56–57.

41. D&C 84:33.

42. Parley P. Pratt, *Key to the Science of Theology*, 9th Edition (Salt Lake City: Deseret Book Company, 1965), p. 101.

43. Alma 13:11–12; Compare Alma 5:54.

44. 3 Nephi 27:20–21.

45. Moroni 10:32–33. Man cannot be sanctified without a full acceptance of the Atonement of Christ, for the Lord explained that "by the blood ye are sanctified." (Moses 6:60) It is only because of the infinite and eternal sacrifice that man is able to be sanctified by the Holy Ghost. See Alma 13:11; 3 Nephi 27:19; Rev. 7:4; Heb. 9:11–14.

CHAPTER X

1. D&C 43:16.
2. *Ibid.*, 133:62.

3. HC 3:380.

4. 2 Nephi 31:20–21; compare D&C 14:7, HC 6:365.

5. D&C 131:5–6; compare this last statement by the Prophet with Nephi's words above that "there is none other way. . . whereby man can be saved in the kingdom of God."

6. Bruce R. McConkie, *Mormon Doctrine, op cit.*, p. 109.

7. HC 5:389.

8. Marion G. Romney, CR, October 1965.

9. D&C 59:23.

10. Mosiah 5:15.

11. 2 Peter 1:5–11; see also Paul's remarks in Eph. 1:14–15, in light of Joseph Smith's statements in *HC* 3:380.

12. 2 Peter 1:17–19; citing the incident in Matt. 17.

13. HC 5:389.

14. D&C 68:12.

15. HC 5:391.

16. D&C 132:49.

17. Bruce R. McConkie, *Mormon Doctrine, op cit.*, pp. 217–218.

18. See D&C 109:15.

19. *Ibid.*, 107:19.

20. Joseph Smith, *Lectures on Faith, op cit.*, Lecture #2.

21. JD 18:363.

22. D&C 93:1.

23. *Ibid.*, 88:68; compare *Ibid.*, 67:10.

24. See Matt. 5:8.

25. HC 3:381.

26. John 14:16, 17, 18, 21, 23. That all of the above refer to the Second Comforter is clear from statements of Joseph Smith in HC 3:380–381 and D&C 130:3.

27. 2 Nephi 11:2–3.

28. Ether 3:13; compare *Ibid.*, 12:39.

29. HC 2:380.

30. *Ibid.*, 1:334–335. In speaking of the nature of a personal visitation by the Lord, President Harold B. Lee explained that "when one receives that kind of visitation, it must be that he has had a vision: for, as Moses said, one couldn't stand in the presence of the Lord except he had been quickened by the Spirit of the Lord." (BYU Devotional Address, September 11, 1973).

31. D&C 93:22. See Harold B. Lee, *Ye Are the Light of the World* (Salt Lake City: Deseret, 1974), p. 49.

32. See Bruce R. McConkie, *Mormon Doctrine, op cit.*, p. 139.

33. D&C 107:19.

34. JD 18:363; compare also a statement by Charles W. Penrose in *Ibid.*, 21:49.

35. B. H. Roberts, *The Gospel and Man's Relationship to Deity* (Salt Lake City: Deseret Book Company, 1966), p. 111.

36. Bruce R. McConkie, *Doctrines of Salvation, op cit.*, II, p. 42. (italics in original)

37. Joseph Fielding Smith, *Man: His Origin and Destiny* (Salt Lake City: Deseret Book Company, 1954), p. 272.

38. Joseph Fielding Smith, *The Way to Perfection, op cit.*, p. 208. Compare the following statement to Brigham Young: "The ordinances of the house of God are expressly for the Church of the First-born." (*JD* 8:154.)

39. Rom. 8:14–17.

40. D&C 84:38.

41. *Ibid.*, 76:55, 59.

42. *Ibid.*, 76:56; 93:19.

43. *Ibid.*, 50:24; 88:67; 93:28.

44. *JD* 6:125.

45. *HC* 5:555.

46. *Ibid.*, 5:527; The Prophet Joseph probably had reference to the realization of the blessings in the Temple when he said: "The anointing and sealing is to be called, elected, and made sure." (*Ibid.*, 5:555)

47. *Ibid.*

48. *JI* 15:111 (May 1, 1880); There is some evidence to indicate that women who are true and faithful (and thus become Queens and Priestesses to their husbands) will exercise authority in the Priesthood. President Charles W. Penrose stated that "when a woman is sealed to a man holding the Priesthood, she becomes one with him . . . , The glory and power and dominion that he will exercise when he has the fulness of the Priesthood and becomes a 'king and a priest unto God,' she will share with him." (CR, April 1921, p. 24; Compare also *JD* 17:119.)

Even more emphatic is a statement by President Joseph Fielding Smith: "Women do not hold the Priesthood, but if they are faithful and true, they will become priestesses and queens in the kingdom of God, and that implies that they will be given authority." (Bruce R. McConkie, *Doctrines of Salvation, op cit.*, III, p. 178)

49. See again President Young's statement above in *HC* 5:527.

50. *JD* 10:355.

51. See D&C 124:28.

52. *HC* 5:424.

53. Bruce R. McConkie, *Doctrines of Salvation, op cit.*, III, p. 131. (italics in original)

54. Joseph Smith, *HC* 5:2.

55. *JD* 25:294.

56. *MS* 13:362.

57. D&C 88:29.

58. Adapted from a statement by John Taylor in "The Mormon," *op cit.*

LIST OF QUOTATIONS FROM MAJOR SOURCES

OLD TESTAMENT

Genesis
22:16
26:3–4

Exodus
3:14
30:30–31
40:13–15

Numbers
30:2

Deuteronomy
8:8

Psalms
110:4
130:5

Proverbs
3:1
3:5–6
23:7

Jeremiah
1:5

NEW TESTAMENT

Matthew
4:4
5:5
5:8
5:27–28
5:33–37
6:2, 5, 16
6:19–21
6:22
6:24
6:33
12:32
14:28–29
16:13–16
16:17
16:21–23
17
18:3
20:16
22:14
26:37
26:50–54
26:69–74

Luke
6:13
12:16–21
16:13
22:31–32

John
1:1–3, 10
1:12
3:1–5
5:43
6:66–69
7:39
10:25
14:16–18, 21, 23
14:27
16:7
17:3
17:6
17:9
17:6, 9
18:10–11

Acts
3:1–8
4
4:12
5

5:27–32
17:24–26

Romans
1:16
1:16
1:17
6:3–5
8:14–17
8:29
9:4

1 Corinthians
2:11
13:4

Galatians
3:11
4:5

Ephesians
1:5
1:14–15
4:11–13
6:18

Colossians
1:15
2:12

2 Timothy
8:16–17

Hebrews
1:2
1:2
5:6
6:6
7:3
7:17, 21
7:20–21
9:11–14
12:24

1 Peter
1:20

2 Peter
1:5–11
1:17–19

1 John
5:8

Jude
20

Revelation
7:4
19:10

BOOK OF MORMON

1 Nephi
2
4:33–37

2 Nephi
4:15–16
9:28–29
11:2–3
31:17
31:20–21
32:8

Jacob
2:17–19

Enos
1–5
4
6–8

Mosiah
3:17
3:19
4:3

4:12
4:26
5:1–5
5:2
5:7
5:15
8:15–17
15:1–4
15:10–12
18:8–10
27:25–26

Alma
5:14
5:54
11:38–39
12:9–11
13:4
13:1–9
13:11–12
37:27, 29
37:36–37
39:5
41:11

Helaman
6:21, 25, 30

3 Nephi
12:5
27:19
27:20–21

4 Nephi
42

Ether
3:13
4:7
8:15, 20
10:33
12:39

Moroni
4
5
7:45
7:47

7:47
10:5
10:24
10:32–33

DOCTRINE AND COVENANTS

1:22
1:38
2:3
8:2–3
9:8–9
13
14:7
20:9
20:31–34
20:60
20:65
20:77–79
21:4–6
25:1
25:10
26:3
28:13
29:1
29:1–3
29:42
34:1–3
35:2
38:27
38:42
39:1–4
39:11
42:12
42:14
42:23
42:24
42:61
43:3–4
43:16
43:34
45:9
46:30, 32
49:5, 28

49:9
50:9
50:24
50:26
50:27
50:27–28
50:36
50:41
58:27–28
59:23
63:23
63:64
64:33
66:2
67:10
68:3–4
68:4
68:12
76
76:15–19
76:24
76:34
76:50–70, 94–96
76:55, 59
76:56
76:60
76:69
77:2
82:3
84:17
84:18
84:19
84:19–21
84:24
84:25
84:31–32
84:33
84:33–44
84:36
84:38
84:43
84:44
84:45
84:85
84:109

85
86:8–10
88:4
88:4–5
88:29
88:67
88:68
88:118
88:131
93:1
93:3–4
93:16
93:19
93:19–20
93:22
93:28
93:29
93:36
93:38
95:5–6
95:8
98:14
101:39
104:18
107:3
107:8
107:14
107:18
107:18–19
107:19
107:20
107:22
107:22
107:53–56
107:99
107:99–100
109:15
110
110:4–5
110:12
121:16–22
121:34, 40
121:34–35
121:35
121:36–37

121:37–38
121:39–40
121:41–45
121:45
124:28
124:58
129:7
130:3
130:12–13
130:21
131:1–4
131:5–6
131:7–8
132
132:4
132:30
132:30–32
132:49
133:5
133:57
133:62

PEARL OF GREAT PRICE

Moses
1:6
1:27
1:33
1:39
4:2
5:29–31
6:55
6:59
6:60

Abraham
2:9
2:9–11
2:10
2:11
3:22
3:23
4:1
4:2

Joseph Smith History
2:34

Articles of Faith
5

JOURNAL OF DISCOURSES
(letters following volume numbers indicate the speaker)

Vol. 1 (1851–54)
45 (BY)
71 (OH)
76 (BY)
77 (BY)
257–258 (PPP)
260–261 (PPP)
261 (PPP)
312 (BY)

Vol. 2 (1843, 1852–55)
31 (BY)
90 (BY)
125 (BY)
157 (HCK)
157 (PPP)
199–200 (WW)
371 (OP)

Vol. 3 (1852–56)
188–189 (PPP)
192–193 (BY)
192 (BY)

Vol. 4 (1856–57)
94–95 (WW)
141–142 (HCK)

Vol. 5 (1856–57)
83 (WW)
173 (BY)

Vol. 6

(1839, 1844, 1852–59)
25 (JT)
100 (BY)
125 (HCK)
161 (GAS)

Vol. 7 (1854–60)
84 (OP)
203 (BY)
289 (BY)
289–290 (BY)
290 (BY)
314–315 (OH)

Vol. 8 (1860–61)
23 (OH)
62 (BY)
129 (BY)
154 (BY)

Vol. 9 (1860–62)
11 (JT)
149 (BY)
150 (BY)
166 (WW)
195 (BY)
229 (BY)
279 (BY)
311 (BY)
324 (WW)

Vol. 10 (1859–64)
5 (BY)
57–58 (JT)
148 (JT)
150 (JT)
173 (BY)
190 (BY)
355 (BY)

Vol. 11 (1859–67)
80 (HCK)
115 (BY)
209 (HCK)
237 (BY)

Vol. 12 (1867–69)
103 (BY)
125 (BY)
163–64 (BY)
157 (BY)
270 (BY)
363 (GQC)

Vol. 13 (1868–70)
55 (GQC)
155 (BY)
312 (BY)

Vol. 15 (1870–73)
127 (BY)
216 (JT)
250 (OP)
365–366 (OP)

Vol. 16 (1873–74)
75 (BY)
240 (DHW)
362–363 (OP)

Vol. 17 (1874–75)
112 (OP)
119 (BY)
247 (WW)
255 (GAS)
372 (JT)

Vol. 18 (1875–77)
2 (JT)
137 (JT)
363 (OP)
363 (OP)

Vol. 19 (1867, 1877–78)
17 (OP)
51 (JT)
52 (JT)
56 (JT)
78 (JT)
137–138 (JT)
142 (JT)

176 (OP)
241–242 (JT)
245 (JT)

Vol. 20 (1878–79)
20 (JT)
22 (JT)
177 (JT)
261–262 (JT)

Vol. 21 (1878–81)
48–49 (CWP)
49 (CWP)
190–191 (WW)
191 (WW)
193 (WW)
284 (WW)
298 (WW)
317 (WW)
318 (WW)
319 (WW)

Vol. 22 (1879–82)
28 (OP)
146 (WW)
209 (WW)
267 (GQC)
308 (JT)
308–309 (JT)
333–334 (WW)
335 (WW)

Vol. 23 (1880–83)
177 (JT)
329–330 (WW)
331 (WW)
341–342 (LS)

Vol. 24 (1879, 1882–83)
55 (WW)
159 (ES)
306 (CWP)
307 (CWP)

Vol. 25 (1878–84)
165 (JT)
290–291 (GQC)
294 (GQC)
367–368 (GQC)

Vol. 26 (1881–86)
62 (GQC)
100 (FDR)
243 (GQC)
245 (GQC)

**HISTORY OF
THE CHURCH**

Vol. 1 (1805–34)
269 (JS)
334–335 (JS)

Vol. 2 (1834–37)
8 (JS)
23 (JS)
31 (JS)
229 (JS)
309 (JS)
380 (JS)
477 (JS)

Vol. 3 (1837–39)
28 (JS)
295 (JS)
295 (JS)
301 (JS)
379 (JS)
380 (JS)
380 (JS)
380 (JS)
380–381 (JS)
381 (JS)
381 (JS)
386 (JS)
386 (JS)
392 (JS)

Vol. 4 (1839–42)
11 (JS)
207 (JS)
209 (JS)
258 (BY, WR)
260–61 (BY, WR)
345 (JS)
360 (JS)
425 (JS)
461 (JS)
575 (JS)
598 (JS)

Vol. 5 (1842–43)
2 (JS)
135 (JS)
136 (JS)
257 (JS)
285 (JS)
389 (JS)
389 (JS)
391 (JS)
424 (JS)
424–425 (JS)
527 (BY)
555 (JS)
555 (JS)

Vol. 6 (1842–44)
50 (JS)
51 (JS)
58 (JS)
78 (JS)
184, 185 (JS)
303 (JS)
305 (JS)
307 (JS)
308 (JS)
308 (JS)
308 (JS)
314–315 (JS)
363 (JS)
364 (JS)
365 (JS)

INDEX

A

Aaronic Order of Priesthood, vii, 9, 11, 12, 23, 24, 122
Abinadi, 115, 116
Abraham
    adoption into family of, 121–122
    blessings of, 121–122
    Father of the faithful, 121
    role in Gospel plan, 121–122
Adoption into the Family of Christ entitles
    men to rich blessings, 120–121
    necessary for all men, 120
Alma, 19, 39, 41, 64, 73, 90–91, 119, 135
Amen to the Priesthood, 69
Ananias and Sapphira, 65
Aspiring to worldly honors, 66–67

B

Ballard, Melvin J., 20–21, 22
Benjamin, King, 120, 130, 132, 133, 139
Benson, Ezra Taft, 24
Birth into Kingdom of God
    seeing and entering the Kingdom, 118
    symbolism related to, 117–118
    through Articles of Adoption, 118
Blessing the family
    through honoring Priesthood, 54
    through training for eternal life, 55
    through bestowal of patriarchal
        blessings, 55
    through transmitting spiritual powers, 56
Blessing the world through the
    Priesthood, 56–57
Born again
    all men must be, 117–120
    meaning of, 118–119
    through overcoming the world, 120

C

Calling and election made sure
    as one meets test of mortality, 138
    as man is sealed to Christ, 139
    as the Lord seals an exaltation
        upon a man, 138–139
    of those who continue faithful, 138
Cannon, George Q., 3, 29, 38, 41, 45, 47, 68, 72, 100, 105, 107, 109, 146
Charity, 71, 75, 135

Christ
as Father and Son, 115–117
received fulness of the
    Father's glory, 115–116, 120
spirit existence exercise of power, 30
the children of, 120–121
Christiansen, ElRay L., 17
Church of the Firstborn
    communion with, 143–144
    membership in, 143–144
Clayton, William, 140
Cleanliness, required for Priesthood power, 59–63
Common Consent, 104
Conversion
    contrasted with testimony, 127–130
    becoming as a little child, 130
    measure of determined by support of
        leaders of Church, 97–98
    of Peter, 127–130
    seeing, hearing, and understanding
        eternal truth, 131
Covenant(s)
    baptismal, 19–20
    importance of keeping, 17
    initiated in pre-earth existence, 18
    meaning of, 16–17
    New and Everlasting, is the fulness
        of the Gospel, 19
    renewal of, 22
    sacramental, 20–21
    temple, 21
Cowdery, Oliver, 9, 88, 123

D

Doctrine of the Priesthood, 1

E

Ego, 113
Elect of God, defined, 140
Election in the flesh, 35–37
Elias, returns to Kirtland Temple, 9
Elijah, returns to Kirtland Temple, 9
Endowment, 21, 22, 144–145
Enos, 85, 131, 132
Eternal life, 114
Eternal lives, 22
Eternity of the Priesthood, 3–6

Evil speaking of the Anointed
  condemned, 106–108
    is breaking a covenant, 107–108
    leads to withdrawal of Spirit, 107–108
    will lead one down to hell, 108
Exaltation, only through Priesthood, 3
Experience, vital in understanding things
    of God, 1–3
Eye single to God's glory
    attained through counseling with the
      Lord in all matters, 73
    attained through setting aside personal
      ambitions, 72–73
    blessings which follow, 73–74
    meaning of, 72

F

Fordham, Elijah, healing of, 50–51
Foreordination
    a specific aspect of election, 38
    of all Priesthood holders, 38–40
    of the prophets, 38
Fulness of the Gospel
    contained in Bible and Book
      of Mormon, 79
    not necessarily the fulness of
      Gospel doctrine, 79
Fulness of the Priesthood
    admits men and women within
      the veil, 145
    entails becoming a King and a
      Priest, 145
    obtained only in the temple,
      145–146

G

Gentleness, 70, 75, 135
Governing the Saints, 70–72
Grand organizational council, 34–35
Grant, Heber J., 110

H

Heirs through Christ, 144
Hyde, Orson, 18, 56, 133

J

Jacob, a royal lineage, 36
Jacob (Nephite prophet), 67, 74, 142
Jared, Brother of, 93, 142
Justification
    obtaining a remission of sins, 131–133
    retaining a remission of sins, 133

spiritual wholeness and peace of
    conscience through, 132

K

Keys of the Kingdom
    are the right of presidency, 8
    held in totality by the Prophet, 99
Kimball, Heber C., 17, 45, 56, 59, 107, 144
Kimball, Spencer W., 55, 85, 103
Kindness, 56, 70, 75, 135
Kingly authority, 6, 145
Knight, Newel, evil spirit dismissed from,
    52–53
Knowledge by faith
    a superior intelligence, 94
    no easy road to learning, 94
    surpasses cognitive processes, 94

L

Learning Priesthood duties
    allows one to stand approved, 46
    brings happiness and peace, 47
    gaining spirit of calling, 46–47
Lee, Harold B., 4, 36, 54, 61, 63, 82, 91, 93,
    98, 99, 101–103, 109, 110, 129, 145
Living by every word of God, 77–78
Living Oracles, 98–100
Living vs. dead prophets, 101–103
Long-suffering, 70, 75

M

Madsen, Truman G., 81
Magnifying callings in the Priesthood
    accentuating details, 43–44
    enlarging upon responsibilities, 43
    holding calling in greater esteem, 44
    magnifies the man, 44–45
    sanctifies by the Spirit, 45
Many called, few chosen
    through failing to live up to pre-mortal
      word of prophecy, 63–64
    through walking in darkness
      at noonday, 64
Marriage, eternal, 17, 21–22, 143
McConkie, Bruce R., 15, 78, 89, 118, 138, 140
McKay, David O., 1, 2, 11, 20, 22, 48, 54,
    55, 60, 61, 62–63, 72, 82, 102, 103, 106,
    119, 135, 163
Meekness, 20, 70, 71, 75
Moroni, 49. 135
Moses, 8, 23, 24, 26, 28, 30, 41, 72, 81, 93,
    94, 122–123, 125

Mysteries
    bring joy, 89
    defined, 89
    God delights to reveal, 89
    withheld from the hard-hearted, 99

N

Nephi, 15, 83, 86, 133, 138, 142

O

Oath(s)
    Christ's denunciation of, 16
    meaning of, 15
    scriptural evidence of, 15–16
    wicked utilization of, 16
Oath and Covenant of the Priesthood accompanies Melchizedek Priesthood only, 24
    fate of covenant-breakers, 24
    God's covenant with man, 24, 26
    man's covenant with God, 23–24, 26
Obedience, a law of heaven, 108
Obedience, intelligent
    blessings of, 110
    consists in gaining divine confirmation of Priesthood leaders' words, 109

P

Patten, David W., 5
Paul, 7, 24, 30, 37, 67, 78, 144
Penrose, Charles W., 44, 47, 104
Personal revelation, 87
Persuasion, 70, 75
Peter
    a member of the First Presidency, 127
    bears testimony of Christ, 128
    boldly declares Christ before the Sanhedrin, 128
    denies Christ, 128–129
    heals the lame man, 129
    not fully converted, 128–129
    speaks on calling and election, 139
    speaks on more sure word of prophecy, 139
Physical life, 113, 114
Pond, Allie Young, 85
Pondering and meditation
    an approach to knowing one's self, 81–82
    leads to a knowledge of God, 81–82
    with the scriptures, 83
Pratt, Orson, 4, 5, 6, 9, 11, 30, 37, 48, 49, 114, 123, 133, 134, 141, 143
Pratt, Parley P., 2, 5, 35, 36, 50, 53, 107, 135

Prayer
    Holy Ghost teaches principles of, 86
    in Spirit, 84–87
    Joseph Smith gives instructions on, 67
    perserverence in, exemplified by Lorenzo Snow, 84–85
Pride, 60, 67, 69, 70, 75, 130
Priesthood
    Aaronic Order, 9
    co-functioning of earthly and heavenly, 6–7
    fulness of, 5–6, 145–146
    keys of, 8–9, 99
    magnifying callings in, 43–57
    Melchizedek Order, 8–9
    Oath and Covenant of, 1, 15, 22–27, 97
    Patriarchal Order, 8–9
    requirements for reception in mortality, 41–42
    a source of power, 11–12
    a source of revelation, 10–11
Priesthood, definition of
    delegated authority to man, 2–3
    God's own power, 1
    Government of God, 2
Priesthood, power in
    dependent upon righteousness, 48–50
    distinguished from authority in, 48
    subject to Priesthood in the heavens, 48
Prophecy, more sure word of
    may be obtained in mortality, 138
    relation to calling and election made sure, 138–139
    the knowledge that one is sealed unto eternal life, 138–139
Prophecy, word of, 4041, 42, 43, 107, 138–139, 140, 147
Prophet, defined, 98
Pure knowledge, 70, 75

R

Renewal by the Spirit, 135
Revelation
    through the Priesthood, 10–11
    growing in the principle of, 87–89
    personal, 87
    spirit of, 87
    the most precious of all knowledge, 92
Rich Fool, 74
Richards, F. D., 56
Richards, Willard, 35
Rigdon, Sidney, 30, 83, 94, 95
Roberts, B. H., 93, 106, 143

Romney, Marion G., 25, 26, 78, 79, 83, 88, 93, 97, 109, 110

S

Sanctification
    comes as the spirit of man reigns, 134
    contrasted with justification, 134
Scripture
    defined, 99
    need for modern, 100–101
    to be declared by General Authorities, 99
Searching the scriptures, 78–81
Second Comforter
    blessings enjoyed in the Americas, 142
    consists of the presence of the
        Son and/or the Father, 141
    promised to Christ's apostles in
        Jerusalem, 141–142
    promised to faithful Priesthood
        holders, 141
Seed of Abraham, defined, 121
Seeking first the Kingdom of God, 74
Seer, defined, 98
Sexual sin condemned, 60–62
Sharp reproof, 70
Smith, Emma, 25, 73, 120
Smith, George Albert, 17, 60, 80
Smith, Joseph, 1, 2, 3, 4, 5, 7, 9, 10, 16, 19, 21, 24, 25, 30, 31, 34, 37, 38, 41, 49, 50–51, 52–54, 55, 59, 66, 67, 68, 69, 71, 72, 79, 80, 81–82, 83, 85, 86, 87, 89, 90, 92, 93, 94–95, 97, 100, 102, 108, 113, 118, 121, 123–124, 125, 131, 132, 133, 138, 140, 141, 145, 166
Smith, Joseph
    a modern Abraham, 123
    a father to Ephraim, 123
Smith, Joseph F., 2, 8, 21, 56, 57, 60, 73, 77, 80, 81, 83, 104
Smith, Joseph Fielding, 2–3, 5, 8, 9, 17, 19, 22, 24–25, 27, 38, 45, 66, 79, 99, 101, 103, 104, 127, 135, 143–144, 145
Snow, Eliza R., 55
Snow, Lorenzo, 18, 34, 84, 146
Sons of Moses and Aaron
    faithful holders of Priesthood
        to become, 23–26, 122–123
    not necessary to be literal descendant in
        order to become, 122
    to offer sacrifice in the New Jerusalem
        Temple, 122–123
Spirit life, 113
Spirit of revelation, 87

Spirituality, defined, 60
Stages of existence, 113–115
Sustaining the Brethren
    is a sacred covenant, 104–105
    through honoring Priesthood in self, 104
    through listening to their counsel, 105
    through praying for them, 105
    through supporting local authorities, 106

T

Tanner, N. Eldon, 24, 105
Taylor, John, 2, 4–7, 29, 34, 41, 45–46, 48, 55, 67, 71, 73–74, 92, 97, 100, 102
Teaching correct principles, 71
Thoughts must be controlled, 62–63
Tyler, Daniel, 67, 145

U

Unfeigned love, 70, 75
Union, only attained through Holy Spirit, 71–72
Unrighteous dominion, 68

V

Vain ambition, 67–69, 75
Vandenberg, John H., 54
Virtue, necessary in using the Priesthood, 59–61, 71

W

Wells, Daniel H., 6
Wells, Rulon S., 18
Whitney, Orson F., 31–34, 105
Widtsoe, John A., 10, 11, 41, 48, 87, 92
Woodruff, Wilford, 6–7, 10–11, 17, 24, 25, 26, 35, 38, 49, 60, 66, 69, 78, 79, 84, 85, 86, 90, 100, 105–106, 110
Words of eternal life, 23, 28, 77, 78, 83, 87, 89, 91, 95, 97, 103, 108, 110, 117, 128, 132

Y

Young, Brigham, 2, 4, 10, 22, 35, 37, 49, 50, 56, 71–74, 79, 82, 86–89, 91, 98, 100, 102, 106, 108, 123, 133, 145
Young, Lorenzo Dow, healing of, 51